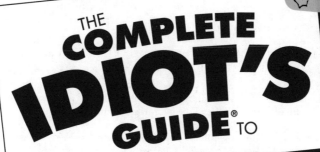

THE COMPLETE IDIOT'S GUIDE® TO

Jewish Spirituality & Mysticism

by Michael Levin

ALPHA

A Pearson Education Company

To my phenomenal wife Suzanne, my ayshet chayil, who inspires me every day.

International Standard Book Number: 0-02-864347-X
Library of Congress Catalog Card Number: 2002101640

04   03   02   8   7   6   5   4   3   2   1

Interpretation of the printing code: The rightmost number of the first series of numbers is the year of the book's printing; the rightmost number of the second series of numbers is the number of the book's printing. For example, a printing code of 02-1 shows that the first printing occurred in 2002.

Printed in the United States of America

Note: This publication contains the opinions and ideas of its author. It is intended to provide helpful and informative material on the subject matter covered. It is sold with the understanding that the author and publisher are not engaged in rendering professional services in the book. If the reader requires personal assistance or advice, a competent professional should be consulted.

The author and publisher specifically disclaim any responsibility for any liability, loss, or risk, personal or otherwise, which is incurred as a consequence, directly or indirectly, of the use and application of any of the contents of this book.

Publisher: *Marie Butler-Knight*
Product Manager: *Phil Kitchel*
Managing Editor: *Jennifer Chisholm*
Acquisitions Editor: *Gary Goldstein*
Development Editor: *Jennifer Moore*
Production Editor: *Billy Fields*
Copy Editor: *Cari Luna*
Illustrator: *Chris Eliopoulos*
Cover/Book Designer: *Trina Wurst*
Indexer: *Tonya Heard*
Layout/Proofreading: *Angela Calvert, Mary Hunt*

Contents at a Glance

Appendixes

Contents

Appendixes

Foreword

The largest single group—if not the majority—of non-native born American Buddhists were born Jewish. It is common knowledge that most American Jews are either minimally involved with Jewish religious communal life, or not involved at all.

Why is this?

While the motives and influences that go into such decisions on a personal or social level are complex, Michael Levin is surely correct when he points to the fact that hardly any American Jews get to learn much about their religion in childhood, and what they learn is—well, childish, and remains so.

Frankly, this book is designed to get the typical American Jew interested in his birthright religion, and to inform those non-Jews who are, for whatever reason, interested in learning something about the tradition that lies at the basis of both Christianity and Islam, and which, unaccountably to some and uncomfortably to others, still exists.

I have a friend who is involved in outreach programs to non- or minimally involved Jews. He insists that the worst advice Jewish parents ever gave their children was the Eastern European Yiddish saying, "It is hard to be a Jew." To his mind, this turned several generations of American Jews away from their heritage.

The fact is, as Michael Levin openly admits, it *is* difficult to live a Jewish life, even as a member of a tolerant society, and even in Israel. In fact, it is less a "religion" than a lifestyle, and regulates nearly every conceivable activity most humans engage in, from eating and drinking and sex to complex Wall Street financing schemes.

Most Americans do not have the patience or acceptance of authority to take such regulation in stride. But for those who do, there are many rewards.

My hat is off to Michael, whom I have known for more than a decade. He wears his learning easily, and he writes in a sprightly, lively, accessible style. I enjoyed reading this book, and I am sure you will, too. You will also be informed of a side of Judaism you may not have been aware existed. And you may decide to go further in your studies.

If that is so, this book will more than have served its purpose.

—Yaakov Elman

Associate Professor of Judaic Studies

Yeshiva University

Introduction

Welcome to *The Complete Idiot's Guide to Jewish Spirituality and Mysticism*. My purpose in writing this book is to provide you with a comprehensive overview of everything spiritual and mystical in Judaism.

I know that's a tall order, so it is inevitable that I will fall short. Nonetheless, I'll do my best to inform, enlighten, and entertain you as we go through the myriad Jewish sources of spirituality and mysticism.

The Kabbalah and the Zohar are incredibly popular today—not just with Jews but even with non-Jewish celebrities such as Madonna and Roseanne. What do these writings contain? More importantly, what's in them for you?

Jews are called "The People of the Book," but even the Bible—the Book of Books—is something of a codebook to most of us. In what way is the Bible still relevant today? How can it be viewed as a textbook on spirituality? What are the ways in which Jews have found themselves nourished by it over the centuries? You'll find all those answers in here.

What does Judaism say about the issue of afterlife? Who is the Jewish messiah, and how will we know when he (or she) gets here? What does it mean to be a good Jew? Can the question of spirituality ever be divorced from the question of character?

The answer to that last question is a resounding "no!" In Judaism, spirituality *is* character. It's impossible to be a "spiritual" person unless one is honorable in his or her dealings with one's fellow human beings. Together, we will fill all the coffers of Jewish spirituality and mysticism, and add to the mixture a few good Jewish jokes, witticisms, and insights to get the ol' noodle working along the way.

And Here's What You'll Find Inside:

When we think of the Bible, we mostly think of stories like Abraham and Isaac, Noah and the Flood, and the Garden of Eden. We also may think back to the time we learned these stories, when we were little children. And it may not occur to us that these stories speak to adults and not just to kids!

The Bible is replete with hidden meanings, spiritual secrets, and mystical moments that really aren't kid stuff at all. The problem, as we'll discuss, is that for many Jews, Jewish education ends with Bar or Bat Mitzvah at 13 or perhaps Confirmation a few years later. So in **Part 1, "Out of the Bible,"** we'll explore the Bible as a Spirituality Sourcebook and see what it offers adults. (Sneak preview: it offers plenty!)

We'll continue our Biblical wanderings in **Part 2, "From Isaac to Sinai,"** and examine everything from the binding of Isaac through the Exodus from Egypt and the giving of the Torah at Mount Sinai. Ironically, Jews seeking spirituality look to other religions, new age philosophies, and the self-help section of the local bookstore without ever realizing that the source of much of the material they find elsewhere—is completely Jewish! We'll examine in depth these Biblical episodes for the wisdom and mystical potential they contain. Prepare to be amazed!

Judaism reveals itself through two forms of contact: between the individual and God, and between people. Character and spirituality are inseparable in Judaism: it's impossible to be "spiritual" if one isn't a decent person. And yet there's much more to Judaism than building one's own character (as important as that is!) In this **Part 3, "Between God and People,"** we'll examine the spiritual and mystical ways that Jews and God contact one another, and we'll also see what it means to be a real *mensch* (stand-up guy or gal) in traditional Jewish terms.

We often think of Judaism as a practical, down-to-earth religion, so **Part 4, "Revelations,"** may be a pleasant and exciting surprise! Here we'll get into the Kaballah, the Zohar, and other aspects of mystical Judaism. We'll explore Jewish concepts of afterlife, the "world to come," the Messiah (yes, there's a Jewish concept of the Messiah!), and the presence of God in the world, the *shechinah*. Straight talk about some perplexing issues!

In **Part 5, "Spiritual Sidenotes,"** we'll take a look at some of the intriguing concepts of Judaism, such as gematria, the study of numbers replacing Hebrew letters, and the role of angels, in Biblical times and in our days. We'll explore why it may be that your Jewish education didn't contain some of the mystical or superrational concepts this book discusses. We'll also plot out a course for you should you like to dig deeper into Jewish thought. And finally, after all of this intellectualizing, you and I can get into a *shmooze* about the number one topic this book is meant to address: *Is Judaism spiritual?* And then, how do you really locate that spirituality for yourself?

Along the way, we'll have four kinds of sidebars for your consideration.

My only regret about this book, aside from wishing that I was a little more learned so that I could make it better for you, is that it isn't catered! Enjoy!

Devine Devarim

Davar is the Hebrew word for "word" or "thing," which indicates the importance of words in Judaism. What we say—the words we choose—speak volumes about *us*. So we'll explore definitions of intriguing Hebrew and Yiddish terms.

High Spirits

What would a Jewish book be without a sense of humor? You may not like all the jokes, but you'll have a great time explaining many of them to your Gentile friends!

Spiritual Citations

In these boxes you'll find outstanding quotations culled from thousands of years of Jewish thought.

Mystical Moments

Here we'll trace fascinating episodes of Jewish history, from the Bible to modern times.

Acknowledgments

I wish to thank Jenna Robbins for her outstanding editing; Jennifer Moore for her excellent work in preparing the manuscript for publication; Howard Zilbert and the staff of Keystrokes for their flawless transcriptions; Gary Goldstein at Alpha for his continuing friendship; and Rabbi Yaakov Elman for writing the foreword. I also wish to thank my teachers: Dr. Haim Agus z'l, Rabbi Robert Block, and Rabbi Chaim Brovender; and special thanks to my wife Suzanne and daughter Chynna Bracha for their love and support. Naturally, all mistakes and inaccuracies belong solely to the author.

Special Thanks to the Technical Reviewer

The Complete Idiot's Guide to Jewish Spirituality and Mysticism was reviewed by an expert who double-checked the accuracy of what you'll learn here, to help us ensure that this book gives you everything you need to know about Jewish spirituality and mysticism.

Trademarks

All terms mentioned in this book that are known to be or are suspected of being trademarks or service marks have been appropriately capitalized. Alpha Books and Pearson Education, Inc., cannot attest to the accuracy of this information. Use of a term in this book should not be regarded as affecting the validity of any trademark or service mark.

Part 1

Out of the Bible

Many Jews, myself included, grew up with a fairly limited Jewish education (if any). In my case, I was 13 and out—as soon as my bar mitzvah was finished, I didn't set foot in a synagogue for the next five years! So, like many Jews, I grew up without a sense of anything spiritual or mystical about Judaism.

In this section, we're going to try to fill in the blanks for those Jews who, like me, didn't get to discover the great spiritual richness of Judaism the first time around. We're going to define the terms Jewish mysticism and Jewish spirituality. We'll also examine the Bible, the ultimate source for the spirituality in Judaism, for clues as to the existence and nature of God and the lessons that we can draw from the stories surrounding Noah and Abraham.

Defining Jewish Mysticism and Spirituality

In This Chapter

- ◆ The purpose of this book
- ◆ Basics of Judaism
- ◆ The difference between spirituality and mysticism
- ◆ Similarities among the various Jewish religious movements

The purpose of this book is to bring together in one easy-to-comprehend volume all of the essential teachings about Jewish mysticism and spirituality that have evolved over the centuries. Together, we'll explore the Bible, the Talmud, the Kabbalah, the Zohar, and Jewish philosophers and commentators of every era in order to develop a complete picture of the Jewish concepts of spirituality.

I said "concepts" and not "concept" because in Judaism, with only a few important exceptions, there's no single acceptable approach to *anything*. There's a common expression in Judaism: Everyone sets his or her own *shulchan aruch*. Shulchan aruch literally means "set table"—the way your plates, glasses, and silverware are arrayed before you at the table. The deeper meaning of the expression is that in Judaism, everyone organizes his or her spiritual life and religious practice as he or she sees fit. Rabbis may guide their congregations, but there is no single central authority, as with the Pope in Catholicism, dictating what to do or how to believe. In fact, the survival of Judaism is one of the miracles of history. We are a people who have survived *without* a central governing body—and even a homeland—for almost 2,000 years!

So Who's in Charge Here?

If everyone gets to pick and choose how to practice Judaism, how has the religion managed to survive all this time? This is a complex question. The bottom line is that Jews have always maintained a deep attachment to their literature, which spells out in many different ways the ultimate Jewish mission: To be spiritual individuals who are part of a spiritual people who demonstrate the presence of God to the world. Amazingly, not all Jews believe in God, and not all Jews believe that we're here to demonstrate *anything*. And yet somehow Judaism keeps moving forward, evolving to meet some demands of the changing times and standing firm in others as a demonstration of commitment to eternal truths.

Devine Devarim

Shulchan aruch literally means "set table"—the way your plates, glasses, and silverware are arrayed before you at the table. The deeper meaning of the expression is that in Judaism, everyone organizes his or her spiritual life and religious practice as he or she sees fit.

Spiritual Citations

"Where there are two Jews, there are three opinions."
—Ancient Jewish proverb

One of the beauties of Judaism is that two Jews don't necessarily have to agree on almost *anything* and yet each is just as Jewish as the other is. Take the concept of *kashrut*—the commandments and traditions regarding the preparation and serving of food and drink. One Jew might consider it essential to eat kosher food both in and out of the home. Another would say that the laws of kashrut were appropriate at one time in Jewish history, but not today. A third Jew would say that it's important to have a kosher home, but it's okay to eat certain dishes in restaurants even though they are prepared in nonkosher vessels and served on nonkosher plates.

Each of these Jews might attend a different kind of temple or synagogue, or not attend at all. And each of them could give you a reasoned, nuanced explanation of why he or she behaves in that particular manner—an explanation that might make no sense at all to the other two people! But are all of them Jewish? You better believe it!

Inside Rashi's Kitchen

While the core elements of Judaism have remained essentially the same for millennia, many aspects have changed. Let's travel back in time 900 years to Troyes, a small town in France. Here we find *Rashi*, Rabbi Shimon ben Yisroel, perhaps the greatest commentator on the Bible and the Talmud that Judaism has ever produced. Virtually every copy of the Jewish Bible published in Hebrew contains Rashi's 900-year-old commentary in the margin. And 20 oversized volumes of the Talmud—the great, vast compendium of Jewish law, lore, custom, and history—offers Rashi's commentary on practically every page. Rashi, many believe, was gifted with *ruach hakodesh*—the holy spirit—as he worked to create his great commentaries. Everyone from schoolchildren to the most learned rabbis use Rashi as a starting point when they seek to understand practically anything in the Bible or Talmud.

> **High Spirits**
>
> A Bar Mitzvah is the day a Jewish boy realizes he's more likely to own a professional sports team than play for one.

Remarkably, if we could be magically transported from the twenty-first century to the time of Rashi and step into his home for a Friday night dinner, we'd recognize the exact same elements that turn Friday nights into the Sabbath in our time. On the table, two candles would be burning. Rashi would say the kiddush blessing, to inaugurate the Sabbath, with the same Hebrew words that a Bar Mitzvah boy or Bat Mitzvah girl of our time would recognize. And the meal would begin with two twisted loaves of challah, the delicious bread on our Sabbath tables.

Let's leave Rashi's home and venture even further back in time, say, 600 years, into the ancient Talmudical academies of Babylonia or the Galilee. We could step into a synagogue and discover that the prayers are virtually the same as those in traditional houses of worship in our day. Chances are, we'd even hear about the latest fund drive for a new building!

Come back to the present moment and skip around the globe: Los Angeles, Shanghai, Moscow, Teheran, Jerusalem, Rome, Johannesburg, Rio de Janiero, Mexico City. The accents might be different, but in traditional congregations the world over, the prayers fundamentally remain the same.

> **Spiritual Citations**
>
> "There is no Judaism without love and fear, wonder and awe, faith and concern, knowledge and understanding."
>
> —Abraham Joshua Heschel

How can this be? After all, according to traditional Jewish belief, the last time God spoke directly to a human being is over 2,500 years ago. That's a long time to go without direct orders!

How could there be such a high degree of uniformity, over the millenia and across the globe?

Jews have tried, as best they can, for 40 centuries, to understand exactly who God is, what God wants, and what we're supposed to do and believe. Naturally there are going to be great differences in opinions, beliefs, and practices, especially in a free society like the United States.

Some Unifying Principles

And yet there are certain core concepts and beliefs that nearly any Jew throughout history could point to and say, "Yes, I agree with that. That sounds very Jewish to my ears." In this book you'll discover what those basic, uniting principles are and why they're so important. Whenever we deal with Jewish history, we're dealing with that fundamental, astonishing fact: Jews have somehow survived. Our literature is all that we have carried down with us through the centuries. Concealed, therefore, in our holy writings is the secret of our survival and our commitment to a spiritual way of life. Together, we'll explore what Jewish writings say about spirituality and how the lessons of Jewish spirituality and mysticism can be applied today by anyone—Jew or non-Jew, believer or nonbeliever—to make his or her life deeper, more powerful, and more meaningful.

What We're Talking About

Let's begin by defining our terms. When I say that an idea is specifically *Jewish*, I mean that the source for that idea can be found somewhere in the literature of the Jewish people, all the way from the Torah to the works of modern-day authors. A *spiritual* idea simply means that the idea pertains to the soul of the human being (as opposed to the intellect or a material aspect of life). When we're talking about *mystical* concepts, we're looking at concepts that are somehow beyond normal human understanding.

Jewish spirituality and mysticism concern themselves with these important questions:

- Why and how was the world created?
- Who created the world and what kind of relationship with the Creator is available to us?
- What kind of people should we be?
- How do we understand our lives—the joyous aspects, the moments of tragedy, and the day-to-day moments in between?
- What happens to us after we die?
- Who is the Messiah, what will He do, and why does He matter?

You could divide these questions into two groups: The first two concern the world we live in, and the last four relate to character. It's not by accident that more spiritual questions relate to character than to the world we live in. The Jewish concept of spirituality can never be divorced from the issue of character. Much of Judaism's spiritual teachings involve what it means to be a good person while living in "the real world" with all its pressures and temptations. Judaism takes a very realistic view of human nature, believing that the human being is essentially born pure and that we live in an impure world.

The soul, Judaism suggests, is a beautiful garment, although it sometimes needs a little dry-cleaning. We are subject to pressures, desires, evil inclinations, and the limitations and complexities of human nature. We have free will and, as such, sometimes choose to do the wrong thing. In Judaism, there's no such thing as a separate "spirituality" from the way we treat other people. You can't be spiritual when you're by yourself and unkind to others. We aren't perfect—we aren't supposed to be perfect. But we are expected to aim high in terms of character, and that is the fundamental expression of Jewish spirituality.

> **High Spirits**
>
> **Zionism**   One Jew talking another Jew into moving to Israel on the money of a third.
>
> —Author Unknown

Ready for Action!

A young man once asked a Chasidic rabbi—a member of an Orthodox Jewish sect—why he always wore black. "You see," the rabbi explained, "the Talmud understands that sometimes people have an incredible urge to do the wrong thing. This even extends to sexual matters. So the Talmud provides an escape valve. Rather than do something wrong in your own community, which could destroy your reputation and your family, if you really find yourself with an uncontrollable urge, the Talmud tells you specifically what to do.

"Dress all in black," the rabbi continued. "Go to a place where no one knows you, do the sin, get it out of your system, and then come back home and resume your normal life!"

The young man looked extremely surprised, so the rabbi explained. "Now, we're expected to practice restraint and self-control," he said. "But who knows when a completely unavoidable urge might come along? So we wear black because when the moment comes—we want to be ready!"

> **Spiritual Citations**
>
> "It is forbidden to buy from a thief anything that is stolen; it is a grave sin, since once encourages criminals, thereby inducing a thief to commit other thefts. If he finds no customer, he will not steal. 'The partner of a thief is his own enemy.'"
>
> —Maimonides, *Mishnah Torah*

You can bet your bottom dollar that the rabbi was not about to go off to another town and perform radical acts. Instead, the story illustrates the fact that Judaism does not expect people to be perfect because we weren't *created* to be perfect. The ideal in Judaism is for people to work hard on their characters so that they pretty much do the right thing if not all of the time, then *most* of the time.

Judaism also has a sense of humor about human nature. After all, the scrapes and predicaments people get into are often quite funny—although maybe not at the time or to them. The essence of being human (and the essence of being Jewish) is to maintain your sense of humor and perspective, even when the world acts like it's going insane.

Coping with Tragedy

The Holocaust was one of the most painful and tragic events in Jewish history. As such, this book examines some of the ways in which Judaism understands tragedy and loss. Perhaps the entire Jewish approach to suffering can be summed up in the words of a Holocaust survivor whose interview can be witnessed at the U.S. Holocaust Memorial in Washington. He says that one day while he was in a concentration camp, a Nazi guard noticed him praying. The guard said, "Hey, Jew, what do you have to pray for? You're stuck in here!"

The Jew responded, "Every day I thank God I don't have to be like you!"

This seemingly simple, though very powerful story, has a few items worthy of examination. First, it should be noted that even though the Jewish man was in the concentration camp, he was still praying. Even in the most dehumanizing situations, Jews never lose sight of their God—even when we don't understand what He's doing or what He's permitting other people to do. We have never entirely lost faith.

Mystical Moments

During the Holocaust, the Jews in the Warsaw ghetto knew that they would soon face an attack from the Germans. Rather than go quietly, the ghetto citizens staged an uprising that was successful in repelling the Germans for nearly a month—longer than it took the Nazis to conquer all of Poland.

Another key element of the story is the courage that the Jewish man displayed in responding so boldly to the Nazi guard's taunt. Jews are a proud people (the Bible describes us as "stiff-necked," meaning stubborn). The Jewish man literally took his life in his hands by mouthing off to the guard. Countless Jews were killed in the concentration camps for the slightest infractions, and this statement was full of disrespect. Miraculously, the guard didn't kill the Jewish man, perhaps out of respect for the bold and honest courage the Jew displayed in summing up his values and beliefs. One wonders how the Nazi guard was affected by that exchange!

Don't Believe a Word I Say

Despite the role God has played in Jewish history, today there are many forms of Judaism that do not even involve a concept of God. Indeed, many Jews don't even believe in the existence of God. There are even plenty of Reform and Reconstructionist rabbis who don't believe in God, many of who practice "predicate theology." This practice involves asking the question, "If there *were* a God, what would God expect from us?" In other words, even if there is no God, we still need to act as if there were one and be the best people we can be.

Many spiritual, thoughtful Jews look at the suffering and unfairness in today's world and conclude that either God set the world in motion and then departed or that the world came into being through some nontheistic means. Of the major Western religions, only Judaism offers a broad highway for the nonbeliever.

Whether you believe that the Torah—the first five books of the Bible—is the irrefutable word of God, a guidebook not to be taken literally, or even a collection of myths lacking divine origin or authorship, there's a place for you among the Jewish people. There are spiritual lessons to be learned throughout Jewish literature and history that hit home whether one is Orthodox, Conservative, Reform, Reconstructionist, nondenominational, or none of the above. Judaism is a very broad tent indeed, with plenty of room underneath for differing approaches and beliefs. Truly, every Jew does set his or her own shulchan aruch at the great banquet of Jewish spirituality.

> **Spiritual Citations**
>
> "Three things to which the Torah is compared: to the desert, to fire, and to water. This is to tell you that just as these three things are free to all who come into the world, so also are the words of the Torah, free to all who come into the world."
>
> —Midrash, Mekhilta

Prophecy, Spirituality, and Mysticism

Judaism, throughout its early history, was a *prophetic* religion. This means that there were a series of individuals who were minding their own business when suddenly they heard the voice of God. Their lives—and ours—were never the same again. An individual to whom God reaches out is called a *prophet*, and the word of God that they hear is their prophecy. A prophet, in short, is someone who has a conversation with God, with God initiating the conversation. The great Jewish theologian Abraham Joshua Heschel described this phenomenon as "God in search of man."

You know the stories. Adam and Eve living in the Garden of Eden under divine instructions what to eat—and what not to eat. (Does that make the Bible the first diet book?)

Noah suddenly receiving instructions from God about how and why to build an ark. (The flood's coming and the wicked will be swept out with the tide.) The AARP-ready Abraham learning from God that he will be the father not just of a son but of a great nation. His grandson Jacob wrestling with an angel (angel is the Greek word for "messenger from God"). Moses spying a burning bush that relays God's message to ask Pharaoh to "let my people go" (release the Jews from slavery).

If we say *prophetic*, we are talking about a situation in which God contacted people who were especially attuned to hearing God's voice. This describes most of the major personnages of the Bible—their spirituality was strong enough for them to "perceive" the presence of God in ways that other people could not. The age of prophecy in Judaism ended more than 2,500 years ago, though, people still wanted to find their own connections to God. The Kabbalists, whom we will discuss in detail in later chapters, felt a powerful urge to unite themselves with the Divine. They were driven by their spirituality to connect with God however they could—through study, song, meditation, and prayer. We'll examine both mystical and prophetic ways that Jews have achieved a sense of oneness with their Creator.

In short, if we use the term *mystical*, we are speaking about human efforts to contact God. When we say *spiritual*, we mean that we are concerned not just with the material world we see around us, but we are also concerned with the unseen aspects of life. So we can say that Judaism is all three. It's a prophetic religion, in that God reached out to individuals like Abraham and Moses; it's mystical, in that people have reached out to contact God in ways we will explore in this book; and it's spiritual, in that it deals with matters of the human spirit.

Prophets and Losses

After the Jewish people entered the land of Israel, God occasionally chose individuals to speak to directly. According to tradition, there were thousands of such prophets. The prophecy (the word of God) as spoken to the most important of these individuals (Isaiah, Ezekiel, Jeremiah, Joel, Micah, and so on) was recorded in the Bible. The Jewish people had an unfortunate tendency to forget their heritage and responsibilities, so God would speak through these individuals to warn what would happen if we didn't straighten out. The punishments the prophets described were as dire as the rewards for observing God's will were desirable.

Devine Devarim

Prophet A messenger of divine will.

Despite these warnings, the "stiff-necked" Jewish people continued sinning. The ultimate result: The loss of our homeland, our monarchy (there were Jewish kings in the land of Israel for centuries), and the loss of the holy temple in Jerusalem.

According to Jewish belief, when the temple was destroyed by the Romans in the year 70 C.E., the gift of prophecy was also lost. No longer did God favor certain individuals with the unexpected gift of His word. Jews had lost that direct pipeline from their Father in Heaven.

Reach Out and Touch …

Two new approaches arose in the absence of direct prophecy. One was the attempt to cod-ify God's law in what we know as the Talmud. The other was the rise of what we can call *mystical* Judaism. If prophecy involves God reaching out to man, mysticism is the opposite: mysticism means that the conversation begins with people reaching up to God.

Over the centuries, the mystical approach resulted in the development of the Kabbalah as well as the writing of the Zohar (both of which I'll discuss in Chapter 16, "Kabbalah: Spiritual Life at a Million Miles Per Hour"). There's a wonderful expression about this kind of Judaism: Those who know about it don't talk, and those who talk about it don't know. So you are stuck with an author who falls into the latter category. Since I'm talking about it, I must not know what I'm talking about! Nonetheless, I've been permitted a few glimpses into these fascinating realms, and I'll share with you what I've learned.

Together we'll explore the Jewish concepts of who or what God is, how and why the world was formed, and where we go from here—the Jewish concept of the afterlife and the Jewish concept of the coming of the Messiah. But above all, we'll delve into the Jewish notion of *character*. As stated earlier, character and spirituality are inseparable in Judaism. In Judaism, it's impossible to be spiritual without being of fine moral character. There is no spirituality in Judaism separate from the question of "What kind of person am I?"

The result of this 3,000-year quest for character is found in Mark Twain's essay "Concerning the Jews," which appeared in *Harper's Magazine* in March 1898:

> *The Jew is not a disturber of the peace of any country. Even his enemies will concede that. He is not a loafer, he is not a sot, he is not noisy, he is not a brawler nor a rioter, he is not quarrel-some. In the statistics of crime his presence is conspicuously rare—in all countries. With murder and other crimes of violence he has but little to do: he is a stranger to the hangman. In the police court's daily long roll of "assaults" and "drunk and disorderlies" his name seldom appears.*

> *That the Jewish home is a home in the truest sense is a fact which no one will dispute. The family is knitted together by the strongest affections; its members show each other every due respect; and reverence for the elders is an inviolate law of the house. The Jew is not a burden on the charities of the state nor of the city; these could cease from their functions without affecting him.*

> *When he is well enough, he works; when he is incapacitated, his own people take care of him. And not in a poor and stingy way, but with a fine and large benevolence. His race is entitled to*

*be called the most benevolent of all the races of men. A Jewish beggar is not impossible, perhaps;
such a thing may exist, but there are few men that can say they have seen that spectacle.*

How did Twain come to these conclusions? What secrets of spirituality does the 3,000-
year-old literature of the Jewish people contain?

Mystical Moments

In the first book of Samuel, the Jewish people find their first king, Saul, unseated
after disobeying an order from God. Saul is replaced by David, who to this day
is lauded by Jews in verse as "David, king of Israel, who lives and flourishes."
It is David who sets Jerusalem as Judaism's capital. Although mainly a detailed
account of David's life, the book of Samuel was named for its prophetic author,
who was instrumental in bringing both Saul and David to power.

I wouldn't have the slightest answer to those questions if it weren't for a test I failed when
I was 11 years old. At the time, I was growing up in the heavily Jewish suburb of Roslyn,
New York. I attended Sunday school at Temple Sinai and, like so many of my peers,
planned on leaving that educational system as soon as I got through my Bar Mitzvah so
that I could sleep in on the weekends. One Sunday, we were given a national Bible quiz
and I did so well that I was to represent my temple at the regional levels of the competition. I was given a section of the Bible to study, the first book of Samuel. I read over the
chapters a couple of times and had virtually no understanding of what was happening.
Nevertheless, on the appointed Sunday, my Dad drove me to a public school in Manhattan to take the next level of the test.

A few hundred kids my age were already waiting. At my table sat a few Orthodox kids—at
least I assumed they were Orthodox because they were wearing yarmulkes, or skullcaps,
on their heads. The monitors came around and we each received our tests. My test was in
English. Multiple choice. The Orthodox kids' tests
were in Hebrew. And they had essay questions, which
they had to answer in Hebrew!

Devine Devarim

The **Torah** is the first five
books of the Bible. The **Talmud** is
the great, vast compendium of
Jewish law, lore, custom, and history, consisting partially of the
Mishna.

I was steamed. I honestly felt a little cheated. How
come they knew so much about Judaism that they could
write answers to essay questions *in Hebrew* while I was
struggling to choose between the four answers handed
to me? Then and there, I decided that one day I would
learn everything they knew about Judaism—and more.
They were so calm and relaxed as they wrote out their

answers. I can still see their Hebrew handwriting flying over the page, while I chanted, "Eenie-meenie-miney-mo."

I didn't pass that level of the test, by the way.

Yeshiva Time

Ten years later, I was backpacking through Europe when I met another guy from the college I attended. He had with him a then-famous *Rolling Stone* article about a woman whose brother had gone to a yeshiva, or school, in Jerusalem and had become Orthodox. She went to visit him and got into big arguments with the rabbis about everything to do with Judaism. This was great—now I knew how I'd go about learning what the other kids knew at the Bible competition a decade earlier. I'd go to that kind of yeshiva, and I'd find out for myself.

Well, I did exactly that. After college, I worked for about six months, then went to Israel to learn in yeshiva. I learned Hebrew, as well as some Aramaic (the language of much of the Talmud). Inside the texts I discovered many secrets of Jewish spirituality that were the traditional province of religiously educated Jews. I've since published five books and have lectured on Jewish subjects across the United States.

Now I'm here to pass on what I've learned to you. Get ready for a 3,000-year ride through Jewish learning and wisdom. If this book succeeds, then you'll have a firm grounding in Jewish mysticism and spirituality. You'll know what Judaism says about where the world came from … and where it's going. You'll know what it means, in Jewish terms, to be a good, spiritual person. When it comes to the great banquet of spiritual living, you'll know better how to set your own table.

The Least You Need to Know

- Jewish beliefs vary from movement to movement within Judaism, and even from individual to individual, although certain common threads exist.
- Despite centuries of tragedy, Jews still maintain a sense of humor.
- Jewish prophets spoke directly with God.
- Spirituality means sensitivity to matters of the spirit, prophecy means God contacting people, and mysticism means people reaching out to make contact with God.

The Bible: Judaism's Spirituality Sourcebook

In This Chapter

- ◆ The Bible's magic recipe
- ◆ Worldwide appeal for scripture
- ◆ The Bible's author
- ◆ The Torah in a nutshell

The beauty of Biblical stories is that they capture the imagination of people of all ages. The tales evoke a sense of wonder and power in children, reminding them that we are heirs to a great tradition stretching back into the mists of time. The stories teach values and demonstrate the difference between right and wrong. We learn of kindness through Rebecca, who gives water to Eliezer at the well. We see Moses moving beyond a sense of unworthiness to the ultimate position of Jewish leadership in his time. These stories have impressed hundreds of generations of Jewish children.

Sadly, if we are exposed to these stories only in childhood, we miss out on the full impact they have on our adult lives. People enjoy moralistic stories much

Mystical Moments

Traditional Jews study the Bible every year, with the cycle beginning again after Simchat Torah, the celebration of the law that concludes the New Year holiday season each fall. Every late September and October, Jews around the world go "back to school" by studying the week's *parasha*, or Torah portion.

more than they enjoy straightforward rules—force creates resistance. This isn't to suggest that the Bible shies away from issuing specific rules. The more we look into the events of the Bible, the more we realize those stories aren't kid stuff. If the situations described in the Bible couldn't be understood on a deeper level than how they're taught to children, there's no way that Jews would have maintained their interest in the Bible for the last 3,000 years.

Most Jews today don't realize just how rich the Jewish Bible is as a source of spirituality, character guidance, for understanding the purpose and meaning of life and the existence and nature of God.

What's Missing from the Bible?

The Bible is thought of as a source of comfort in times of need, a text whose every page contains thoughts to inspire, assuage your doubts, and get you through the night.

The Bible can therefore be a very disappointing book to read. It can be hard to follow. It often jumps from topic to topic, story to story. There are gaps—a lot of what you think you'll find in the Bible isn't there.

For example, many of us grew up hearing the story of young Abraham and his father's shop of clay idols. Even as a boy, Abraham knew that idols were powerless and that there was only one God, who could not be depicted in clay. To make this point to his father, Abraham smashed all but the largest of the idols in the shop and put a hammer in the hands of the biggest idol.

Spiritual Citations

"Intense study of the Bible will keep any writer from being vulgar."

—Samuel Taylor Coleridge (1772–1834)

His father returned. "What happened to my idols?" he asked angrily. "Abraham, did you do this?"

"Don't look at me," Abraham responded, calmly hooking a thumb at the big idol. "*He* did it."

Abraham's father, of course, is stuck. If he replies that idols can't break each other, then he's acknowledging that his whole enterprise—and idolatrous worldview—is a sham. So he can't punish Abraham, even though it's completely obvious that Abraham, and not Big Idol, did the destructive work.

Remember that Bible story from your childhood? There's only one problem. It isn't in the Bible! It's actually in a book called the midrash, a collection of stories the rabbis culled about the various personalities and events in the Bible. As to Abraham's childhood, the Bible itself is silent.

Frequently, even the tales we *think* are in the Bible aren't. Just as important, much of the knowledge we *hope* to find within its covers is also conspicuously missing. It would be great if the Bible contained any of the following:

 ♦ A chapter on explaining the nature of God

 ♦ A detailed section on how to pray

 ♦ A definitive list of what you need to do in order to be a good person

Unfortunately, the Bible contains none of these. Anyone dipping in to find spiritual nourishment may find himself or herself disappointed.

So the question is this: What is in the Bible, and why has it succeeded in speaking to generation after generation for almost 3,000 years?

> **High Spirits**
>
> "To what do I attribute my longevity? Cool mountain water. That and a stuffed cabbage."
>
> —Mel Brooks as the 2,000-year-old man

The Magic Ingredients

You can think of the Bible as a combination of four elements: mystery, history, poetry, and law. Let's look at each element in turn.

Mystery

The Bible contains many extraordinary, inexplicable, or supernatural events: the creation of the world; the first times God spoke to human beings (Eve and Adam, Noah, Abraham, Jacob, and Moses, to name a few); the creation and destruction of the Tower of Babel; Noah and the flood; Abraham's near-sacrifice of Isaac; Jacob wrestling with an angel; the Exodus from Egypt; survival for 40 years in the desert; and the deliverance of the land of Israel to the Jewish people. Each of these events—and so many others—is so thought-provoking that millions of readers have thumbed the Bible's pages, making it the best-selling book *of all time*. Fascinated devotees and skeptics alike find themselves asking the same questions: Did these events really happen as written? What impact do these stories have on our lives today? How much should I believe?

Almost 30 centuries after it was written, the Jewish people continue to render the same verdict: *Can't put it down.*

Devine Devarim

In Hebrew, the words **Aseret ha-Dibrot** are commonly known as the Ten Commandments. However, a more exact translation would probably be the "Ten Statements." "Ten Commandments" in Hebrew would read as "Aseret ha-Mitzvot." The exact translation of the first commandment actually reads more like a statement— "I am the Lord your God who brought you out of the land of Egypt, the house of bondage."—so in Hebrew, the word "commandment" does not quite fit as readily as in English. The commandments can be found in two locations in the Bible, Exodus 20:2–14 and Deuteronomy 5:6–18, each slightly different in wording.

History

The Bible contains the history of the world and the founding and early history of the Jewish people. It's less an encyclopedia of spirituality organized by topic than it is the saga of the Jews, the key to understanding the personality of our nation, our role in the world, and our future. It's a work of history that spans hundreds of years, extraordinary personalities, and the best and worst of human nature.

One of the key aspects that makes the Bible so credible as history is that it never sugar-coats the facts about the Jews in order to make us look good. So much negative material about the Jews appears in the Bible—incest, rebellion, idolatry, illicit sexual relations— that you might even wonder whether it was written by the Jews' worst enemy!

The Bible pulls no punches. When we were bad, we were very, very bad. The Bible presents all of our forefathers' faults in glaring detail. We have never claimed to be descended from a race of morally pure, physically strong, and psychologically healthy supermen. We were scared, we were treacherous, we were stiff-necked and stubborn.

Spiritual Citations

"If Moses had been paid newspaper rates for the Ten Commandments, he might have written the Two Thousand Commandments."

—Isaac Bashevis Singer

For a people who are supposed to be the epitome of faith, we had a hard time believing in God or in our leaders. Take the story of the golden calf. Moses ascended Mount Sinai to receive the Ten Commandments from God. He was to be gone for 40 days. On the fortieth day following his departure, he failed to reappear. Well, of course he failed to reappear: he'd only *been gone* for 39 days. Moses and the Jewish people were using two different ways of thinking of "forty days."

Thousands of Jews who only days earlier had witnessed the splitting of the Red Sea in their escape from Egypt were certain that Moses had abandoned them and that the whole "God" story was a ruse. They melted their wives' jewelry into a golden calf (a symbol of idolatry) and danced around it in worship, much to Moses' disgust when he returned, on schedule, the next morning. No faith at all.

Take the rest of the Jews' time in the desert. This generation escaped slavery in Egypt, crossed a Red Sea that miraculously split to allow them passage yet drowned their enemies, and received delicious food (*manna*) that descended from heaven every single morning (except on the Sabbath, so they would get double portions on Fridays). How did they react? By complaining that Moses was a poor leader; that they were better off enslaved in Egypt; that in Egypt they got to eat meat and in the desert they got no meat; and on and on and on. It sounds less like the epic story of a spiritual people and more like a vacation tour that fell apart.

At the end of his life, Moses was so certain that the Jews were likely to forget God and commit every conceivable abomination that he actually took up a good-sized chunk of the book of Deuteronomy (*Devarim* in Hebrew) to threaten them with horrible curses should they go astray. The remainder of the Bible tells the history of the Jews repeatedly going astray—worshipping other gods, praying but acting poorly, committing murder. Even King David, the great leader from the most humble of beginnings, was no role model. He coveted a beautiful woman and sent her husband to die in battle so he could snag his babe. It's just wrong, I tell you, but it's all in the Bible.

Poetry

From the blessings Jacob bestowed on his 12 sons to the Songs of the Sea sung by Moses and his sister Miriam in gratitude for Jewish survival and escape from Egypt, the Bible is replete with some of the greatest poetry the world has ever known. Of course, the text was originally written in Hebrew, a terse, powerful language that lends itself to poetic expression. (Not every language is lovely to the ear; the Dutch, for example, write all their love songs in French.) We'll explore the poetry of the Bible and examine what relevance it may have to our post-millennial lives in later chapters.

Law

The Bible is, among other things, a law book, establishing a legal system for the Jews both in the desert and for their entrance into the land of Israel. The Bible sets forth everything from criminal and civil law to observance of Sabbath and the planting and sowing of crops. Christianity and Islam use the laws of the Jewish Bible as the starting points for their own legal systems.

While the Bible is often quite specific about how people are meant to live, it is often more like the U.S. Constitution in that it lays down general principles that are to be interpreted in the light of changing circumstances. Just as the American Founding Fathers could not have predicted (or legislated) traffic lights or speed limits, so the Bible does not seek to predict the discovery of electricity or the invention of the telephone. Yet both of these concepts are regulated for Sabbath use by principles laid down in the Bible.

Just Like Us

Part of the allure and appeal of the Bible is that even 3,000 years later, we can still relate to the people it describes. At times they're contentious, egotistical, dishonest, self-serving and cruel, while elsewhere they are courageous, bold, shockingly honest, self-sacrificing, humble, and ingenious.

In short, they're just like people today. The stories of their triumphs and tragedies have been powerful enough to speak to readers for millennia. We live in a self-help world where we expect that books will solve all our problems with neat, simple solutions spelled out for us in bite-sized informational chunks. That's not the Bible. The Bible wasn't written with the sole intention of speaking to our generation. It's had to be useful for thousands of years.

The Bible has the awesome responsibility of speaking to people who have lived in every situation in human history, from times when most people rarely ventured outside their own village to a day when we routinely travel into outer space. In December 1968, when the first manned Apollo mission circled the moon (landing there wouldn't happen for another seven months), what do you think the astronauts read aloud to the folks back home on Earth? "In the beginning, God created the heavens and the Earth."

When the Bible was written, information traveled slowly. The ancient Israeli version of the Internet consisted of signal fires set at the top of hills so that Jews across the land could know that a new month had been declared at the court in Jerusalem. (Even back then, there were hackers: Residents of Shomron, or Samaria, would sometimes set misleading signal fires to throw people off.) The Bible made sense to the Jews who lived back then, when news traveled by fire; and it still makes sense today, when modern telecom tools like e-mail and cell phones convey information across the planet in milliseconds.

The Bible might not be as instantly rewarding to the reader as the average instant guru's guide to spirituality that you can buy in a bookstore. But you've got to admire its track record (and if you're a publisher, you've got to admire its sales record). Its longevity attests to the fact that it has much to offer … even if it takes some digging and delving to discover what those spiritual secrets might be.

"In the Beginning ..."

Let's take a look at that first sentence, one that was written approximately 3,000 years ago and was read aloud on that first manned mission to the Moon: "In the beginning, God created the heavens and the earth."

The key to good writing is to insinuate questions and avoid answering them immediately (or perhaps ever). Unanswered questions stop readers in their tracks. Take Charles Dickens's *A Tale of Two Cities*: "It was the best of times; it was the worst of times." Wait a minute, the reader shouts. How can that be? It's one or the other, never both. Or could it be the best of times for some people and the worst of times for others? What exactly does the author mean by that? By the time you've figured out the answer, you're so deeply engaged with the novel that there's no putting it down.

> **Spiritual Citations**
>
> "God's gift of the power of speech was as important as the creation of the world."
>
> —Rabbi Hama ben Hanina, third-century Talmudic scholar

Or try this: "Call me Ishmael." The first three words of Herman Melville's *Moby Dick*. Here are the questions those three little words raise: Who's talking? Why are you talking to me? Why aren't you telling me your real name? Where are we? What's going on? Why'd you choose Ishmael as your false name? (If you know your scripture, you know that Ishmael was the son of Abraham by his wife Sarah's handmaid, Hagar, and that the scorned Sarah expelled the adulterous couple from the home.) Why associate yourself with that name?

If the first lines of two novels written more than 100 years ago can raise that many inquiries, imagine how many questions fire off in a reader's mind with that first Biblical sentence: "In the beginning, God created the heavens and the Earth." Here are just a few of the questions that have been raised in readers' minds for 30 centuries: Who is God?

Why did He (if it is a He) create the heavens and the Earth? How could it be the "beginning" if God already exists? How did God create everything, with *The Complete Idiot's Guide to Creating Time*? More recently, since Darwin, people have been asking about the fossil record. What about evolution? Are we meant to take those words literally or are they meant in some allegorical way? How do we know there's a God in the first place? How do we know the whole universe didn't just start on its own? And who's the author of this book? On what evidence does the author base his bold opening statement?

All good questions. There's a wonderful expression: "Where you stand depends on where you sit." In other words, how you feel about an issue depends on your position, whether we're talking politics, religion, sports, or the break-up of the Beatles. As we noted in the previous chapter, the difficulty in writing about Judaism is that there are almost as many types of Judaisms as there are Jews. There are Jews who believe that every word of the Bible is literally true. There are Jews who believe that the stories were knit together over a period of generations or even centuries. Some Jews think the whole Bible is myth, and the sooner disposed of, the better.

There are still others who believe that the Bible is holy not because it's "true" but because Jews have considered it holy for centuries. And there are other Jews who accept that portions of the Bible are accurate and true while others borrow from contemporaneous cultures. For example, the Mesopotamians had a book called the *Enuma Elish* in which a flood story not unlike Noah's is detailed. The story of Joseph's temptation by the wife of Potiphar (Pharaoh's minister) has many parallels in world literature. In short, 10 Jews, 20 opinions.

In this book, I'm going to be as open as I can to presenting all sides of every issue because I don't want anyone to say, "This guy doesn't share my point of view! I'm outta here!" But I do want to suggest that the more you're open to challenging your own personal beliefs about the Bible (and the rest of Jewish literature that we'll explore), the more you'll learn and the more deeply you'll be able to experience Jewish spirituality yourself.

Author! Author!

Who wrote the Bible? A vexing question indeed. No one knows for certain—even within Orthodox Judaism there are varying opinions. The primary Orthodox opinion is that God dictated the first five books of the Bible to Moses, who wrote them down in the form we read today. Those first five books are commonly called the *Torah*, which literally means "instruction" or "enlightenment." According to one tradition, the Hebrew word *ohr* ("light") is at the heart of the word "Torah." (Alternatively, the Torah is also referred to as the Pentateuch or Five Books of Moses.)

The book of Genesis (*Beraishit* in Hebrew) begins with Creation and proceeds through the lives of Cain and Abel, Noah and the flood, and the patriarchs and matriarchs (Abraham and Sarah; Isaac and Rebecca; Jacob and his two wives, Leah and Rachel; and Jacob's 12 sons). The book concludes with the Israelites (they aren't called Jews just yet) in Egypt, where they have traveled due to famine in what will later be called the land of Israel.

Devine Devarim

The fourth book of the Bible, **Bamidbar** in Hebrew, is known as **Numbers** in English because events open with a census taken of the entire Jewish people.

Exodus (*Shemot* in Hebrew) picks up the story in Egypt. The Jews are now slaves to Pharaoh, who orders the deaths of the firstborn Jewish boys. Moses is born to a Jewish woman who puts him in a small raft on the Nile; the babe is found by a daughter of Pharaoh who unwittingly hires Moses' mother as a wet nurse. Moses grows up in the home of the Pharaoh and eventually is chosen by God to lead the Jews out of Egypt. After repeated pleas—and plagues—Pharaoh relents. The Jews leave Egypt in haste (no time for baking bread; hence matzah), traverse the Red Sea thoughtfully split by God on their behalf, and enter the desert. There, as we discussed earlier, Moses goes up to get the law from God, comes down a day late by his people's calculations, and discovers thousands of Jews worshipping a golden calf. This is only the first infraction against the will of God detailed in the Torah. You get the sense that many of the Jews want to go back to Egypt and fire their travel agent.

Then comes Mount Sinai and the pronouncement of the Ten Commandments (discussed in detail in Chapter 10, "The Main Event"). The book of Exodus concludes with a brief overview of civil law that's quite sensitive to the needs of the individual both in its time and in ours; and a lengthy description of the *mishkan*, the prefab tabernacle that accompanies the Jews for their 40 years in the desert. The mishkan also houses the tablets on which the Ten Commandments are inscribed.

High Spirits

A 17-year-old asks his father for a car. "I'll make you a deal," says the dad. "For the next semester, you have to get good grades, attend temple every week, and cut your hair. If you can do all that, then we'll see." The son agrees.

Three months later he comes back to his dad, his straight-A report card in hand. "Hmm," says the father, "and you've attended temple as well. However, you haven't cut your hair."

"I've been thinking about that," says the son. "All those guys we learn about in temple—Moses, Abraham, David—they all had long hair."

"Yeah," his father replies. "And they walked everywhere!"

Next comes the book of Leviticus (*Vayikra* in Hebrew), which is mostly given over to the animal sacrifices to be offered in the great Temple in Jerusalem, built 480 years after the Jews enter the land of Israel. The laws of kashrut are also described in detail in Leviticus, as well as an overview of the various Jewish holidays and the Sabbath, and more of the rules for life in the land of Israel, which the Jews are shortly to attain.

The fourth book is Numbers (*Bamidbar* in Hebrew), which contains the Jews' further misadventures in the desert. After various laws are set forth, we find a number of dramatic situations. Moses' sister Miriam criticizes him behind his back and is punished for doing so. The rebel Korach and his followers challenge the authority of Moses … with disastrous results. The Jews go to war against Sichon, the king of the Moabites, and Og, the king of Bashan, and win. Some Jews commit immoral acts with women from the surrounding peoples, worship their gods, and pay a huge price. A group of Jewish spies secretly enter the land of Israel … but 10 of the 12 return only to tell lies that the land is unfriendly and is possessed by a race of giants. A lot happens in Numbers.

Finally we come to Deuteronomy, which literally means "Second reading or Repetition of the Law." In Hebrew, the book is called *Devarim*. Here Moses addresses the entire Jewish nation as it stands ready to enter the land of Israel, recapping their entire 40-year history in the desert. He prepares the people to enter the land, admonishes them against breaking God's law, and sets forth the blessings and curses that await if they obey or disobey their Creator. Moses dies at the end of the book, destined to be buried in an unmarked grave in a location described only as "opposite Baal Peor."

Mystical Moments

You won't find Baal Peor on Mapquest. Baal Peor was the name of a heathen god who stood for the concept of randomness or chaos. Baal Peor is code for the idea that everything in life happens by chance. That Moses' resting place is "opposite Baal Peor" implies that he stands for the proposition that life isn't random or chaotic or driven by chance.

Question: What about the last eight lines, which describe the death and burial of Moses? Who wrote those lines? There are two schools of thought within Orthodox Judaism: the first that God dictated those lines to Moses, who wrote them with tears streaming down his cheeks because he knew his time had come. Other biblical scholars suggest that Joshua, Moses' second-in-command and the leader who took over after his death, commandeered the pen.

There you have it: a very brief overview of what is contained in the Five Books of Moses, the beginning of the Bible, what Jews call the *Torah*. But we still don't have answers to any of the initial questions we posed: Who is God; why did he create the universe, if he did; who wrote the Bible; and what spiritual guidance does it offer us today. Let's tackle the first of those questions—who is God?—in the next chapter.

The Least You Need to Know

- ◆ Despite being 3,000 years old, the Bible still has relevancy in modern society.
- ◆ The Bible's popularity is due in part to the key ingredients of mystery, history, poetry, and law.
- ◆ The true author of the Bible is still subject to debate, although most Orthodox Jews believe Moses wrote the Torah.
- ◆ Events depicted in the Bible contain the moral and ethical codes by which Jews live their lives.

Who Is God?

In This Chapter

- ◆ Believing in God
- ◆ Characteristics and will of God
- ◆ The (bad) luck of the Jewish people
- ◆ Judaism's definition of sin

There is no absolute proof for the existence of God. If anyone tells you otherwise, ask to see evidence. It just doesn't exist.

This may seem like a strange way to begin a discussion of the Jewish concept of God, but it really makes the most sense. The whole concept of a connection to God starts with the idea of faith. If there were absolute proof of God's existence, faith wouldn't be necessary. Traditional Judaism believes that God has provided enough clues to His existence for us to discard all doubt. But each of us has to come to a conclusion about the question of God's existence for ourselves.

Is There Somebody out There?

For millennia, it was unthinkable to be a Jew who didn't believe in God. While Jewish history is replete with Jews who ignored the Bible, the commandments of God, and even direct contact from God (witness Jonah, whom we'll discuss in detail), until the last few hundred years, nearly everyone believed.

What changed? The Christian world in the eighteenth century entered the Age of Reason, during which time everything—even the existence of God—had to be proven absolutely in order to hold water. Jews were not immune to this turn in philosophical events, and many Jews came to doubt the existence of God.

It's not hard to doubt that God exists. Look around. We see wars, killings, crime, tragedy, sick children, innocents dying for no reason, and so many other sad, inexplicable events.

> **High Spirits**
>
> Q. How many Orthodox Jews does it take to change a light-bulb?
> A. Change?! There will be no *change.*

And yet, it's also hard *not* to believe that God exists. Once again: Look around! We see beauty, the orderliness of the planets and the seasons, the extraordinary complexity of the world, repetition of design patterns in nature such as the veins on a leaf and the veins on our hands, the ability of humans to create and enjoy art and music, our capacity to love and be loved, the wonder of sex, and on and on. There's a fascinating saying: The believer only has to explain the existence of God. The atheist has to explain everything else.

To Believe or Not Believe

Do you have to accept the idea of God to be a good Jew? The answer to this question depends on the branch of Judaism to which you adhere. For the Orthodox, the existence of God is a given. It's where everything in Judaism begins. God spoke to Moses on Mount Sinai and gave the Jewish people their basic marching orders, which we follow to this day: to be a symbol of God in the world. One of the worst titles you could bestow upon an Orthodox Jew is *cofer ba-ikar,* one who denies the basic point of Judaism that God exists and gave us the Torah to follow.

Reform Judaism is a two-century old movement that seeks to blend Judaism with modern times. Conservative Judaism is a middle ground, combining adherence to tradition with awareness of modernity. Reconstructionist Judaism, the newest movement, focuses on the cultural aspects of Judaism.

> **Spiritual Citations**
>
> "God is of no importance unless he is of supreme importance."
> —Abraham Joshua Heschel

Maimonides, the great twelfth-century Egyptian Jewish codifier of law, wrote 13 principles of faith, later incorporated into the *Yigdal,* that are still sung each week at the conclusion of Sabbath services. The first principle in the Yigdal is that God exists. The very basis of

Orthodox belief is that you can't have Judaism—or even a universe—without God. Even so, no Orthodox Jew would interrogate his brother over his 100-percent faith in God and the Torah. Faith is a personal matter. In Orthodoxy, it's expected that you believe, but no one's going to spring a pop spirituality quiz on you.

I once asked a *rosh yeshiva* (the head of a school) in Jerusalem whether he believed absolutely that God existed. He responded, "I'm 85-percent intellectually convinced. My momentum carries me the rest of the way." His words showed me that even in Orthodoxy, the most traditional of today's approaches to Judaism, there's room for a little bit of uncertainty. After all, how can we be absolutely sure of something we haven't seen with our own eyes? And besides, few of us live our lives with 100 percent proof of *anything*.

Other branches of Judaism, such as Reform and Reconstructionist, do not make belief in God a tenet of faith. Indeed, many Reform and Reconstructionist rabbis do *not* believe in the existence of God for the reasons we discussed previously. Their position is that even though we might not have a complete scientific explanation for the creation of the world, it's highly unlikely that some kind of Being created it and it's even more unlikely, given the messy state of human affairs, that a God could be in charge. Where was God during the Holocaust? they might ask. Why would he allow the World Trade Center attack, or even the starvation of a single child in Africa? Why would he permit any of the darkest moments in human history?

Traditional Judaism does not claim to have definitive answers to these questions, for the simple reason that God hasn't come down lately and issued a policy paper on the subject. Traditional Judaism believes in the concept of *bechirat hofshi*, or free will. In other words, God essentially gave humankind the freedom to do as they pleased, right or wrong. However, he also gave them a conscience in the hopes that it would curb their wrongdoings.

Devine Devarim

bechirat hofshi   free will

Another traditional explanation is that God is like parents who sit in the bleachers and watch their kids make all kinds of errors. The natural urge for a parent is to run onto the field and say, "No! You're holding the bat wrong! Do it this way!" But unless parents restrain themselves, their children will never learn. According to this approach, human history consists of humans making their own mistakes and trying the best they can while God stands on the sidelines hoping they will choose right over wrong.

Good vs. Bad

If you don't have to believe in God to be a "good Jew," then what exactly is a good Jew? And for that matter, are there bad Jews? At this point in Jewish history, where we've been through so many travails and nightmares as a people, I don't think you'll find too many cases of Jews declaring their brethren "bad." There are isolated, unfortunate examples, such as those Jews in Israel who do not accept the right of Conservative Jews to worship as they please and harass their services. Otherwise, Jews live in a sometimes uneasy truce with each other.

Orthodox and non-Orthodox Jews have few points of contact, rather like members of a large extended family who have little contact and don't know much about each other. The point of this book is to make all Jews and all people interested in Judaism knowledgeable about Judaism, so they can make informed decisions for themselves.

Spiritual Citations

"As one thinks of God in his heart, so does God think of him."

—The Rav of Medzibezh

Let's return to the subject of just what we know about God. We cannot be absolutely sure that God exists, but traditional Jews have little if any doubt about the subject. What makes them so certain?

Richard Feynmann, the Nobel Prize-winning physicist (and a Jew!), made the point in his essays that he just didn't think God existed. He believed that the universe simply exists as a backdrop to the battle between good and evil. Traditional Jews believe the exact opposite—that the universe is a very beautiful, complex, aesthetically stunning landscape for the battle between good and evil, which rages on in each of us every single day.

According to traditional Jewish belief, God predated and created the universe out of a sense of cosmic loneliness. The Jewish concept of God is of a loving, creative Being who (if we may anthropomorphize) felt frustrated at having no one else in the universe upon whom to bestow his love. For thousands of years, Jews have believed that God created the universe out of a sense of love and a need to share that love with others.

He Speaks, We Breathe

How did God create the world? Through the power of speech. God spoke, and things— big things—happened. "In the beginning, God created the heavens and the earth," the book of Genesis begins. It's possible to interpret that line in a different manner: "In the beginning, God created the physical world and the spiritual world." How did God's speech cause the world to come into being? How did God further speak and cause darkness and light to separate, oceans to form, continents to appear, mountains to rise up, forests and streams, animals, and finally people to appear? God knows. We sure don't.

Certainly, until the European Age of Reason three centuries ago, virtually everyone in the Western tradition took for granted that God created the universe. They might have had different names or concepts for that "God force," but there was never a culture that posited that the universe somehow spontaneously came into existence. The ancient

Greeks believed that God created the universe. Aristotle called God the "Prime Mover." The Romans believed in God—actually, in lots of gods. All three of the major Western religions—Judaism, Christianity, and Islam—believed. Doubt has only crept into the picture relatively recently in human history.

Mystical Moments

Science may yet find a way to verify exactly what happened millions of years ago, but right now only theories exist. It's important to recognize that no theory about the creation of the world currently accepted by the leading men and women of science conflicts with the first few lines of the book of Genesis. If anything, science is limited to determining the *mechanisms* by which the world and all its constituent parts came into being. Who put those mechanisms in place? You'll need more than a radio telescope to determine that answer. In fact, you'll need faith. So far, there's no absolutely certain way to prove or disprove that God set the whole thing in motion.

You might argue that people today are much smarter than people hundreds of years ago. My college class once asked our Greek history professor whether he would like to have lived in ancient Greece. "Are you kidding?" he asked disdainfully. "Do you know what dentistry was like back then?" In many ways human history has evolved. We no longer burn witches at the stake, we have the Internet and jet planes, and we have all the tools of modern communication.

And yet, in other ways, humanity has taken major steps backward. The twentieth century was the bloodiest in human history because of our ability to mechanize the process of killing people. We have the greatest levels of universal education the world has known, and yet there exists as much xenophobia and bigotry as ever before. Our economic system permits the greatest number of people in human history to live in comfort, and yet most of the people on the planet live in the direst poverty with no chance of escape. We have never understood nature so well or been able to harness its energy, and yet we have never been so destructive of nature for our own selfish uses.

Spiritual Citations

"True worship is not a petition to God. It is a sermon to ourselves."

—Emil G. Hirsch, German-Jewish industrialist

So maybe we're not quite as wise and all-knowing as we think we are!

Other generations might not have known as much, or have traveled as much, or communicated with the ease that people of our era do. But they made up for those deficiencies, if you will, with a certain level of intellectual modesty. They were not as quick to dismiss the possibility that Something was responsible for the creation and continued existence of the universe. Jews have always called that Something God.

God's First Mistakes, Er ... Humans

Let's travel back once again to the dawn of creation. God brings the universe into existence out of an all-too-human need to share love with others. His first two human creations are Adam and Eve. Note that their souls were pure and untainted.

Mystical Moments

Traditional Judaism believes that, although it cannot be seen or examined or touched, the soul is the essence of a person. It's the part of us that lives on in this world after the body dies. It's the point of connection between God and people, between the physical and spiritual worlds, between the visible and the unseen.

Everything's just swell in Eden, until along comes the snake with his recipe book, *1001 Ways to Serve Fruit from the Tree of Knowledge*. Eve takes a bite, Adam follows suit, and suddenly the game's over. The Garden of Eden is closed: "You'll have to leave now; drive home safely."

The story of Adam and Eve offers an important clue to the nature of the Jewish concept of God: *There are rules.* We have a glorious world in which to live, but we also have responsibilities. God is fair and loving, Judaism posits, because he makes clear what those rules are. God didn't trick Adam and Eve into eating the fruit; they knew that they had to live not by the Ten Commandments but by the One Commandment: *Thou shalt not eat the fruit from the tree of knowledge of good and evil.* And yet they violated that one simple rule, and there was a price to pay.

Are You in God's Will?

In Judaism there is a concept of doing God's will. The Talmud says that if we unbend our will to do God's will, then God will likewise bend the will of others to do our will. In other words, if we follow the rules God lays down for us, life will be meaningful. If we don't, there will be a price to pay. How do we know what God's will for us is?

God doesn't send individuals letters saying "Dear Dave, here's my will for you today." Instead, God places a soul within each of us to act as a moral compass. When we're not headed in the right direction, it triggers a sense of guilt or remorse. The rabbis believe that God sometimes arranges suffering in this world to get our attention. We don't always know when we're doing God's will, but we frequently know when we aren't.

High Spirits

One day Adam was kicking around the Garden of Eden feeling rather lonely. God, in all of his infinite wisdom, noticed and told Adam that he would make him a companion, which he called "woman."

"This 'woman,'" Adam said with some skepticism, "what will she be like?" God described her as beautiful, intelligent, and full of humor—the perfect companion. "Hmm," said Adam. "How much is 'woman' going to set me back?"

"An arm and a leg," God replied.

Adam contemplated this, then counter-offered. "What can I get for one rib?"

What do we mean by "will"? The same thing that's meant by the phrase "last will and testament." Your last will is your last thinking on a given topic, in this case, the disposition of your assets. To do God's will, therefore, is to study the feelings we get when we do right and wrong, notice which feels better, and act accordingly. Jewish spirituality could be described as becoming in tune with God's thinking for us.

Rather than thinking of the world in terms of rewards and punishment, it may be easier and more acceptable to think in terms of actions and consequences. According to Judaism, actions in the physical world have repercussions on the spiritual plane. Adam and Eve's action of eating the fruit triggered negative consequences: expulsion from the Garden.

What do we have to do to return to the Garden of Eden, which in traditional Judaism is a synonym for living with God, both in this life and in the afterlife? (Yes, traditional Judaism believes in an afterlife! More to come later on that important topic in Chapter 17, "The End of Time: The Messiah and the World to Come") The answer is straightforward: We must surrender our will, our self-centered thinking, and resume a sense of connection to God's will.

Born with a Clean Slate

A key belief in Judaism is that the soul begins its life perfect and untainted. One morning prayer begins this way: "God, the soul you placed in me is pure." Unlike Christianity, we do not accept the doctrine of original sin, which states that the soul of every human being born is somehow less than perfect because of Adam and Eve's sin. Traditional Judaism believes that each person's soul is purer than Ivory.

Spiritual Citations

"The righteous are called living even when they are dead, and the wicked are called dead even when they are living."

—Author Unknown

However, as we err during the normal course of our lives, the soul is affected. Rabbi Yisroel Deren compares the soul to a garment. We wear the soul here and there and sure enough it gets a little dirty. Thus the importance of Yom Kippur, the Jewish Day of Atonement. This High Holy Day is God's dry cleaning shop, Rabbi Deren says. In by six, out by seven the next night ... and the soul is as clean as if it were brand new. (Obviously a lot of prayer, sincerity, and devotion are key to that cleaning process—it's just a metaphor.)

A popular prayer recited in Jewish houses of worship on the High Holidays describes God as "compassionate and gracious, full of kindness and truth ... forgiver of sin." The whole idea in Judaism is to become more like God—not in the sense of dispensing justice or "playing God," but by taking on the qualities Judaism believes God possesses. Those qualities are

- Compassion (as opposed to judgment)
- Graciousness (as opposed to harshness)
- Kindness (as opposed to cruelty or thoughtlessness)
- Truth (as opposed to dishonesty)
- Forgiveness (as opposed to holding a grudge)

This is the Jewish God and these are the qualities Jews seek to emulate on the path to spirituality.

Incidentally, the God of the Jewish Bible sometimes gets a bad rap. You hear people say "Old Testament God" and your first reaction is to duck under a chair lest you get hit by lightning. Jews don't call the Jewish Bible "The Old Testament" because the Christian Bible or New Testament is not part of our religion—it's part of Christianity. They are welcome to refer to the Jewish Bible as the Old Testament, but Jews are not obligated to rename their holy book because of a decision made in another religion. The God of the Jewish Bible is all the wonderful things in the previous paragraph ... and is also quite demanding. God expects a lot from the Jewish people, as we shall see in later chapters.

Devine Devarim

The **Old Testament,** in Christianity, is the term used to refer to the Jewish Bible, to distinguish it from the holy writings specific to Christianity. The **New Testament,** in Christianity, is the sequel to the Jewish Bible. The New Testament does not constitute a book of the Bible in Judaism.

Traditional Judaism believes that God has the traits that you want to possess in your own life: a giving nature, compassion and graciousness, kindness, truthfulness, and forgiveness. Those are the traits of the Jewish God ... and those have *always* been the traits of the Jewish God.

Misery Loves Our Company

If God loves the Jewish people so much, why has so much misery befallen the Jews? From the destruction of the first and second Temples in Jerusalem, through the entire history of European anti-Jewish oppression culminating in the Holocaust, it becomes entirely fitting to ask where God fits into the picture. Fair enough. Let's examine these events and see how spirituality and history meet.

> ### Mystical Moments
>
> The Jews were readmitted to the land of Israel after 70 years and rebuilt the Temple at that time. However, 420 years later, after their increasingly corrupt leadership continued to set a poor example for rank and file Jews, the second Temple was destroyed, this time by the Romans in the year 70 C.E. Historians view the destruction of the Temple as a byproduct of Roman Imperialism. The Talmud, on the other hand, viewed the destruction of the Temple as a function of the misbehavior of Jews yet again. In this case, there was one primary sin that the Jews were committing, and for which we lost our temple and our homeland: the sin of senseless hatred.

In *History of the Jews*, Paul Johnson writes that Jews have been considered outsiders by the Christian world because we wouldn't accept Christ, and by the Moslem world because we wouldn't accept Mohammed as a prophet. Across the ages, Jews have suffered, often at the cost of their lives, for adherence to the belief that God is God and that we don't need anyone else's concept or representation.

We can't blame God for the actions of individuals (or even of governments, in the cases of the Crusades, the Inquisition, or the Holocaust). As mentioned earlier, God created people with free will. If followers of any faith choose to act against people who believe or worship differently, we can't hold God responsible. Yes, it's God's world, and we can *ask* for an explanation of why God permits cruelty and even savagery. But we aren't likely to get an explanation. Free will means just that: No one is keeping us from doing the wrong thing. God gave us consciences, but God did not implant in us anything that keeps us from committing a sin. That's as true for you and me as it was for Hitler and Torquemada.

Just Shy of a Bull's-Eye

Let's take a moment to define "sin." The word was taken from an archery term that literally means, "missing the mark." When we say we have sinned, we just mean that we've fallen short of our goal. We don't give up; we just try again. Most Jews are familiar with the *avinu malkaynu* prayer chanted on Yom Kippur. Avinu malkaynu translates as "Our father, our king," or if you prefer a gender neutral translation, "Our parent, our ruler."

The prayer's message is that if we decide to act in accordance with God's wishes, God relates to us as a parent to a child. If we rebel and give God too much grief, as it were, God relates to us as a ruler. Therefore, a Jew's relationship with God is entirely up to him or her.

> **Devine Devarim**
>
> The **avinu malkaynu** is a prayer chanted on Yom Kippur. *Avinu malkaynu* translates as "Our father, our king." The prayer's message is that if we decide to act in accordance with God's wishes, God relates to us as a parent to a child. If we rebel and give God too much grief, as it were, God relates to us as a ruler. Therefore, a Jew's relationship with God is entirely up to him or her.

Creating the world and its people took a staggering amount of courage on God's part (again, if we can ascribe human emotions to God). Traditionally, Jews have believed in the concept of *gam zu l'tovah*, that everything happens with a sense of ultimate good. It's often hard to see where that good will comes from but, as God told Moses, "My thoughts are not like your thoughts." We're not expected to understand God—we just don't have the tools. Rabbis sometimes use the analogy of God as a great army general who doesn't share his specific plans with the troops (that would be us).

A friend of mine says that he feels like he's on a two-seater bicycle. God's up front steering, and my friend is behind pedaling. Every so often he'll tap God on the shoulder and say, "Where are we going?" To which God just smiles and replies, "Keep pedaling."

In short, we don't know exactly where we're headed, although we have a few ideas, which we will discuss in later chapters. The main thing to know is that Judaism sees God as a loving, caring, giving, generous, forgiving, truthful, fair-minded Being who wants—above everything else—that we set aside any selfish thoughts of our own and emulate those character traits we ascribe to God. God isn't out to get us or forget us. God "suspends the universe on nothingness," as the Yom Kippur prayer says, because the universe would be too lonely for God if we weren't here. That makes each of us pretty important.

The Least You Need to Know

- If there were absolute proof for God's existence, it wouldn't be faith.
- Adhering to God's will results in a happy, prosperous life.
- Humans are endowed with free will and are born with a clean slate.
- "To sin" comes from the archery term meaning "to miss the mark."

Chapter 4

Noah and the Flood

In This Chapter

- ◆ Noah's finer points
- ◆ ... and not-so-fine points
- ◆ The ark as a metaphor for society
- ◆ Jewish argumentative tradition

Two by two the animals of the world made their way into the ark.

The biblical story of Noah's Ark and the Flood has captivated children for almost 3,000 years. Perhaps you grew up with the Bill Cosby comedy routines about the ark. Neighbors asking Noah what he's building in his driveway, and Noah refusing to answer. The neighbor demands a hint. "You want a hint? Okay. Here's a hint: How long can you tread water?"

We can learn a lot about character and responsibility from the life of Noah. In Judaism, character and responsibility are inseparable from the concept of spirituality.

Noah, This Is Your Life!

Let's begin with the way Noah is first described. The Bible is pretty terse, so you've got to come prepared to analyze its words for the hidden meanings.

Noah, according to the Bible (Genesis 5:9, if you're playing along at home), was "a just man, perfect in his generation, and Noah walked with God." What are we really saying here?

Noah was a just man: so far so good. Any one of us would do well to merit being called "just," or *tzaddik* in Hebrew.

To be called a just man in the Bible is no small honor. Now what exactly does it mean to "walk with God"? The Bible doesn't specify, but it sounds as if Noah was conscious of his Creator and had a strong sense of right and wrong and thus strove to do the right thing. That's high praise as well.

But what about the middle piece of the description? Noah was "perfect in his generation." Uh-oh. Sounds like faint praise when you think about it. Why couldn't it have just said "perfect"? Why does the Bible, which, traditional Judaism believes never wastes a word, have to add that "in his generation" disclaimer?

After all, Noah's generation couldn't have been that morally upright—God was about to wipe them out with a flood! They were the most evil generation up to that time in human history—and maybe since then as well. Certainly there has been no shortage of evil in the world, but God hasn't seen fit to break his covenant and wipe the slate clean again with another flood. So it's hard to tell exactly how the evil of Noah's time stacks up with the worst generations of modern man.

Nevertheless, there are those words staring us in the face: Noah was "perfect in his generation." And his time, according to Genesis 5:11, was nothing to write home about: "The earth was corrupt before God and filled with violence. And God looked at the world and behold! It was corrupt, for all beings were corrupt in their ways on the earth." So that's the backdrop against which Noah was described as "perfect in his time."

The Bible, therefore, is implying that Noah had good qualities—he was a *tzaddik*, a righteous man who walked with God. But he must not have been absolutely ideal, because of that oblique reference to the fact that he was pretty much the best of a bad lot. When God looked at that generation, the story implies, Noah was simply the best he could find.

> **Devine Devarim**
>
> The Hebrew word **tzib-bur,** or community, is considered an acronym or abbreviation for three Hebrew words: **tzaddik** or righteous person; **benoni,** or average person, and **rasha,** an evildoer. What makes a community? The presence of all three types of people—good, bad, and middle-of-the-road.

> **Mystical Moments**
>
> Need more proof that Noah was nowhere near perfect? Noah is the first Biblical figure to get intoxicated. After the 150-day cruise package God books for him, Noah stumbles off the ark with wobbly sea legs and plants a vineyard. It's not long before the Bible has its first drunk. Lucky for us the ark wasn't named the Exxon *Valdez*.

Noah's Lesser Traits

God tells Noah that the world is so filled with violence that He will destroy the entire population. "Make yourself an ark of gofer wood," God commands (Genesis 5:14), and then provides the dimensions. God then explains that the flood will destroy all living creatures. Noah has been charged with the task of bringing on board two of every kind of animal, as well as his wife, three sons, their wives, and enough food for all concerned.

So what does Noah do when he hears that God is going to destroy the world? I've had plenty of time to think about this. If I were suddenly fingered as Ark Builder Number One for my generation, I'd try to talk God out of it. "Hey, God, are you sure? You really want to destroy *everybody?* Don't get me wrong. I'm deeply honored that you've chosen my family to save. This is better than winning the Powerball. But are they all really that bad? That Chad guy down the block is rather nice. Can't he just get a time-out?"

After all, other Biblical figures aren't shy about arguing with God. Adam, that morally imperfect progenitor of humanity, turned to God and tried to blame his wife.

Devine Devarim

The Hebrew word for violence in that quotation from Genesis is **hamas**, which followers of current events recognize as the name of the Palestinian organization deeply opposed to the state of Israel. Hebrew and Arabic are remarkably similar in grammar, syntax, and vocabulary, a painful reminder of the close historical relations shared by the two peoples who struggle so tragically in the Middle East.

Abraham tried to bargain when God declared His plans to destroy the evil cities of Sodom and Gomorrah. He managed to get God to spare the cities if he could find a certain number of righteous citizens, whittling the number from 50 down to 10. (He missed his calling as a car salesman.) Moses tried to talk God out of using him to convince Pharaoh to free the Jews: "I have a speech impediment, I'm the wrong guy, pick someone else." Other religions have "conversations with God." Jews have confrontations. It's their longstanding tradition.

But did our ark-builder try to convince God not to destroy the world? No, not Noah.

What about this: You're too afraid to talk God out of the plan, because, after all, God's God and you're just some guy with a stack of gofer wood and a yardstick that measures in cubits. So you figure, I'm going to tell the world about this impending catastrophe. I'll take out ads, make speeches, go online, e-mail all my friends, wear a signboard—anything at all to get the word out: If we don't get our act together, we'll all be doing the eternal backstroke. Did he try that? No, not Noah.

How did Noah respond to God's threat to destroy the world? He didn't remonstrate, and he didn't demonstrate. Instead (open your Bible to Genesis 6:22), "So Noah did *everything* God commanded him."

High Spirits

Lessons from Noah's ark:

- Always travel in pairs.
- Remember that we're all in the same boat.
- Realize that termites inside the boat can be more worrisome than the storm outside.
- Respect all animals as if they were the last ones on Earth.
- Remember that "professionals" built the Titanic. The ark was Noah's first watercraft.
- Keep in shape. Even a 600-year-old man can be called upon to do the service of God.

Now, normally you can't fault a person for following the explicit word of God. But let's remember what's happening here: Everyone Noah has ever met has just received a secret death sentence that only Noah and God know about. That means all of Noah's relatives, friends and neighbors with the exception of his immediate family. That means his neighborhood, his country, his whole world. He accepted all too easily the idea that destroying the planet was an acceptable response on God's part to the violence and evil his generation fomented.

There's a spiritual lesson here. You can't just follow laws blindly. You've got to use your own judgment. The extreme example of failing to consult one's own conscience is the Nuremberg defense the Nazis gave: "We were just following orders." Noah was a righteous man, or else God would have never have chosen him to build the ark and continue, through his lineage, human history. But Noah was only "perfect" in relative terms. In a generation where violence and depravity was the norm, Noah was a cut above. But he could have done so much more, had he only stopped to think through the implications of what was happening around him. Noah's attitude was, "Hey, my family's taken care of. That's all I have to worry about."

Spiritual Citations

"Such is the human race. Often it does seem such a pity that Noah and his party did not miss the boat."

—Mark Twain, *What Is Man?*

So we've now seen two sides of the Jewish argumentative tradition. On the one hand, there's Abraham, who is praised for his (ultimately unsuccessful) attempt to negotiate with God on behalf of Sodom and Gemorrah. On the other, there's Noah, who accepted without question God's decision to wipe out the entire planet (except for Noah's immediate family). No wonder the Torah lavishes praise on Abraham and stints on praise for Noah.

Later we'll see the full flowering of this tradition of arguing with God—the life of Moses. But let's not get ahead of our story. We still have more to learn from Judaism's first pleasure boat builder.

Beyond the Ark's Doors

Most of us stopped thinking about the Noah story when we were in single digits. My daughter, who is 15 months old, has a picture book about Noah and the animals filling the ark, and she loves it when my wife and I read her that book. But the story offers sophisticated lessons that far exceed the way we viewed Noah when we were kids. The main lesson is this: *It's not enough just to take care of ourselves.* The lesson of Noah—his downfall or spiritual blind spot, if you will—is that we've got to be responsible for more than just our immediate families. There's a whole world out there, and as citizens of the planet we're responsible for our whole world, not just for our own little corner of it.

Rabbi Abraham Twerski points out that Noah might have been considered one of the patriarchs of Judaism, along with Abraham, Isaac, and Jacob, if only he'd been a little less passive in allowing the destruction of the world. Instead, Noah is on his own in Biblical history, and he's not even considered the first Jew (that distinction belongs to Abraham). So we see that being Jewish implies not only a right, but a responsibility to challenge authority—even the highest levels of authority—if a greater good is being ignored. That's not a lesson for kids. That's the Bible speaking to you and me, thousands of years after it was written. There's another aspect of the story worth mentioning: Noah didn't enter the ark until the rains had already begun to fall. Some say that Noah didn't get on board until the rainwater was actually up to his neck! This indicates that he was so busy hammering away that he

> **Mystical Moments**
>
> A popular rabbinical story tells of a man sawing a small hole in the floor of a boat. The others on board ask him to stop and he replies, "What do you care? The hole is under *my* seat." So it is with society. We can't be selfish and only look after our own families. We've got to take a broader view of our responsibilities.

> **Spiritual Citations**
>
> "I hope I can love a tzaddik as much as God loves a wicked man."
>
> —Baal Shem Tov

forgot his overall *purpose*. What was Noah's purpose in life? To be righteous, to walk with God. The lesson for us: We can get so carried away in the doing of our jobs that we forget the big picture. We can be so overwhelmed by our work that we forget to love and cherish our families. This is what I mean when I suggest that Biblical stories that seem suitable only for children actually have important spiritual ramifications for adults.

The Hebrew word for rain is *geshem*. The Yiddish word for material goods is *gashmiyus*, which is based on the plural of the Hebrew word for rain. In other words, the Jewish tradition compares material blessings to rain. We need them, and we enjoy them, as farmers (and even city dwellers) enjoy the rain. The problem comes when we become overwhelmed by *gashmiyus*, or material things, just as Noah's generation was overwhelmed by *geshem* or rain. We can literally drown in a sea of abundance. How do we avoid doing so? By placing our primary emphasis on the spiritual, not the material, side of life. You can't get to heaven in a Mercedes-Benz. Judaism is about perspective, balance, and responsibility. Our job is to build an ark big enough for the whole world to enjoy. Anything less, and we're not living up to our mission.

The Least You Need to Know

- Noah was not perfect; he was human.
- Abraham was the first Jew, not Noah.
- Judaism prizes perspective, balance, and responsibility.
- Challenging authority is a responsibility and a long-standing Jewish tradition; it's best to do so from a position of knowledge.

Chapter 5

Lessons from Abraham

In This Chapter

- How to achieve a balanced life
- Layers of meaning in Biblical text
- The lessons of Sodom and Gomorrah
- Secrets to a successful marriage

The Hebrew Bible devotes more space to the life of Abraham than any other individual except Moses. Abraham had a rich, full life—he lived 175 years and attained astonishing wealth. According to rabbinic tradition, he left his family because they practiced idolatry and he believed in the existence of one God, not many. He joined up with neighboring kings to make war and had a child when he was *100 years old* (his wife was 90). Famously, he nearly sacrificed his son on an altar, at God's command. And he is remembered as the father of the Jewish people.

Leaving Home

It takes enormous courage to act on your own beliefs, especially when what you believe runs counter to popular opinion. Ultimately, Abraham stands for the proposition that you've got to be your own man (or woman). Greatness as a human being doesn't come from following the crowd. In Abraham's place of

Mystical Moments

What is prayer? What is worship? The Hebrew word for prayer (one of them, actually. Hebrew has words for prayer the way Eskimo languages have words for snow) is *l'hitpalel*, which is a reflexive verb meaning "to judge oneself." Does God hear prayer? We believe so. Prayer is the opportunity to remind ourselves of our priorities, of what's important to us, of what we consider most vital.

birth, people worshipped a multitude of idols. One idol controlled the weather, another crops, still another childbirth, and so on. Abraham perceived that idols, which were nothing but clay figures, controlled nothing. The conflict between his beliefs and those of his father (an idolmaker) and the community was simply too great, so Abraham did what he had to do. He moved.

What's Your God?

The story of Abraham reminds us that we need to make choices about what's most important in our lives. Take the following expression: "Your idea of God is whatever you think about the most." Whatever you spend most of your time thinking about is your Higher Power, your concept of divinity.

Whatever we think most about, whatever we *remind* ourselves most frequently about, that's our God. That's what we concentrate on. That's the focus of our lives. When we are focused exclusively on work, money, sex, school, or what have you, it's very hard to achieve balance in life.

The Nature of Obsession

You may have heard the expression, "Obsession is a mask for fear." The difference between obsession and thought is that you have thoughts ... but an obsession has *you*. Any time we're deeply and consistently focused on one particular obsession, there's a very good chance that deep down, we're afraid of something. If we're obsessed with money, we may be afraid of running out of money, of losing love because our partner won't respect us if we don't make enough or have enough. If we're obsessed with work, we may be afraid to have a real life—one that involves more of ourselves than simply getting up and going to the office every day.

If we're obsessed with our health, we may well be afraid of dying. Few people *want* to die, but the fear of dying can be so strong that we forget to live fully. You may know runners who devote so much time to running that they don't have time to have a relationship. They may have 8 percent body fat, but they unlace their running shoes in an otherwise empty home.

In our society we have television, which is basically a device we place in our kitchens, living rooms, and bedrooms to remind us how crummy our stuff is. Television spends approximately 16 minutes of every hour pointing out that our car is too old, our clothes are *so* last year, our health (and sex life) is at risk because we don't take certain pills that smiling people are holding up to the camera, and that everything else in our lives—from our teeth to our hair to our beer—needs to be fixed, thrown out, or replaced. Television interrupts those 16 minutes per hour with sitcoms, dramas, and football games, in order to entice us to sit through the commercials.

So in many ways, in our society today, what we think most about is *stuff*. Cars, clothing, home improvement items, soda. If we watch, on average, four hours of TV a day, that's an hour a day of commercials. Anything we spend an hour a day thinking about is going to have an enormous amount of power in our lives. It's possible that the single most important thing that we remind ourselves about every day is how inadequate our *stuff* is. So we're obsessed with getting more money so we can get more stuff. In our society today, it's not too much of an exaggeration to say that stuff … is God.

> **Spiritual Citations**
>
> "Death is nature's way of telling you to slow down."
> —Woody Allen

> **Devine Devarim**
>
> *l'hitpalel*   to pray (literally, it is a reflexive verb meaning "to judge oneself.")

Balancing the Material and the Spiritual

Abraham shows us how to achieve a balanced life by thinking most not about stuff, but about God. Everything he did, every action he took—from leaving home as a child to the negotiations over Sodom and Gomorrah (which we'll discuss presently), from the hospitality he showed strangers to the way in which he found a wife for his son Isaac—every action he took showed that his entire focus in life was on the spiritual. Did he therefore miss out on the material blessings of life? Not at all. He enjoyed great wealth, long life, political power, a successful marriage, fatherhood and grandchildren, and eternal remembrance in the Bible.

This demonstrates one of the key spiritual secrets of the Bible: *You don't have to give up the material benefits and blessings of life in order to enjoy a powerful spiritual life.* In Judaism, it isn't a matter of choosing between the material *or* the spiritual. That's a false choice. Judaism does not define materiality and spirituality as mutually exclusive. You get to live a spiritual life while enjoying all of the benefits of material existence. Not a bad deal, wouldn't you agree?

When you keep the focus on God, when your primary focus is on the spiritual, everything else falls into place. Judaism has never required its adherents to spend their lives behind

Spiritual Citations

"Woe to those who get up at dawn to chase after liquor, who tarry into evening while wine inflames them ... The deeds of God they do not regard, and the work of his hands they do not see."

—Isaiah, 5:11–12

cloistered walls or eschew sex or any of the other pleasures of life. Indeed, there is a midrash, a rabbinical tale, that when you die and go to heaven, God will say to you, "I offered you so many opportunities for legitimate pleasure—why didn't you take more advantage of them?"

The rabbis aren't suggesting that you go out and sleep with your neighbor's spouse or joy-ride down the highway in a stolen car. Obviously there are certain limits! But just like in the Garden of Eden, there is still plenty to be enjoyed within the limits set down for us. Later in this chapter, we'll look more closely at Abraham's story and see what it means to us today. First, though, let's take a look at how Jews view the Bible.

Layered Is "In"

The Bible was never meant to be read strictly on a surface level. The rabbis teach that there are four levels of meaning to every line in the Bible. There's the level of *pshat*, which refers to the most basic, literal meaning of the text. Next, there's *remez*, Hebrew for "hint." This suggests that each line hints at deeper meanings. The third level is *drash*, the Hebrew word for "analysis" or "explanation." When you get to the level of *drash*, you're able to examine the situation and find analogies and connections to other aspects of life. The deepest level of meaning is *sod*, Hebrew for both "foundation" and "secret." In Israel today, if something is "classified top secret," it's called *sodi*, from the same word. There are deep secrets contained in every line of the Bible, accessible only to those who study it the hardest.

Devine Devarim

pshat   the most basic, literal interpretation of Biblical text.

remez   a second layer of deeper textual meaning. (In Hebrew, literally "hint.")

drash   the textual analysis of text in which analogies and connections to other aspects of life can be found.

sod   the deepest level of contextual meaning containing the Bible's greatest secrets.

pardes   the "garden" of connotations, created by using the first letter from each of the levels of meaning. From this word comes the English "paradise."

Hebrew loves acronyms. If you take the first four letters of *pshat*, *remez*, *drash*, and *sod* (or P, R, D, and S) and throw in vowel sounds to create a word, you get the Hebrew word *pardes*, or garden, from which we derive the English word "paradise." In other words, when we truly devote ourselves to understanding Biblical texts or other aspects of Jewish law and lore, we don't just gain wisdom and knowledge. We attain paradise. Jews believe the key to paradise is study. In particular, we study the lives of the great figures in the Bible and Jewish history to derive lessons about how to live our own lives.

Abraham left his home to get away from the influence of the belief system there. In today's world, Abraham probably wouldn't watch much TV. For one, he'd be too busy living his life. Second, he wouldn't stand for the commercials bombarding him with the material aspects of life. For Abraham, what was most important was the *unseen*—the God of his understanding and his relationship with that God.

Sodom and Gomorrah

Early in Abraham's life, he attained great wealth as a landowner and owner of cattle. He became aware that God was on the verge of destroying two cities known for their utter wickedness: Sodom and Gomorrah. These cities were sort of like Las Vegas before Steve Wynn or Times Square before Disney. In contrast to Noah, who was content to let destruction reign down upon the Earth as long as he was taken care of, Abraham threw himself into negotiations with God to save the twin sin cities.

"What if there are 50 righteous people in those cities?" Abraham asks God. "You'd kill them along with the bad guys? What are you, kidding me?" (Yes, I'm paraphrasing.) God sees his point and relents: If Abraham can identify 50 righteous individuals in the two cities, they'll be spared.

Abraham wasn't simply headstrong. He also possessed an ability to negotiate that would put Monty Hall to shame. *Okay*, Abraham thinks, *I've got God down to 50. How low will He go?* "What if there are 45 good people there? Would you destroy the cities even though you'd be taking down 45 good guys along with the evil-doers?"

God considers the proposition and goes along. For 45 righteous people, the city won't be destroyed. Now Abraham's feeling momentum shifting his way. "Hey, God, how about … *40?*" He eventually succeeds in talking God all the way down to 10.

"And that's my final answer," says God.

> **Mystical Moments**
>
> A tourism organization in the Middle East once suggested that Sodom be turned into a modernized city of sin, complete with casinos and strip joints. However, the chief Rabbinate of Israel reminded them what had happened the first time around, and pointed out that there was nothing to stop the Almighty from destroying the city a second time. The plan was dropped.

The story continues with an unsuccessful search for even 10 righteous people in Sodom and Gomorrah. They're *all* sinners. It's like Studio 54 in there. The cities are destroyed as Abraham, his nephew Lot, and Lot's wife make their successful escape.

Lessons of the Sin Cities

What exactly are we supposed to learn from this episode? What part of paradise is gained by understanding the story on a deeper level? Rabbi Yitzhak Etshalom, a noted Biblical and Talmudic authority in Los Angeles, offers an intriguing answer. Rabbi Etshalom quotes Rabbi Ovediah Sforno, a fifteenth-century Biblical commentator, physician, and philosopher who lived around 1470–1550 in the northern Italian city of Bologna. (It's highly common for observant Jews today to study Biblical commentaries that are hundreds of years old, and "the Sforno," as the rabbi is colloquially called, is one of the most frequently read authors, even 500 years later.)

The Sforno writes that punishing wicked people *isn't* God's highest motivation. God wants to see people who are doing the wrong thing *change*. That's why the process of *teshuva*, or repentance (to be discussed later in detail), is so vital to Judaism. It's why Yom Kippur, the least fun of all Jewish holidays, is the one that even lapsed Jews are most likely to observe. God doesn't want to see wicked people die for their wickedness; God wants to see people have a chance to change. So God was in effect playing along with Abraham. Abraham understood that God wanted to give the people of Sodom and Gomorrah one last chance to live with integrity.

Rabbi Etshalom suggests that the story shows the importance of the individual. Abraham is saying that a small number of people can influence a great majority. We see this is true throughout human history: Joan of Arc, the framers of the U.S. Constitution, the Freedom Riders in the American South, all were individuals or small groups who "spoke truth to power" and had influence far in excess of their numbers. Even evildoers can be influenced to change, Abraham's actions suggest. *"Hakol holaych achar hasiyum"*—everything depends on the conclusion, not necessarily on where things stand in the early going. We don't give up on individuals and we don't give up on people.

> **Spiritual Citations**
>
> "On Yom Kippur, instead of striking your heart at the mention of every sin, your heart should strike you."
>
> —Chofetz Chaim, theologian

> **Devine Devarim**
>
> Hakol holaych achar hasiyum   Everything depends on the conclusion, not necessarily on where things stand in the early going. We don't give up on individuals and we don't give up on people.

The case of Sodom and Gomorrah is extreme. Granted, the world is full of people who do the wrong thing, but even in Las Vegas you'll find a large percentage of the population who don't gamble, don't cheat on their spouses, and who live blameless lives. Even in our crazy world, there is no such thing as a city entirely populated with evildoers. Keep in mind that when the Bible includes a story, it's got to be something that will stand the test of time. It's still intriguing, 3,000 years later, to think of cities so evil that not even a handful of decent people live within their gates. It's a wild idea, when you think about it. In Hollywood terms, it's very high concept.

Don't Look Back!

There's one more brief story to examine with regard to the cities of Sodom and Gomorrah. God told the escaping trio of Abraham, Lot, and Lot's (unnamed) wife not to look back on the destruction of the cities. There's no specific reason given. Maybe the volcano-like eruptions of fire, sulphur, and brimstone might have damaged their retinas. Lot's wife looks back nonetheless and she is transformed into a "pillar of salt." What exactly does that mean?

On the pshat level of Biblical interpretation, it's hard to say. She was given an explicit command and violated it, which was something people sought to avoid in those days. Dig down a bit to the remez level and we can derive an intriguing spiritual lesson: It's all too easy for us to dwell in the past, in what might have been.

When we spend too much time dwelling on what might have been instead of focusing on what's happening now, we're missing out. Judaism is about the here-and-now, enjoying the moment, and recognizing that life is a very temporary gift. Even though traditional Judaism believes in an afterlife (which you can read about in Chapter 17, "The End of Time: The Messiah and the World to Come"), most Jews don't spend all that much time thinking about it.

Judaism is a religion that keeps you busy. From observing the *mitzvot* (the commandments) and preparing for Shabbat, to keeping kosher and donning your *tefillin*, the Jewish agenda is constantly full. It's a religion of action and not just philosophical reflection (although we have plenty of that, too).

Devine Devarim

tefillin   a system of leather straps and boxes containing excerpts from the Torah, worn by Jewish men and boys during weekday morning services.

Mystical Moments

There is an Eastern European custom to eat hard-boiled eggs on Passover, as a symbol of mourning. It's similar to breaking a glass at a wedding—we still recall the destruction of the Temple even at the joyous event of Passover.

If your approach to Judaism is less involved with ritual and Jewish law and more involved with the concept of *tikkun olam* (improving, literally *fixing*) the world, you're busy with social action. Your focus might be anything as worldly as the environment or world peace, to volunteering at the hospital or getting the city to put in a stop sign at a busy intersection. But one way or another, you're busy. Judaism is grounded in the belief that it's better to wear out than to rust out.

The One-Sentence Guide to Happy Marriages

The Bible was the first self-help book for relationships. The key to a happy marriage can be found in the life of Abraham. The setting: After Isaac is born, Sarah is unhappy. That's because Hagar, Sarah's handmaid who had a child with Abraham, is mocking her. Who needs that? Sarah tells Abraham to have Hagar and her child, Ishmael, leave the family compound.

This doesn't play well with Abraham, who loves his son. Since Abraham didn't have a therapist or marriage counselor at his disposal, he took his concern straight to the Big Guy.

Unofficial marriage counselors (a.k.a., rabbis) have often quoted God's response to Abraham's dilemma: "Everything she says to you, listen to it." The implication: Do it. Do everything Sarah says.

High Spirits
"Sex is the most wholesome, beautiful, and sacred act that money can buy."
—Jack Benny

There you have it: The entire Biblical guide to happy marriages. Husbands, do exactly what your wives say. Don't grumble, don't backtalk, just *do it*. In the Jewish way of thinking, marriage is just one big Nike ad. *Just do it*. The comedian Dennis Miller says that wives usually have to say things three different times to get their husbands to do what they want. "The first time, we just don't hear it," Miller says. "The second time, we don't believe it."

So there you have it. You can ignore your spouse (ladies, this works just as well for you as it does for men, even though the commandment falls squarely into the laps of males), and you and your spouse can be angry and miserable. Or you can do things your spouse's way *right now* … and everybody's happy.

Abraham, who doesn't hesitate to argue with God over the fate of strangers in Sodom and Gomorrah, doesn't say a word in his own defense. He doesn't justify, reframe the argument, or try a new approach. He simply obeys God. There is no indication in the Bible that Abraham and Sarah had anything but a very happy marriage. I know, I know. Some of you guys are thinking, "What about *my* needs?" Judaism's response: Sorry, pal. Everything your wife says, you do. That's your responsibility.

We live in a time when men are encouraged to get in touch with our feelings. For most, that usually means they feel like having a beer. The typical male would be content with a bed, a flat surface to eat off, and cable. The rabbis recognized this trait (they were males themselves, you know). Think back to the story of creation. Every day, upon completing the day's creations, God would look upon the new additions to the world and say, "Behold, it is good." According to the *midrash*, special (sometimes fanciful) commentaries on the Bible, on the sixth day, when God said, "And it was *very* good," He was actually talking about the sex drive! What did the rabbis mean by that? "If it weren't for the [sexual] inclination, no man would build a house, or plant a vineyard, or go to work."

In other words, if it weren't for the desire to find a woman to spend time with, to fall in love with, or to marry, guys would give in to their natural tendencies to be total worthless slobs. So the price men pay for love is the surrender of the tendency to live selfishly (and often somewhat sloppily). Women are different and generally don't share the genetic proclivity of men to live comfortably surrounded by pizza boxes and beer cans. When a man overcomes his (somewhat selfish) nature and understands that the happier he can make his wife, the better a life he'll enjoy, he'll jump to do what she wants without having to be told several times.

(Please don't show this section of the book to my wife, who would laugh out loud when she read it and wonder when I would start applying this rule to myself.)

Devine Devarim

midrash   The collection of rabbinical insights into Bible stories.

High Spirits

Why do Jewish men die before their wives do?

Because they *want* to.

Intriguingly, the language of the Hebrew text doesn't just say "Do it." Rather, it says, *Shma b'kolah.* (Genesis 21:12.) That translates literally as "Listen *in* her voice." On a deeper level, it's saying, "Don't just listen to what she's saying. Listen to *how* she's saying it." The tone and the unspoken message are just as important, if not more so, than the actual, specific request. In Judaism, it's understood that to be a good husband, a man must constantly be asking his wife what she's thinking about, what she's doing, and what she's feeling. A man who loses touch with those three vital aspects of his wife's day is on the road to destroying his own marriage without recognizing how he's doing so.

So there you have the one-sentence Biblical handbook to happy marriages: Husbands, get busy (or look busy!). And wives, please don't abuse this truly unlimited power you hold over us guys! We're doing the best we can!

In sum, had Abraham been alive today, he might have had his own radio call-in show—he was that attuned to world events, relationships, spirituality, and parenting. No wonder he's considered the father of Judaism, because he still has so much to offer us today! Let's see what other spiritual lessons can be drawn from the Bible ... in the next chapter.

The Least You Need to Know

- What you focus on the most becomes your God.
- One person can make a difference.
- Biblical text contains four layers of meaning.
- The secret to a successful marriage is communication and listening carefully to what your partner says.

Part  2

From Isaac to Sinai

We continue our Biblical *tour d'horizon* and examine the lives of Isaac, Jacob, Joseph, and Moses. One of the keys to Jewish Bible study is that the Bible can be read on more than one level. There are often hints at spiritual secrets that only the learned can discern. What are those secrets? What lessons is the Bible trying to impart between the lines?

We'll also turn to the Sinai story and see what mystical secrets we can learn about how God spoke to Jewish people, what was said, and what the atmosphere was like at that time. As the Big Guy might say, Thou Shalt Not Skip This Section! Enjoy!

Chapter 6

The Son Also Rises

In This Chapter

- ◆ Abraham's most famous test of faith
- ◆ The importance of hospitality
- ◆ The age of Isaac
- ◆ Putting God first

The most famous, and most troubling, episode in the life of Abraham relates to the great test God set before him, the sacrifice of his son Isaac. Consider: When the story of the binding of Isaac was already several hundred years old, the first Olympics in ancient Greece had yet to take place (776 B.C.E.). The Trojan War had not yet been fought. Homer hadn't written a line of the *Iliad* or the *Odyssey*, nor had Plato and Aristotle written a word of philosophy. The Parthenon was still a parking lot. We're talking *old*, here, my friends.

The Big Test

The story takes place after Abraham, at Sarah's insistence, sends his son Ishmael and his concubine Hagar away from the family home. God has vouchsafed to Abraham the safety of the mother and son. Abraham is puzzled by the promise of God that he will be the father of a mighty nation when he cannot have a son by his own wife and the son he has with his wife's handmaiden is no longer in contact. And then, one fateful day, three visitors arrive.

Warm Welcomes ... Even for Strangers

Even though Abraham is unsure of their identities, his hospitality to these strangers is limitless. He literally runs around the homestead, choosing a fine animal for a feast for the guests, instructing his wife to prepare a meal, and in general making the guests feel comfortable. This in itself is one of the most important spiritual teachings of the Jewish Bible—the importance of hospitality. You can walk into a temple or synagogue anywhere in the world on a Sabbath and find either an invitation for a meal at the home of one of the congregants, or as lavish a *kiddush* or after-service collation as the community can afford. This is as true in the twenty-first century as it was in first. Hospitality is the hallmark of the Jewish people, and if you haven't availed yourself of it after a service, you don't know what you're missing. Where did we develop that practice? From the example of Abraham, as he prepares a feast for his unexpected guests.

The unexpected visitors bring amazing, almost incredible news: By this time next year, Abraham and Sarah will be parents. This news makes Sarah break down in laughter. "Are you kidding me?" she asks through her laughter. "My husband's 100! And at 90, I'm no spring chicken either."

And yet, sure enough, the strangers' prophecy is fulfilled a year later with the arrival of Isaac. (In Hebrew, his name is *Yitzchak*, which means laughter.) At last, God's promise to Abraham that he will be the father of a great nation can now come true. Abraham's happiness is cut short 12 years later, however, by a new message from above. God tests him—the Bible uses the language of a test—by insisting that Abraham sacrifice his son.

> **Devine Devarim**
>
> **kiddush**   The prayer said over a vessel of wine in order to inaugurate the Sabbath and on Saturday morning after services; the collation after Sabbath services; a holy act, as in a *kiddish haShem*—a sanctification of God's name. All derived from the Hebrew root word meaning "holy" or separate.

> **Spiritual Citations**
>
> "One who deceives his fellow man deceives his Maker."
> —The Talmud

The Two Faces of Abe

Abraham's response: Nothing. He simply obeys. What's more, the Bible tells us that he wakes up early the next morning to complete the task. Along with two young field hands, the distraught father and loyal servant of God takes his son Isaac, a knife, rope, and provisions for the journey. With the gear packed on the back of donkey, the quartet sets off.

When Isaac asks his father, "Here's the knife and the rope, but where's the animal that will be sacrificed?" Abraham responds, "God will provide one."

The modern mind has a very difficult time with this story. If we are parents, the idea of committing such an act on our own children is so abhorrent as to be unspeakable and even unimaginable. Once again, we have to go below the surface level of the story in order to extract meaning. Why exactly would a story like this be given such prominence in the Bible—and what spiritual guidance, if any, are we expected to find in it?

Mystical Moments

The message is not, on any level, that it's okay to sacrifice your children. Judaism was practically unique in its formative days in that it made it a crime to sacrifice children. A local god called Moloch could only be satisfied with human sacrifice; Judaism outlawed such offerings. Interestingly, a large portion of the Torah is given over to specific descriptions of animal sacrifices to be made daily, at the new moon, on festivals, and at New Year's, as well as during specific situations that befell individual Jews. Judaism felt obliged to include animal sacrifice because it would have been too much of a leap for the first Jews to make—religion *always* included animal sacrifice. If you had no animal sacrifices, Judaism wouldn't have looked like a religion to most of its early adherents. So animal sacrifices were *in* … but human sacrifices? Never.

The moral implications of this story have perplexed even rabbis for centuries. They dig and delve to find some explanation of how a father could commit such an act without protest. Presumably the individuals of Sodom and Gomorrah whom Abraham bargained for were strangers to him. How can we understand—or even respect—a man who can argue with God to save the lives of people he doesn't know, while being ready to take the life of his own son?

In his book *Explorations*, Rabbi Ari Kahn suggests that whenever any nation goes to war, the parents of that nation are in effect sacrificing their children's lives. But there's a difference between permitting or encouraging your child to fight for his or her country, and physically taking part in their slaughter.

Some commentators believe that Abraham knew that he wouldn't be asked to go through with it. I think he sensed that God was testing him, and that God wouldn't ask him to go through with an act clearly contrary to morality in virtually all times and places. Jewish parents, like all parents, treasure their children. We don't put them in harm's way. If anything, we're overprotective as parents, perhaps because we know how cruel and cold the world can be.

There's no way that Abraham could have gone through with the killing of Isaac. It just wasn't in him. This observation is based on part of an earlier verse in the story, where Abraham asks the two young field hands to stay with the donkey while "we shall go there [to the place of the sacrifice]. We shall worship and *we* shall return to you." (Emphasis added.) Either Abraham was lying to Isaac and the field hands, perhaps to keep them in the dark about his true intentions, or Abraham knew that he would have to participate in this test and would return shortly with his son to the two young men. Abraham hasn't told a lie anywhere else in the long account of his life and it would be too far out of character for him to do so now.

A fascinating sidebar to the Isaac story is that he might not have been the little boy we always imagine. According to Judaism's leading Biblical commentator Rashi, whom we have already discussed, Isaac wasn't a little boy at all. He was 37 years old!

How is this figure arrived at? The next episode in the book of Genesis tells of the death of Isaac's mother, Sarah. Backtracking from her age at death leads Rashi to the conclusion that Isaac was already rather old! The idea of Isaac at 37 accompanying his father to the scene of the sacrifice puts an entirely different spin on the story.

High Spirits

My mother loves to tell the story about the Jewish mother who is carrying her 10-year-old son across the street. "Can't he walk for himself?" a stranger asks.

"Of course," the Jewish mother replies. "But thank God he doesn't have to!"

They reach the mountaintop together (some rabbis believe the location to be the Temple Mount behind the Western Wall in Jerusalem) where Abraham binds Isaac to the altar. Some believe that Isaac himself figured out what was happening and insisted that Abraham bind him lest he flinch when the ax flies to kill him. At the last moment, an angel stops Abraham from doing the deed. God tells Abraham that it was all a test and Abraham has proven himself.

Bound to God

And there you have the most important message of the *akeida*, the Hebrew name for the story of the binding of Isaac: God is loving, kind, compassionate, caring, and present—but often hard to fathom. And yet God never implies that life is a free ride and that we can do whatever we want regardless of the feelings (or property) of others. Judaism sees life as a privilege that brings in its train responsibilities. And the primary responsibility of a Jew is to put God first in his or her life, whatever his or her conception of God may be.

Again, it's not my role to tell you what to believe. That's your choice and your decision. Rather, I'm here to describe as best I can the traditional Jewish approaches to spirituality so that you can create your own *shulchan aruch*, your own "set table" for the banquet that is life.

Mystical Moments

The moment that Abraham addresses the field hands bears brief analysis. It says (Genesis 21:4–5) "And on the third day Abraham lifted his eyes and saw the place in the distance." And *then* Abraham instructs the young men to remain with the *hamor*, the donkey, while he and Isaac go off to worship together. Here's what's interesting. Biblical commentators going back a thousand years or more preserve an ancient tradition about what happens between when Abraham first lifts up his eyes and sees the worship place in the distance, and when he instructs the two young men to remain with the donkey. In that missing space (and now we're operating on the level of drosh, the interpolation of important details), Abraham says to the young men, "Do you see the place, too?" They respond negatively. These young, anonymous field hands are not on the same spiritual level as Abraham and Isaac. There's no way that they can "see" spiritual visions that can only come to someone as committed to the spiritual path as Abraham.

So Abraham says to them, "Stay here with the *hamor* [donkey]." When studying the Bible, the rabbis have traditionally resorted to plays on words to determine deeper meanings. The word for material things is *homer*, which sounds a lot like hamor. According to this interpretation, based on a slight play on words, Abraham is really saying, "You stay here in the material world while Isaac and I go off into the spiritual realms. We'll worship and then we'll return to your level."

The akeida was actually the final of 10 spiritual trials that God had applied to Abraham to test his mettle. When a potter makes a vessel, he doesn't test the weakest ones. He knows they're too weak to send out into the world with his name on them. Abraham was strong enough to take—and pass—every test God put his way. The most important test was to determine whether Abraham would put God first.

The akeida also demonstrates how power brings responsibilities, not rights. Despite the knowledge that he would father a great nation, Abraham did not become overly arrogant. A true leader must live humbly and display humility even when no one else is watching. Keep in mind that Abraham and Isaac were alone at the time of the near-sacrifice. Even then they lived by the belief that one should commit one's sins in public and one's good deeds in private. Abraham didn't let the presumed power God gave him go to his head.

What can we learn from this? We need to place the spiritual above the material in our own lives. If we believe in God, we must make our commitment to God infuse every action we take, even when those actions run counter to our own desires, which are so often ego-driven or about self-gratification. If we don't accept the idea of God, we need to practice what Reform Jewish rabbis call "predicate theology"—we need to *act as if* there were a God in the world who will one day hold us accountable for our actions.

If I may speak of God in this context, it's as though God still has an altar, the same altar on which Abraham was ready to sacrifice Isaac. God says to us, "Put whatever you value most on My altar. Put your family, your career, your money, your health, even your sex life; put everything of importance to you on My altar. And just as I gave back Isaac to his father Abraham at the right moment, so I'll give you everything you need—exactly when you need it. You don't have to rely solely on your own efforts. I'll be there to help you through the days and nights of your life ... but only if you're willing to put Me first, and to put everything else second. And ultimately all will come out just fine for you and for those you love."

High Spirits
Why was Isaac 12 years old when God ordered Abraham to sacrifice his son?
Because if he had been a teenager, it wouldn't have been a sacrifice.

The Least You Need to Know

- ◆ God's tests are for our own benefit.
- ◆ Hospitality is a fundamental characteristic of the Jewish faith.
- ◆ The Bible is subject to many "correct" interpretations.
- ◆ Ultimate faith in God results in happiness.

Chapter 7

Nobody's Perfect

In This Chapter

- ◆ How Isaac finds a wife
- ◆ The power of the spoken word
- ◆ Bad blood between Jacob and Esau
- ◆ Why tragedies happen—even to good people

Perfection Not Necessary

Some of the leading figures of the Bible, from Isaac and Rebecca through Jacob and his son Joseph, were flawed in significant ways. The stories about these individuals more often than not revealed their shortcomings instead of the heroic aspects of their personalities. You have to give the Jews a lot of credit. We never seek to whitewash our history, or cover up for the sins and errors of our founding fathers and mothers. Instead, we present their foibles in clear, powerful ways, teaching that you don't have to be perfect in your practice of Judaism to be an outstanding human being. We're not angels, and we're not expected to *become* angels.

The irony about most of the stories in the Bible, and certainly the ones that we will consider in this chapter and the next, is that the Bible uses stories of character flaws as well as stories of heroism to teach people how to develop character strengths. Why did the Bible resort to depicting human weakness instead of heroism? Although there is a certain amount of heroism to be found, it practically has to sneak in between the moments of complete and utter dysfunction.

Perhaps the Bible was not written for the benefit of the angels, but for the benefit of human beings. We humans have a nasty tendency to do and say the wrong thing, to make the wrong choice, to do things we regret. If the Bible simply told the stories of another 10 Abrahams instead of the all-too-human individuals who populate its pages, no one could relate. In many ways, the Bible is not a book for the righteous. They don't need it. The Bible is a book for people who fall short of the mark.

The Bible is about people striving to perfect themselves. Righteousness is the goal—not the starting point. The Bible thus becomes a guide to living in the real world, not a Pantheon of unattainably heroic lives.

How to Marry Well

One of the most beautiful and touching stories, familiar to countless generations of Jewish children, is the manner in which Abraham instructed his servant Eliezer to find a wife for his son Isaac. It might have been funny if, after the binding of Isaac, the young man had said to his father, "Dad, I don't think I'm ready to get married just yet. I really don't want to be tied down. Again." Fortunately, the Bible was written in the land of Israel and not in a comedy club in Miami Beach, so we are spared that sort of remark. Abraham tells Eliezer to bring his camel to the watering place and wait and see which young woman, if any, offers water to both Eliezer and his ride. So Eliezer devised a test for the young woman: Eliezer was to ask for water for himself, and the right young woman would bring water not just for him but for the camel as well.

Abraham also stipulated that Eliezer should return specifically to Aram, the place from which Abraham came, and bring back a young woman from that place. Sure enough, Eliezer reaches the watering hole, and a young woman named Rebecca appears just as he says a prayer to God: "Behold, I'm standing here by the well and the daughters of this town come out to draw water. May it happen that the young woman to whom I say, 'May I have some water to drink?' says, 'Let me give you some water, and let me give your camel water as well.'" At that very moment Rebecca appears, and plays out the scene to the letter.

> **High Spirits**
>
> "Is it not easier for a camel to descend through the eye of a needle than to find a rent-controlled, two-bedroom apartment in New York City?"
>
> —Gary Goldstein

A Lesson in the Power of Speech

There is a spiritual lesson here, and it has to do with the power of speech. In Hebrew, the word *davar* has two meanings: "word" and "thing." In other words, in Hebrew, words have weight. They have heft. They matter. The words we say are extremely important, and we can actually influence our reality by the way we speak.

The ultimate example of this is the Jewish mystical belief that God created the world by "speaking." One of the most important morning prayers of traditional Jews begins, "Blessed is the One who spoke and the world came into being." In the Jewish mystical tradition, God created the entire world simply by pronouncing the Jewish letter *hay*, or H. A breath of the Almighty was enough to set into motion the entire universe.

So it is, surprisingly, with us. We have enormous power to shape our world, according to Jewish mystical tradition, by the words we speak.

Eliezer had absolutely no hesitation in speaking his needs to his God, and the result was that the right person suddenly appeared. Many people think that the concept of affirmations is a New Age development. Affirmations, the concept of speaking about the reality one wishes to create in order to make it come true, actually goes back more than 3,000 years.

Prayer is where we learn to "affirm" the important things we truly need: wisdom, renewal, health, peace in the world, and other vital matters. The story of Eliezer seeking a wife for Isaac is one of the first examples in recorded history or literature of an affirmation. In short, words have a huge amount of power, and when we use words to express our gratitude or our needs, we are putting ourselves in touch with a source of unparalleled power.

> **High Spirits**
>
> A husband decided to check his wife's hearing. From the kitchen he called, "Florence, can you hear me?" No answer. He walks into the living room about 15 feet away. "Florence, can you hear me?" Still no answer. Finally, he stands right behind her as she sits watching television. "Florence, can you hear me?"
>
> Finally, she answers. "For the third time, Irving—yes, I can hear you!"

The Key to Rebecca

How did Eliezer know that Rebecca was the right woman? Because she displayed kindness. It wasn't in her resumé; it was in her character.

Human nature has not changed very much in the 3,500 years or so since this story took place. When you look at all the murder and mayhem in the Bible, it certainly seems as though very little about human beings has changed. If anything, the shortcomings of the characters give the Bible its timelessness.

By this time in his life, Abraham was wealthy and extremely powerful in his region. He could have arranged the marriage for his son based on similar qualities in the family of the young woman he might have chosen. He could have told his servant, Eliezer, "I want you to go out and find a young woman from a very rich and powerful family. I want to create a financial and political alliance that will mean even greater wealth and prominence for my family. Be sure to get a printout of the Dunn and Bradstreet report on the family, a picture of their net worth, and specifics as to their holdings. Catch my drift?"

Abraham did nothing of the sort. He simply asked Eliezer to find a young woman who had excellent character. The test that he set forth was simple: Water for you, water for the camel, too. Eliezer gets to the well, says his affirmation, and lo and behold, Rebecca appears.

The story continues with Eliezer going to the family of the young girl and asking them—and then her—if she would like to marry young Isaac. The family agrees, and Rebecca consents. At no point in that conversation does Eliezer inquire into the family's wealth, land holdings, or political power. All of that is irrelevant, because character is what matters.

> **Mystical Moments**
>
> Judaism prohibits marriages during certain times of the year and on certain days. The weeks immediately following Passover are forbidden for marriage. Weddings are also prohibited during the "three weeks," which normally falls between mid-July and mid-August and is a remembrance of the time that Romans ransacked Jerusalem in 70 C.E.

Yeah, Baby, She's Got It

The particular form of character that Rebecca displays is known as *simchat laiv*, or a joyous heart. An unhappy person has trouble sharing. When we think of hoarders or misers, we think of people who are so scared to share with others or let anything go that they miss out on life. Rebecca is the opposite: What she has, she willingly, freely, and without prompting shares with others. This is symbolic of a joyous heart, which is a highly praised trait in the Jewish tradition. In other words, Rebecca symbolized *chesed*, loving kindness, to balance Isaac's *gevurah* or judgmentalness.

The psalms say, "Serve God with joy." The term for the holiday on which we finish reading the Torah and start reading it anew is Simchat Torah, normally translated as "The Celebration of the Law," but more accurately translated as "The Joy of the Law." In the same vein, the Talmud asks, what is the best quality that a person could possess? The Talmud suggests qualities

> **Spiritual Citations**
>
> Rabbi Noach Orlowek says that if a young woman has to choose between marrying an incredible Torah scholar with a morose personality, and a joyous carpenter, she should choose the carpenter every time.

such as generosity, kindness toward one's neighbors, foresight, and unselfishness. But above all is a good heart, which encompasses all of those other character traits. Certainly Judaism, with all there is to learn and consider, is a religion that relies on and appeals to the intellect. But Judaism is primarily a religion of the heart.

Throughout the Bible, the Prophets castigate the Jewish people for the practice of *avodat hats'fay-tiyim*, literally "lip service"—saying prayers that they don't really believe. The Prophets direct the people to re-engage in *avodat haliv*, or "service of the heart"—prayer and worship that has genuine feeling behind it. The heart is all-important, and a joyous heart is prized above all.

Devine Devarim

avodat haliv Reciting prayers with belief and convictions; literally "service of the heart."

avodat hat'sfaytiyim Reciting prayers one doesn't believe; literally "lip service."

Brotherly Love?

Isaac and Rebecca have two sons, Jacob and Esau. The two boys are about as different as humanly possible. Esau is a man of the field, loves to hunt, and brings his father delicious game. Jacob, on the other hand, is more of a studious child, and according to rabbinical tradition actually studied in the yeshiva, or religious school, established by his relatives Shem and Ever.

Jacob also happens to be a trickster. In a famous Biblical tale, he dupes his older brother out of his birthright when Esau returns from the field one night ravenously hungry. Taking advantage of the situation, Jacob offers him a bowl of red lentil soup in exchange for his birthright—not a very good deal from Esau's point of view, but he's too hungry to resist.

The trickery doesn't stop there. Later, when Isaac is on his deathbed, Jacob and Esau visit their blind father seeking a blessing. Rebecca favors Jacob over the first born, Esau, and helps him deceive his dying father. Rebecca makes the tasty meat dish that Isaac loves so much and associates with his hunter son, Esau. Rebecca also helps Jacob into a costume, dressing him in Esau's clothing and putting goatskin on his hands and the smooth of his neck. That way, Isaac is more likely to mistake Jacob, who is smooth-skinned, for his hairier older brother.

Sure enough, the trick works: Isaac gives Jacob the blessing of the first born, much to the consternation of Esau, who cannot believe that his brother tricked him and that their mother made it all possible.

Mystical Moments

Is Isaac aware of the switch? It's entirely possible. Isaac first wonders aloud how Jacob, disguised as Esau, could have arrived so quickly with the food. Jacob's response: "I made good time." Isaac's reaction to that comment is not recorded. He's obviously not sure though, because he asks Jacob to step up close so that he can feel Jacob's skin and tell whether or not it is Esau, as it is supposed to be. So Jacob approaches his father, who feels his skin, and utters the famous words, "The voice is the voice of Jacob, but the hands are the hands of Esau." (Genesis 27:22) Some scholars suggest that Isaac believe Jacob to be more befitting of continuing the family tradition and so allowed the deception. However, it is an unanswered question whether Isaac knew that he was actually blessing Jacob.

Once again, we are confronted with a morally ambiguous story. However, it's clear to see that people aren't perfect. They make mistakes in judgment, sometimes huge mistakes. Some might believe that it was wrong for Jacob to deceive his father, as it was wrong for Rebecca to participate in the fraud. Jacob does not go unpunished for his deception. He pays mightily for his mistake when he is in turn deceived at his own wedding (and you wonder why men have cold feet about marriage?). Jacob falls in love with Rachel and works for seven long, grueling years to win her hand. However, after going through the whole wedding ceremony, he's shocked to find Leah under the veil—now his legal wife. He still wants to marry Rachel as well, so he must work for his father-in-law for another seven years before he can win her hand.

Yes, friends, there is such a thing as Jewish karma. (The Hebrew term is *mazal*, which means luck—in the sense of constellations in the sky going your way. Mazal tov!) What goes around comes around. We may not be perfect people, but if affections radically impinge on the rights of others, we can expect to pay a severe price. Jacob tricks his brother and his father; before long, he finds himself tricked as well.

These stories offer a clear-cut case of actions and consequences. Today, life is not that simple. So often, we see good people suffering (*tzaddik v'ralo* in Hebrew, meaning a righteous person to whom evil occurs), and we see morally questionable people doing everything from dating a supermodel to winning the presidency. What lessons are we expected to draw from a world where badness apparently goes unchecked much of the time?

Judaism is not silent about these issues. First of all, we are not really expected to understand everything that goes on in this life. There is simply no way for a human being to fully comprehend the meaning of tragedy, whether it is the tragedy that befalls an individual or tragedy that befalls millions. Sociobiologist Edward O. Wilson wrote in his book *Consilience* that the human brain is wired for survival, not for self-understanding. We never truly understand ourselves: We are not always clear on our motives in a given situation, we certainly don't understand where some of our thoughts come from, and we have no idea how dreams are formed or what they mean. There is such a vast amount of uncharted territory within our own brains that we can't possibly grasp every little nuance outside of ourselves—especially tragedy.

The existence of tragedy does not preclude the existence of a living God. So many of the events that we consider tragedies or "acts of God" are actually the results of actions taken by human beings. Although an earthquake may wipe out a large number of people, just about every one of those people knew that they were choosing to live in an earthquake zone. Is it truly an "act of God" if a distracted driver on a cell phone hits another person? Or is it simply another case of free will? If we misuse the free will that was granted to us, we shouldn't point the finger at the Being that gave us that free will.

Moreover, in times of spiritual turmoil, everyone is liable to suffer tragedy and loss. It's as if the world reaches a certain level of moral instability, and then all of a sudden the rules about reward and punishment are struck inoperative. When the world is a moral mess, bad things can happen to just about anybody. The rabbis of the Talmud who formulated that belief would not be terribly surprised by today's current events, where we have a combination of a slippery moral climate and a high level of indiscriminate suffering.

The rabbis offer a third explanation to cope with suffering: Suffering both purifies and ennobles us. Traditional Judaism has long taught that people who suffer unjustly in this life will be more than compensated in *ha'olam haba*, the next world or the world to come.

The bottom line in Judaism is that suffering always has meaning, even if we can't always understand its meaning at the time. It may serve as an atonement, it may help a person prepare to help someone else, or it may be for the benefit of the entire generation. Yet it is never viewed as random.

Devine Devarim

tzaddik v'ralo A righteous person to whom evil occurs.

ha'olam haba The afterlife; the next world, or the world to come.

Mystical Moments

The first mention the Bible makes of the afterlife is in the book of Samuel (28:15–19). Long after the judge Samuel has died, King Saul seeks his advice in his battle with the Philistines, who greatly outnumber his own army. Samuel appears and tells him, "Tomorrow, you and your sons shall be with me; the Lord will give the army of Israel also into the hands of the Philistines."

In short, Judaism struggles with the concept of why bad things happen to good people. The straight line between Jacob's tricking his father and then finding himself the victim of similar behavior illustrates that on a spiritual level Judaism does believe we get back what we put out measure for measure. It's just that in uncertain moral times like these, the concept of divine retribution becomes somewhat cloudy. Judaism doesn't offer any simple, pat answer to the question of the presence of evil in the world—because there are no pat answers. This is something that all of us struggle with.

The Least You Need to Know

- Many Biblical figures struggled with their flaws as they developed their greatness.
- Character matters above all.
- Jews believe in karma, too!
- Even the good experience tragedy, but they shall be rewarded in the afterlife for their suffering.

Chapter 8

The First National Bank of Pharaoh

In This Chapter

- ◆ The story of Joseph
- ◆ The reunion of Joseph and his brothers
- ◆ The difference between arrogance and self-confidence
- ◆ Coping with loss

It's a good thing that they didn't have Hollywood pitch meetings back when the Bible was written. Imagine the reaction of a cynical Hollywood producer to a screenwriter's pitch of the story of Joseph. "You got a guy with no last name, in clothing that's out of fashion, and you want to shoot it on location in Egypt?"

For those of you unfamiliar with the story of our pal Joe, here it is in a nutshell.

Talk About Sibling Rivalry!

Joseph is the second youngest of 11 brothers. As his father's favorite, he earns the jealousy and wrath of his siblings, who only become more enraged when little Joey decides that his dreams are telling him that he is superior to the other members of his family. One day, while out wearing the coat of many colors that his father gave him, Joseph meets up with his jealous brothers. The unruly mob throws him in a pit, hoping that he'll fall prey to a wild animal. In a strange fit of conscience, one of the brothers declares that it's not right to kill family. Instead, they opt to sell him into slavery to a passing caravan. The brothers return to their father, feeding him the tale that Joseph was attacked and killed by a wild animal and showing him the tattered bloody coat as evidence.

Joseph eventually finds himself in Egypt, where he becomes a servant in Pharaoh's house. The wife of Potiphar, one of the Pharaoh's top aides, takes a liking to Joseph and is irate to be turned down by our virtuous hero. As revenge, she tells her powerful husband that Joseph put the moves on her and Joseph soon finds himself in jail. Behind bars, Joseph takes to interpreting dreams for the other prisoners. He tells one cellmate that he will reclaim his old position as assistant to Pharaoh. Two years after his prediction comes true, Joseph finds himself recommended as a dream interpreter for the Pharaoh himself.

Pharaoh tells Joseph his dream: Seven skinny cows eat seven fatter cows. Joseph explains that the dream means that Egypt is going to enjoy seven years of excellent economic growth followed by a famine. He further instructs Pharaoh that the time is now to start putting away grains for those seven lean years. Pharaoh goes along with this, and puts Joseph—a Jew, by the way—in charge of the entire Egyptian economy.

While Joseph is the head of the Egyptian economy, the famine comes, just as he predicted. Twenty-two years after having sold him into slavery, Joseph's 11 brothers come down from the land of Canaan looking for assistance. Now in a seat of power, Joseph tests his brothers

Mystical Moments

Who was the deceived father? Give yourself a cookie if you answered Jacob. The bad karma curse didn't end with his deceptive wedding. To make matters worse, his beloved Rachel—for whom he toiled 14 years, if you count the 7 he was swindled out of when he mistakenly married Leah—dies in childbirth.

Spiritual Citations

"When arrogance appears, disgrace follows."
—Proverbs 11:2

Mystical Moments

Jacob sired 12 sons, from which the 12 tribes of Israel (i.e., the entire Jewish race) descend. In fact, after Jacob wrestles with an angel and wins, he is bestowed a new name: Israel (in Hebrew, "Yisra'el"). It's a wonder the WWF hasn't commandeered the name yet.

to see if they have learned their lesson for the evil they did to him. When they pass the test, Joseph reveals his true identity to them, prompting a joyous family reunion. The brothers go back to tell their father, Jacob, that Joseph is still alive, and that he's running Egypt. The entire family picks up and moves to escape the famine in Canaan.

Arrogance vs. Self-Confidence

Rabbi Abraham J. Twerski offers powerful commentaries on these and other Biblical events in his book *Living Each Week*. With regard to Joseph, Twerski points out the balance that he eventually learned between arrogance and self-confidence. When the story begins, Joseph is a conceited 17-year-old who believes his family should bow down to him. Most 17-year-olds I know have a hard time taking anything seriously, especially their families. In that sense, the story of Joseph inflicting his dream interpretations on his family squares with everything I remember about being that age. However, through his harsh and trying experiences, Joseph learns to shed his arrogance and grow into a confident man.

In short, Joseph moves beyond fear. Arrogance minus fear leaves self-confidence, a trait that only comes from proving over time that you can succeed at a given task. For Joseph, that task was simple survival. His ability to withstand these traumatic events and experiences left him with a strong degree of self-confidence, which in turn manifested itself when his two cellmates told him their dreams. Joseph eventually parlayed his self-confidence into a stint as Pharaoh's right-hand man—an enormous accomplishment for someone who was both an ex-convict and a Jew.

Joseph's story also demonstrates, once again, that actions have consequences, as evidenced by the fate of his vengeful brothers. When passion or emotion blinds us, we more often than not make hasty decisions that have huge ramifications down the road. In the Jewish marriage ceremony, the husband—or sometimes the husband and the wife—step on a glass. The third interpretation, the one most germane to our discussion here, is the notion that a relationship is very much like a glass—it appears strong, and yet it is incredibly fragile. One false step and it could be shattered. It's almost impossible to fit the pieces back together after it's been broken. So the breaking of the glass is reminder to both parties in the marriage that a relationship can actually be shattered with a false step.

> **Spiritual Citations**
>
> "It is impossible to have a dream that does not contain worthless information."
> —The Talmud, Berachot 55B

The Jews' History Begins

In traditional Jewish belief, the consequence of the selling of Joseph into slavery was the descent of the nascent Jewish people into the land of Egypt, where they would serve in slavery for hundreds of years. In other words, his brothers' actions not only affected arrogant little Joey, but an entire nation.

It should be noted that, throughout all of his trials and tribulations, Joseph never complains—not when he's sold into slavery or even when Potiphar's wife bears false witness (a Biblical no-no if ever there was one). Joseph displays an extraordinary degree of acceptance. People of faith tend to believe that there is a reason behind everything that happens, even though we cannot always identify what that reason is. We mentioned earlier the Hebrew expression *gam zu l'tovah*, meaning "this too is for the best." We can never understand exactly why we are suffering in a given situation. The Jews personify the notion that what doesn't kill us truly does make us stronger.

Devine Devarim

gam zu l'tovah   this too is for the best.

Jewish scholarship finds the details that are omitted to be as important as the ones that are made plain. The fact that Joseph is nowhere found to complain has been understood by Jewish scholars down the centuries as a lesson in spiritual acceptance of unpleasant and even life-threatening circumstances. Acceptance doesn't mean liking a situation; it just means acknowledging that this is the reality, and that we hope it will pass.

There's one final lesson to draw from Joseph, and also from the Book of Genesis, according to Rabbi Twerski, and that's this: Don't take revenge.

When Joseph sees his 11 brothers arraigned before him in the court of the pharaoh's palace in Egypt, he could so easily have had them locked up, punished, or even killed. At that moment, Joseph held all the cards. Traditional Judaism strongly opposed the concept of carrying a grudge, because when we fail to "drop the rock," we are very likely to take revenge at the earliest opportunity. The Bible admonishes this: "Don't hate your brother in your heart."

Joseph did not reveal his identity immediately, for which he perhaps could be faulted. One might accuse him of a little bit of gamesmanship with his brothers. He also caused his father additional pain when he demanded the youngest brother, Benjamin, be brought down to Egypt before he revealed his identity. His father, Jacob, was convinced that not only would Joseph be lost but now his youngest son, Benjamin, would die as well. Joseph could have spared everyone a whole lot of anguish if he had simply revealed his identity at the first possible moment instead of schlepping it out.

> **High Spirits**
>
> A husband and wife are flying over the Pacific when the pilot comes over the PA system. "Ladies and gentlemen, I have some good news and some bad news. The bad news is the engine is out and we're going to have to make an emergency landing. The good news is I see an island. However, it's uncharted so the likelihood of being found and rescued is slim."
>
> The husband turns to his wife and asks, "Sarah, did you mail that check to that Jewish charity?"
>
> Sarah replies, "No, Irving. It completely slipped my mind!" When Irving laughs, she asks, "What's so funny about that at a time like this?"
>
> Irving replies, "They'll find us."

The whole point of the Book of Genesis is that the founding fathers and mothers of Judaism, with the exception of Abraham, were not perfect people. They suffered from the same sorts of character flaws and weaknesses that trouble us today. The Bible is not a record of how perfect people led blameless lives. Rather it is the story of how individuals, much like ourselves, faced with hardship overcame weaknesses in order to establish a beautiful religion for themselves and the generations that followed them.

The Least You Need to Know

♦ Arrogance minus fears equals self-confidence.

♦ Apparent tragedy often leads to greater spiritual success.

♦ We cannot always understand why we suffer, but suffering is never random.

♦ Judaism teaches that everything is for the best.

Spirituality Secrets of Sinai

In This Chapter

- ◆ The importance of Passover
- ◆ The mass revelation of the Exodus
- ◆ The early years of Moses
- ◆ The hardening of Pharaoh's heart

Talk show host Johnny Carson defined Thanksgiving as "the day when entire families gather around the table once a year to thank God for the fact that they only have to gather around the table once a year."

Passover is another matter. Jewish families that may have little contact with Judaism throughout the rest of the year almost certainly come together for a Passover *Seder*, the festive meal marked by the telling of the Exodus story or the recounting of some other movement toward human freedom. Of almost all the Jewish holidays, we find Passover the most compelling and emotionally stirring. Perhaps only Yom Kippur has the same amount of force to touch the hearts of Jews, even those not otherwise affiliated or active in Judaism.

The central claim of the traditional approach to Passover is that God freed an enslaved people from one of the most powerful nations the world has ever known. In doing so, the freed people earned a special relationship with God.

Hitting the Road

Traditional Judaism places the Exodus story at the absolute heart of the religion. It is impossible to imagine traditional Judaism without the story of Moses leading the children of Israel away from Pharaoh, across the Red Sea, and into freedom in the desert. Orthodox Jews not only believe the story as written, but follow a dictate from the Talmud which suggests that "it is incumbent upon every Jew to consider himself or herself as having been present at Sinai." So for the Orthodox, God's gift of the Torah at Mount Sinai is not simply an historical event that happened three millennia ago. Rather, it is an event at which each of them was present … if only in spirit. Sinai is a vital and living experience for traditionally minded Jews.

> ## High Spirits
>
> Not all Jewish holidays are well known—even to observant Jews. My cousin Bob, who lives on West 72nd Street in Manhattan, emerged from his apartment one day to find that alternate side of the street parking, a staple of life in the Big Apple, had been suspended that day. He turned to the building superintendent, who was from Puerto Rico, and asked what the occasion was. *"Shemini atzeret,"* the superintendent matter-of-factly replied, naming a little-known Jewish festival day. Imagine that! Some Jewish holidays are better known to building superintendents and the parking department than to Jews.

The question of whether Mount Sinai happened as written has troubled Jews for generations. In the twelfth century, a writer named Rabbi Yehuda Halevi wrote a book called *The Kuzari* about the Turkish king of the Khazars, one of the tribes that made up Russia in the eighth century. The king had a recurring dream in which God told him that although his thoughts were in the right place, his actions were all wrong. The king of the Khazars therefore brought to his court a Greek philosopher, a Moslem cleric, a Christian leader, and a rabbi. He interrogated each as to the beliefs of his faith and ultimately decided that Jews had the religious approach that most clearly comported with his feelings about the Almighty. Not only did the king of Khazars convert, but so did all his people.

Spiritual Citations

"How I should love to cuddle with the Sabbath queen."

—Julius Lester, an African-American 1960s revolutionary who converted to Judaism

One of the questions that the king poses to the rabbi is how he can be certain that the Exodus happened as written in the Bible. The rabbi responds that no other religion in the history of the world has ever claimed to have come into existence via a mass witnessing of the voice and presence of God. In Christianity, the belief is that Jesus demonstrated miracles to a relatively small number of people, and that God's revelation to him was a one-on-one affair. Similarly, when Buddhism and Islam were founded, they began when their leaders (Buddha and Mohammed, respectively) went off on their own and experienced a series of divine prophecies or revelations. Only Judaism, by contrast, claims that God spoke not to one person or even a handful but to several million people all at the same time. This claim of mass revelation sets Judaism apart from the other faiths of the world.

The rabbi asks the king, "How could so many million people have seen this and yet there nowhere exists a minority report? How could it be that no one in the thousands of years since the Exodus has refuted this charge?"

The Serendipity of Moses

In the beginning of the book of Exodus, the Jews have been living in Egypt for quite some time and have become an extremely numerous group. Initially, there were 70 individuals who came down with Joseph and his family. But that was generations ago. Once Exodus begins, the Jews are so numerous that they trigger fear in the mind of Pharaoh, who tells his advisors, "Come, let us do wisely with the Jews, lest they multiply, and if there is a war, join up with our enemies, and fight against us."

Anti-Semitic paranoia? Intelligent projection? You be the judge. Either way, Pharaoh enslaved the Jewish people and made them build storehouses. Whether the Jews actually built the great pyramids is a matter of historical and archaeological conjecture. The great pyramids associated, at least in the minds of Jews, with the period of Jewish slavery were not built at the time when Jews were serving as slaves, according to the book of Exodus. So we're not quite sure exactly which great storehouses the Bible is describing, although it appears not to be the great pyramids of Egypt that we can visit today.

Once the Pharaoh who enslaves the Jews dies and a new Pharaoh takes his place, the Jewish people's hopes of freedom are dashed. The new Pharaoh makes life even tougher for the Jews, increasing their workload to the point where the Jewish male slaves must remain at their work sites even at night because they do not have time to travel home. According to the mystical tradition, the Jewish women actually come out to the work site at night to make love with their husbands so as to insure the continuation of the Jewish people.

> ### High Spirits
>
> "I thank God for my sons," said an elderly man. "My firstborn is a doctor. The second is a lawyer; the third, a chemist; the fourth, an artist; and the fifth, a writer."
>
> "What do you do?" he was asked.
>
> "I," said the man, "have a dry goods store. Not a very big one, but I manage to support them all."
>
> —Author Unknown

Then comes the edict that Jewish baby boys must be put to death as soon as they are born, in an effort to eliminate the possibility of a later generation of Jewish fighters. This prompts a Jewish mother to put her son in a small raft of reeds and float the child down the Nile, believing her son has a better chance at surviving. The infant is discovered by the daughter of the Pharaoh, a kindly woman who then unwittingly hires the same boy's mother as a wet nurse in order to ensure his survival. Thus, Moses grows up in the house of Pharaoh, surrounded by all the accoutrements of wealth and power that the Pharaoh's home can provide.

The fact that Moses grows up in such splendor offers yet another key to Jewish spiritual thinking. What sets Moses apart from his fellows is not only the fact that he does not have to work like a slave. What distinguishes him is his attitude. Moses grows up in an atmosphere conducive to the development of power and leadership. Although possible, it is highly unlikely that a Moses-type leader could have emerged from the ranks of the slaves. If not for Moses, it's entirely possible that the descendants of Joseph would have served as slaves until the point where any trace of non-Egyptian identity would have been eliminated. The Jewish people might never have come into existence.

Spiritual Citations

Any leader who can't see a distance of 500 miles is no leader.
—The Stoliner Rebbe

Devine Devarim

Nisan The first month of the Jewish calendar and the month of the Jewish Exodus from Egypt. Ironically, Rosh Hashanah, the Jewish New Year, falls during the seventh month, **Tishrei,** the month during which God created the world.

Moses' story illustrates the importance of expectations. In spiritual terms, we generally get what we expect. Today, expectations for Jewish kids runs so high that, according to Woody Allen, the definition of when life begins is upon graduation from medical school.

Moses grew up with the mentality of a winner. And yet, he did not achieve greatness until he went out to see what his fellow Jews had to do for a living. Rabbi Twerski draws our attention to Exodus 2:11, which says, "And Moses grew up and went out to his brothers and saw their suffering." Interestingly, the Hebrew verb for "grew up," *vayigdal,* can also be understood as "became great." The root of the verb is *gadol,* which Hebrew school survivors may recall as meaning "big." In other words, the verse can be read on two levels of biblical interpretation—pshat and remez. The standard way, pshat, suggests that once Moses grew up and was of a certain age, he went out and saw the suffering of his brothers. You could also understand it this way: Moses *only became great* when he went out and saw the suffering of his brothers.

In other words, we do not maximize our own potential when we think solely of ourselves. When we don't recognize the fact that others in the world may not have it as good as we do, we are not all we could be. The power of the story of Moses is that the suffering of others transformed him. If you've seen the Disney movie *The Prince of Egypt,* you get the sense that until Moses went out and saw how hard his fellow Jews were forced to work, he was, in comparison, training to be a greeter in Tomorrowland.

Far from Perfect

Moses went from being a trust fund baby to the potential leader of his people practically overnight. But even this fearless leader has character flaws. When Moses sees an Egyptian taskmaster beating a Jewish slave, he kills the tormenter, looks both ways, and buries him in the desert. Certainly his heart was in the right place when he saw his fellow Jew being beaten, but killing the taskmaster is probably not the most ideal form of dispute resolution. Moses clearly had a lot to learn about leadership.

The next day, Moses witnesses the same mistreatment. The taskmaster this time challenges Moses and says, "Are you going to kill me the way you killed that other guy?" Moses is shocked: He can't believe that word has gotten out. Now he's got to make a run for it. You can't go around killing taskmasters. The Teamsters won't stand for it. Moses makes a run for it. He goes to the desert, marries, and is tending a flock of sheep when he comes upon a burning bush, a bush that "burns but is not consumed." This becomes the signal by which God first speaks to Moses and tasks him with the mission of getting the Jews out of Egypt.

> ### Mystical Moments
>
> Why a burning bush? Elie Wiesel, the author of Pulitzer-winning works related to the Holocaust, suggests that if there had been a bolt of lightning, Moses probably would have run and hid from it. If the sign had been something else that was vast, other people might have seen it as well. But a bush that burns and is not consumed—now that's an attention-getter. It was a one person-sized miraculous event, exactly right for attracting the attention of young Moses.

It might sound surprising, but Moses does not warm to the task at all of being the leader of the Jewish people. Maybe he'd been to some Federation meetings and knew what he was in for. Like most trust fund babies, he had developed a slight allergy to real work and tries like heck to get out of the job. Moses tells God, "You don't want me to do it. I have a speech impediment." God replies that Moses' brother Aaron can do the talking. Moses tries another tact: "I don't know what your name is, God. When the Pharaoh asks me what 'God' sent me, I won't know what to say." God replies, "Let them know that 'I will be whatever I will be' sent you." This is the intriguing name by which God asks to be identified. Thus comes the Jewish belief that God can handle any situation and will take on the form that is most appropriate.

God is very patient as Moses goes through these objections—and why not? God has a lot more time than Moses. Finally, Moses says, "You know, I just don't want to do it. Send somebody else." That really ticks the Almighty off. God replies, "Moses, I'm not asking you, I'm *telling* you. Go to Pharaoh now. Tell him to let my people go that they might serve me in the desert."

By now, Moses is a married man, having wed a woman he encounters while on the lam earlier. Moses now goes to his father-in-law, Jethro (no, not the one of *The Beverly Hillbillies* fame) and asks for permission to leave the camp and return to the home of Pharaoh. Couldn't Moses just tell Jethro, "See ya!"? Of course he could. However, according to Rabbi Twerski, divine ordinance does not make you exempt from the responsibilities of being a decent person. Were he alive today, Moses would have explained his important mission to his wife and asked if it was okay with her. However, 3,300 years ago, the world worked slightly differently. Moses felt obligated to discuss the matter with his father-in-law. Rabbi Twerski suggests that it was simply out of respect (*derech eretz*, as connoted in Hebrew) that Moses went to Jethro. In political terms, it would be described as a courtesy call. Jewish tradition does not look kindly on the arrogance of power.

Devine Devarim

Haggadah The scripture read at the Seder during the first two nights of Passover that recounts the plagues Moses brings upon Egypt and the Jewish Exodus.

Moses now makes repeated trips to Pharaoh, his brother Aaron in tow, requesting that Pharaoh let the Jewish people go. Pharaoh refuses to the point where Moses, acting at God's behest, brings down a series of plagues on the Egyptians, which are recounted in the traditional Passover *Haggadah*. Changing the water of the Nile to blood is no small matter; the river is the chief god of the Egyptian people. The plagues increase in severity and Pharaoh continues to refuse the Jews' egress. Finally, the killing of the Egyptian firstborn children proves too much for Pharaoh, who finally relents.

To Err or Not to Err

This story would not be morally problematic except for one not-so-minor detail: In between each plague, we are told that God "hardened Pharaoh's heart." The implication is that Pharaoh might have been willing to let the Jews go, but God would not allow him to act on that willingness. How can the plagues that God brought down on Egypt be reconciled with a loving and fair deity if, in fact, God was "hardening Pharaoh's heart"?

There are two mystical responses to this question. One is that the Egyptians had so enslaved and embittered the lives of the Jews that this level of punishment was appropriate. Another, deeper answer requires an examination of the concept "hardening one's heart."

There's a simple truth about human nature: We can become used to just about anything. Initially, when we err, it feels wrong. We might not be able to sleep that first night. But if we persist in our actions, no matter how wrong they may be, the astonishing capacity of the human mind to rationalize anything kicks in. We become inured to the nagging of our conscience.

> ### High Spirits
>
> Humor columnist Art Buchwald once wrote a column purporting to be a mock interview with a Mafia hit man. Buchwald asked how he was able to go around killing people for a living. The man replied, "To be honest, I had some trouble sleeping the first night, but after that I got used to it."

Pharaoh wasn't above the law. He *was* the law. God instructs Moses and Aaron to see Pharaoh early in the morning at the banks of the Nile because this is the time when Pharaoh, ahem, relieves himself. In order to perpetuate his godlike persona, Pharaoh must keep such matters secret from his followers; gods don't have the same physical requirements as the rest of us, if you catch my drift.

So Pharaoh would sneak down to the Nile first thing in the morning, do his business, and spend the rest of the day performing his Pharaonic duties. People who consider themselves gods and are seen by others as gods do not consider themselves bound by the same rules as the rest of us. Pharaoh, like many an absolute ruler before and after him, was an absolutely corrupt individual. As such, he had become so used to following his own pleasures that the feelings of others—such as the million slaves he had sleeping in the fields every night—meant nothing to him. Like the Mafia hit man, he had become used to doing the wrong thing.

Rabbis traditionally believe that the "hardening of Pharaoh's heart" actually meant that Pharaoh acted as if he were *addicted* to doing the wrong thing. A drug addict could be described as hard-hearted in that he or she is totally incapable of putting the feelings of others ahead of anything but using drugs. So it was with Pharaoh: Doing whatever came into his heart, no matter how much pain it caused others, was his standard mode of behavior.

> ### Spiritual Citations
>
> "Power corrupts and absolute power corrupts absolutely."
> —Lord Acton, English historian

In Jewish terms, the notion of spirituality is utterly inseparable from the notion of character. Pharaoh himself might have been the most spiritually minded person on the planet. When he wasn't oppressing Jews, he might have spent the entire day praying to Isis and Osiris. However, spirituality cannot be separated from the actions we take in the real world. How we treat people is at least as important as how we try to relate to God.

On Yom Kippur, we seek to repent for our wrong actions. "Repent" simply means to change one's mind. When we do something that hurts someone, we generally don't think too much about it, then or thereafter. Yom Kippur asks us to go back through the year and review our actions to see where we might have hurt someone. The magic of Yom Kippur—in mystical terms, the holiday during which we cleanse our souls for the New Year—cannot take effect until we have asked forgiveness from individuals we have harmed. The Talmud, where it discusses Yom Kippur, is quite explicit: Forgiveness cannot be granted by God until it is sought from our fellows. The Jewish tradition teaches that prayers disconnected by action are of no meaning in Judaism. Actions matter. The actions we take don't just change the world—they change us. Striving to live a decent life strengthens our Jewish karma. If, on the other hand, we repeatedly harm others, we will become used to a life of indecency and reach a point where, like Pharaoh, it just doesn't bother us. That's when we risk taking down not just ourselves but our loved ones and even our community and our world. In Judaism, actions speak louder than words.

Pharaoh allowed the Egyptians to endure numerous plagues before relenting to Moses' demands. In order, the 10 infamous plagues were: the Nile turning to blood, frog infestation, lice, wild animals, cattle disease, boils, hail, locusts, three days of darkness, and the deaths of the firstborn. After the tenth and final plague, Pharaoh released the Jewish people. However, they still faced an arduous 40-year journey ahead of them.

The Least You Need to Know

- Passover is one of the most holy of the Jewish holidays.
- Judaism is the only religion to claim mass revelation of God.
- No matter how important we perceive ourselves to be, we must always be respectful.
- Actions speak louder than words.

The Main Event

In This Chapter

- The parting of the Red Sea
- The deliverance of manna
- The mass revelation at Mount Sinai
- The Jews were chosen by God

And so we come to the "main event" in Jewish history, God's gift of the Torah at Mount Sinai. Judaism has drawn from the Sinai experience, as described in Exodus and as amplified in various commentaries, as a wellspring of information about spirituality.

Follow Your Own Leader

When we last saw the Jewish people, they were fleeing in haste after the tenth plague, at which point Pharaoh finally allowed them to depart. They had no time, according to tradition, even to bake bread before they left; hence the *matzah*, or unleavened bread, that the Jews eat on Passover. By the time the Jews reached the Egyptian border at the Red Sea, Pharaoh's army had practically overtaken them. (Pharaoh, still caught up in his addiction to evil, had changed his mind about releasing the Jews.)

The unarmed Jews were trapped between the devil and the deep blue—or in this case Red—sea. At this point, for the first time but certainly not for the last, the Jewish people were highly critical of Moses, asking him, "Because there were no graves in Egypt, have you taken us away to die in the wilderness?" (Exodus 14:11)

Moses turns to God, not quite sure how to handle this rebellion. God tells Moses to stretch out his rod over the water, and it will divide; the Jews will make it across and the Egyptians, to complete their punishment for the abuse they have heaped upon the Jews for all these years, will not. According to the midrash, the collection of rabbinical insights into Bible stories, the Jews huddle en masse at the water's edge, fearful of entering it. One Jew, Nachshon, the leader of the tribe of Judah, takes the plunge—literally. He dives in, at which point the water suddenly parts.

Devine Devarim

An error made during early translations of the Bible may have accidentally made a mountain out of a molehill. According to some scholars, the original written version meant "Reed Sea," which would have been considerably easier to part than water. However, this translation does not account for the drowning of the Egyptians after the Jews safely pass through.

Nachshon's action illustrates the Jewish belief that we cannot rely on other people to do the hard work for us. We must be as spiritually self-reliant as Nachshon, the Mark Spitz of his generation, and dive right in.

Today there is a tendency to look upon rabbis as the spiritual torchbearers for their communities. It's almost as though rabbis were the spiritual equivalent of stockbrokers: We might check in once in a while to see how our account is, but by and large we let them make the trades.

Mystical Moments

In Judaism, there are very few moments—such as Rosh Hashanah and Yom Kippur—when a rabbi actually speaks to God on behalf of his or her community, acting as a middle person or go-between. The rest of the time, we are truly on our own in prayer and in our lives, in the sense that we are expected to be responsible for our own spiritual well-being.

A rabbi's role in a community is, as we all learned in Sunday School, that of a teacher. A rabbi teaches us how to pray, how to understand concepts in Judaism, and how to behave ethically and morally in the world, but the role pretty much ends there. Certainly, rabbis are expected to lead by example in terms of exemplifying good character. But the salvation of an individual Jew is his or her own business, not the responsibility of the rabbi, no matter how prominent or learned. This idea explains why several million people—not a lone representative—received God's word on Mount Sinai: Just as we are responsible for our spiritual lives now, so were all the Jews given a peek at the true nature of God.

High Spirits

A yeshiva in England created a rowing team to compete in regattas. This one particular yeshiva trounced all its competition in the Jewish world and decided that it would take a chance and enter a regatta that included teams from secular schools as well.

The Jewish team came in dead last. When asked why they did so poorly, the captain said, "Well, on all the other boats, they had one person shouting directions and six people rowing. On our boat, it was the other way around."

It is said that the only thing Jews like more than gefilte fish is a title. Jews love to think of themselves as leaders and not followers. The Talmud offers the following axiom: "Better to be a tail to lions than a head to foxes." In other words, we're much better off keeping the right company instead of running with a group that's only going to get into trouble. Nonetheless, leaders don't have all the answers. Sometimes it's up to us to take the plunge.

Woodsy Would Be Proud

The Jews make their way across the water to safety in the desert. What exactly is the purpose of the desert? Why do the Jews end up spending 40 years there? In spiritual terms, a desert is a place of material emptiness. It's a place where we are able to develop ourselves spiritually. You can almost think of the 40 years in the desert as the spiritual boot camp the Jews underwent prior to entering the land of Israel. This is where our people developed the cohesion, national self-hype, and confidence that was lacking when we were slaves in Egypt.

Recently, some rabbis have raised questions as to whether the Jews actually lived in the desert at all, let alone for 40 years. They argue that no archaeological evidence exists to support the proposition. Traditionally minded Jews respond by saying that a desert region, consisting mainly of sand, is not conducive to leaving an archaeological record for a people who essentially camped for brief periods and built nothing to last. They built no permanent structures, the foundations of which could be discovered. They traveled by foot, and so left behind no chariots. How could we possibly expect the desert to yield clues that a people had traveled there for that long?

Spiritual Citations

"If a Jew breaks a leg, he thanks God he did not break both legs; if he breaks both, he thanks God he did not break his neck."

—Yiddish proverb

Think back to Woodstock, in the summer of 1969. A quarter of a million people attended the famous music festival in upper New York State. If you were to examine the farmland where the festival took place, you might find some historical markers, but you would not find any specific trace of the festival itself. You would find no Coke cans, no pieces of the stage, not even any roach clips. Just as 250,000 people left no archaeological record of themselves at Woodstock, so it is that several million people left no archaeological record in a desert over a 40-year window more than 33 centuries ago.

While the Biblical account of the Exodus may be difficult to prove, fairness dictates that it is equally hard to disprove as well.

What's the Manna with You?

Celebrations ensue now that the Jews have escaped Egypt and are safely on the other side of the sea. Moses and the men sing; Miriam, Moses' sister, leads the women in song and dance as well. It doesn't take long, however, before the Jews start to chatter about Moses and his brother Aaron. As with any Jewish touring group, they start complaining about the food. "Back in Egypt," they say, "we had meat and bread. Now we've got nothing to eat—nothing good, anyway. And such small portions!"

Thus we come to the story of the *manna*, an important chapter in Jewish mystical belief that explains how the Jews managed to survive in the harsh desert climate. At dawn, when they awaken, the Jews find enough food to last for the whole day. What's more, their fare tastes like practically anything they want it to taste like—sort of a Biblical tofu, if you will. God essentially says to the Jewish people, "If you walk in my ways, I will take care of you. If you just stick with me, everything is going to be okay—*spiritually and materially*."

Every morning thereafter, the Jews awaken and go outside to collect their manna, which you could also call the first airdrop of food supplies in recorded history. On Friday mornings, the manna would come down in a double portion so that there would be enough for the Sabbath without having to gather it that day as well. The Sabbath, as a day of rest, featured no gathering of food in the desert … and no shopping for food today. We buy enough on Friday to get us through!

Devine Devarim

manna (1) The food, obtained by way of miracle, that the Jews lived on during their 40 years in the desert. (2) Divine or spiritual nourishment.

There is a very significant message here about how we are provided for. The Jewish spiritual belief is that individuals—a boss, a client, a customer—are only the vehicles by which we are taken care of in a financial or material sense. The real source of our supply is our creator. The Jews in the desert were asked to have faith in the same God who got them out of slavery, out of Egypt, and into the relative safety of the desert. They were asked to believe that this God would protect them and meet all their needs. They had a choice: If they acted with faith, the manna would descend and they would be completely taken care of.

This reminds me of the experience of many of the Holocaust survivors immediately after World War II. Many of them were not repatriated to the countries from which they had come. After all, the Jewish communities where they had lived were pretty much destroyed by that point. Not only that, anti-Semitism lingered on even after the war, and many Jews were killed in Poland and other Eastern European countries even after World War II had officially been declared over.

Some Jews went directly to Israel or America, if they had either family or an intense desire to travel to those places. Yet thousands upon thousands of Jews who had been in the concentration camps spent as many as four years, or in some cases even longer, in "Displaced Persons camps," or DP camps. In the DP camps, the survivors had all their needs met: Comfortable bedrooms in which to sleep, all the food they could eat, even entertainment in the form of hobbies such as photography or amateur theatrics.

The DP camps were staffed by servicemen and women who knew what the survivors had undergone at the hands of the Nazis and who could not do enough to treat them with dignity and respect, as DP camp attendees later testified. Their time in the camps gave them the ability to rest, get their strength back, and begin to deal with the emotional trauma of the horrors they had witnessed and the losses they had suffered along the way.

In many ways, the desert experience of the Jewish generation that had escaped Egypt was much like a DP camp. They did not have to work. All their material needs were met. They were free to develop their lives as they saw fit. It was a time when they could release the slave mentality that had haunted them in Egypt and begin to contemplate new lives in the land of Israel.

The difference between the DP camps after World War II and the desert experience was that little, if anything, was expected of the refugees in the DP camps. They were completely at leisure to rebuild their lives at their own pace. In the desert, God had other plans for the Jews: Here, God would fashion them into a spiritual people as opposed to a slave people. They would learn to move their reliance from the Egyptian taskmasters to the one God, as God spoke directly to them.

What, exactly, did God expect? We've seen earlier in this book that the Jewish concept of God is of a loving, present, caring, and listening Deity, yet One who has high expectations about character and behavior. God gives us much, but expects much in return. The spiritual lesson of the manna is that when we place our trust in our Creator, we don't have to struggle on a material level. We will be given what we need, and we will neither starve nor need to beg. As it is written in the Psalms, "I have been young and now I am old, and yet I have never seen a righteous person begging for bread." If the world is acting out of faith, then all our needs are met. That's the lesson of the manna.

Unfortunately, human beings tend to act out of fear at least as often as they act out of faith; the fear that they would not be taken care of evidences itself over and over throughout the Jews' time in the desert. However, the fact that at no time was the Bible expunged of all the fearful, negative, critical moments when the Jews were at odds with Moses and with God indicates that there is a certain amount of faith in the accuracy of the stories. Why would a people manufacture stories about its creation in which they deliberately come off badly? Jews have historically exhibited a painful accuracy about themselves and their shortcomings.

Taking Egypt out of the Jews

After the deliverance of *manna*, we find the Jews at their next pitstop along the way, a location called Refidim (Exodus 17:1). Now that the food situation has been handled, the Jews turn to complaining about the lack of water. You start to wonder whether Moses, in the privacy of his thoughts, ever wondered if he should have taken one look at that burning bush and just kept walking. Who needs such *tsuris?* Moses may have been slightly daunted by the continuing negative behavior of the Jewish people, but God certainly was not. God says to Moses in Exodus 19:4: "You have seen what I did to Egypt, and how I carried you on eagle's wings, and brought you to myself. And now if you will certainly obey my voice, and keep my covenant, you shall be my own treasure from among all peoples, for all the Earth is mine. And you shall be to me a kingdom of priests, and a holy nation."

This run-up to Mount Sinai brings up one of the thorniest issues in all of Judaism: The question of chosenness. Traditional Judaism believes that God essentially chose the Jews to be a model community in the world, to be an example of exactly what God wants in terms of behavior, character, and morality. The theory was supposed to work this way: God would give the Jews instructions as to how to live exemplary lives, the rest of the world would see this, and would act with an awareness in their lives that God existed in the world.

As the anti-Semitic rhyme puts it, "How odd of God to choose the Jews." (Although the less well known response is this: "But not so odd/As those who choose/A Jewish God/But spurn the Jews.") On the face of it, the Jews *were* a rather odd choice for this particular mission. With the exception of Abraham, none of the previous leaders or founders of the Jewish people were rather exemplary human beings. They had their good points, but they sure got into some serious ethical scrapes. (We haven't even talked about Judah and Tamar; you can look that one up in your own Bible.) The Jews were a slave people with a slave mentality, and as soon as they tasted a little bit of freedom, all they could do is complain: "Moses, we can't cross the water! Where's our food? Is this the best you can do? Where's my Evian?" And that's only the beginning.

According to Rabbi Irwin Kula, "It was easier to take the people out of Egypt than to take Egypt out of the people." The behavior of the Jewish people, even after the giving of the Torah at Mount Sinai, was so bad that God decreed that with a few exceptions the entire generation would have to die—even including their leader Moses. Only their children, the following generation, would have the privilege of entering the land of Israel.

And yet, despite all their shortcomings, God must have seen something in the Jewish people. This is one of the extraordinary mystical secrets of Judaism: God has even more faith in us than we have in God or in ourselves.

Mystical Moments

During the Civil War, Harriet Tubman became known as the "Moses of the Underground Railroad" for her efforts in helping slaves escape from the South into the "promised land" of the North, much as Moses himself helped the Jews escape from Egypt into the desert.

You Make the Call

Then comes the moment when God actually speaks to the entire Jewish people at Mount Sinai. It must have been quite a sight: The entire mountain "smoked in every part, because God descended upon it in fire, and the smoke ascended like the smoke of a furnace, and the whole mountain quaked greatly." (Exodus 19:18) The people could hear the blast of the *shofar*, a ram's horn blown in remembrance on the High Holy Days even today. Thunder and lightning shook the mountain. Under these circumstances, God then spoke the words of the Ten Commandments.

The Bible could have been written under a different title: *Everything I Needed to Know I Learned from the Legal Codes I Received at Mount Sinai*. The Ten Commandments, by themselves, constitute enough of a system of laws for an individual or a society to live by: One God, no other gods; don't take the name of God in vain; keep the Sabbath; honor your parents; don't murder, practice idolatry, steal, bear false witness, or covet. When you think about it, if each of us could get through the day doing even that much, the world would be a much better place.

On a surface reading, God spoke, and it is understood that the Jews basically agreed. In fact, there is a moment where the Jews say *na'aseh v'nishmah*, meaning "We will do and we will hear." The mystical understanding of that phrase is that the Jews will perform practices as they have been instructed, and only after will they question why they are doing

what they're doing. In other words, the Jews are saying, "You got it, God, whatever you want. If we have any questions, we'll get back to you with them." In traditional Judaism, na'aseh v'nishmah is code for acting with faith. We may not always understand what we're doing, but we know we are in fact doing the right thing, and we'll try to keep doing it.

The intriguing question is whether or not the Jews actually obligated themselves at Mount Sinai to follow God's word. Picture yourself there (traditional Judaism suggests that we all do). You've been a slave all your life, which means that you haven't made a decision or even had too many original thoughts from the time you emerged from the womb.

How hard did the slaves work in Egypt? Rabbi Saul Berman, then of Lincoln Square Synagogue, once told his congregates, many of whom worked on Wall Street as attorneys and bankers, that they worked longer hours than did the slaves in Egypt. Nevertheless, the Jewish slaves in Egypt worked hard enough, and without so much as a retirement plan or HMO.

Picture the scenario: You're just getting your work done, and suddenly the city is infested with frogs. The Nile's an unsightly shade of red. Citizens unknowledgeable in the basics of cosmetology suffer uncomely boils. Then there go locusts. There go wild animals. And finally, there *you* go—you and the entire Jewish people, leaving in the middle of the night, following some random guy. Then, after narrowly escaping the entire Egyptian army, you end up in the desert, which has a sorry excuse for a cafeteria. By this point, you're probably feeling a bit confused and conflicted about the whole situation.

> **High Spirits**
>
> The whole of Holland is proof of what man can create on the most thankless soil.
>
> —Theodor Herzl

And then you are confronted with the greatest laser show in the history of the world. You can practically hear Pink Floyd. There's thunder, smoke, earthquakes, lightning, shofars blowing—and then all of a sudden you hear the voice of God, "Thou shalt not yada yada yada …."

The question is this: As witnesses to such an awesome phenomenon, did you and your fellow escapees agree to take on those Ten Commandments—not to mention the other 603 in the Torah—of your own free will? In law, a contract that is attained under duress is not enforceable. Were the Jews essentially pressured by God, with all this sound and light extravaganza, into accepting the Torah, or did they willingly agree?

This question is complicated by a mystical understanding of Exodus 19:17: "And Moses took the people out in the midst of the camp to meet God, and they gathered at the foot of the mountain [Mount Sinai]." The intrigue is found in the Hebrew word for "at the foot of," *b'tachtit*. This word is closely related to the Hebrew word *tachat*, which means "under." The Talmud, the great compendium of Jewish law composed approximately 1,400 to 1,700 years ago, contains an understanding of this verse with the word "under" plugged in where "at the foot of" normally goes. The rabbis of the Talmud read the verse this way: "And they stood *under* the mountain." In other words, in mystical terms, God actually *held* Mount Sinai over the heads of the Jewish people.

This is not something that you might have heard in Sunday School because mystical approaches are generally not taught to children. Nevertheless, Jewish thought holds that God physically holds the entire mountain over the Jews.

Mystical Moments

Canaan, or the "Promised Land," is the name of the Palestinian region that today lies between the Jordan and the Mediterranean. After leading the Jews out of Egypt, Moses sends forth spies to survey the land of Canaan. The men return and report of a wondrous place, a "land of milk and honey." However, they are too frightened of the inhabitants to try to claim the land as their own. As punishment, God subjects the refugees to 40 years of wandering the desert, ensuring that the generation that escaped Egypt will have perished and that a new generation will enter the Promised Land.

However, an opposing approach interprets the act as God saying, "You've got two choices. If you accept the Torah and the laws that I am giving you today, you will go freely into the land of Israel. If you don't accept, it's been nice knowing you!" That's a rather bold interpretation of the Almighty, so the rabbis who hold this belief came up with another explanation for when the Jewish people freely accepted the Torah. That time is actually Purim, when the Jews were so happy and grateful to have been saved from the clutches of evil Haman that they now willingly accepted the rules that God had first pronounced centuries earlier at Mount Sinai.

If you're scratching your head wondering which interpretation is correct, join the club. The essence of Judaism is that multiple interpretations of any given event in the Bible are not only accepted but welcomed. The Talmud tells the story of two rabbis who were at odds with each other over the interpretation of a particular Biblical verse. So they asked God to explain who was right. A voice came down from heaven, saying, "These *and these* are the words of a living God." In other words, Judaism is a religion that is extremely open to interpretation (within the limits, of course, of each of its movements). Therein lies Judaism's great appeal.

Spiritual Citations

A spiritual connection to Mount Sinai is not strictly the province of orthodox Jews. Ellen J. Lewis, writing for the Union of American Hebrew Congregations' Department of Adult Jewish Growth, a Reform Jewish organization, offered the following commentary. During a five-day hike through the Sinai desert that she had undertaken 20 years earlier, she and her group reached the base of Mount Sinai early on the afternoon of the second day. She found herself thinking, "So this is where it happened!

"Then I shook myself. This is where what happened? Never before had I believed that an actual revelation of Torah had occurred in the Sinai wilderness. I was, after all, a rational person. Yet somehow in that moment, an unexpected and powerful spiritual current opened me up to a new way of experiencing God's presence. For the first time in my life, I felt the power of divine revelation." (Shevat of May 30, 1998, *UAHC Torah Commentary*, pp. 1028–1043.)

Jews who have visited the mountain believed to be Mount Sinai have often experienced a deep and moving feeling. The question to ask is this: If there had been no Mount Sinai experience, then how exactly did the Jewish people come into being? Not only that: Why does half the world, roughly a billion Christians and two billion Moslems, accept as fact the revelation at Sinai?

Although I obviously cannot provide an eyewitness testimony, I do believe that there must have been something awfully big that directed this people on its path of spirituality and lapses from spirituality. What exactly the form was of that "big bang" experience, I cannot definitively say. But there is indeed something holy about the story of Mount Sinai and the escape of the Jews from Egypt, simply because the story has been treasured for thousands of years by our fellow Jews. No matter how rational we are, the story of Mount Sinai is, even in our generation, a burning bush: It's something for which we turn aside from our normal day-to-day pursuits and examine for ourselves. It is the source of an eternal flame that neither time nor rational thought has ever managed fully to extinguish.

The Least You Need to Know

- Leadership is a revered Judaic characteristic.
- We must be spiritually self-reliant.
- Countless Christians and Moslems agree that God spoke to the Jewish people at Mount Sinai.
- The revelations at Mount Sinai are the pinnacle of the Jewish faith.

Part 3

Between God and People

In Judaism, the soul is the contact point between the divine and the human. What is the Jewish concept of the soul? How is the soul activated? How do we use our spiritual nature to connect with the sublime?

In this section, we explore the nature of Jewish prayer in practice and see exactly how Jews seek to build the muscle of spirituality in its adherence. And we also examine the mystical nature of human character—and discover what it means to be truly human and approach the Divine.

Chapter 11

Making Contact

In This Chapter

- ◆ Contacting your spiritual side
- ◆ The three types of prayer
- ◆ The three types of spiritual actions
- ◆ The importance of Torah study

In this chapter, we are going to begin to examine the ways that Jews have traditionally made contact with their spiritual side and with God. The spiritual side does not necessarily refer to the afterlife or another plane of existence. This can refer to your own spiritual conscience, with which you can have daily spiritual contact if you only let it.

Too Jewish?

The topic of making contact with one's spiritual conscience reminds me of a story about a young rabbi who preaches his first sermon on a Friday night. The topic: The importance of Sabbath observance. It's a great talk, but there's a problem: The following week, only half the congregation return. So he tries again, this time with a stirring sermon on the importance of keeping kosher, obeying the laws related to food and drink. The following week, only about a quarter of the congregants return.

The young rabbi is feeling desperate, so he launches into a powerful sermon about the importance of observing the laws of *taharat mishpacha*, the guidelines regarding sexuality and marriage. The following week, only eight people show up. They don't even have a *minyan*, an official quorum for prayer.

The young rabbi, distraught, goes to see the president of the congregation after the service. "What did I do wrong?" he asks.

The president, an older man, shrugs. "Well, a lot of our congregants are business people, and they have to keep their businesses open on Saturday in order to survive. Thus, the talk about Sabbath observance wasn't exactly what they wanted to hear."

The young rabbi nods quickly and says, "Oh. I get it."

The president continues. "The biggest donor to our synagogue runs the largest non-kosher steakhouse in the county. Everybody in our temple loves that steakhouse. So the talk about keeping kosher wasn't exactly a rousing success."

The young rabbi nods again. "Oh, I get it," he says.

The president continues. "And when you talked about the laws of sex and marriage …" He doesn't even continue the sentence.

The young rabbi ponders for a few moments and says, "I guess I understand. Well, then, next week what should I talk about?"

The president of the congregation bursts into a broad smile. This is the question he thought the young rabbi would never ask. "Just talk about Judaism!" he exclaims.

Devine Devarim

taharat mishpacha
The guidelines regarding sexuality and marriage.

minyan   Official quorum for prayer.

Mystical Moments

Traditionally, rabbis only gave two sermons: On the Sabbaths before Passover and Yom Kippur, to remind people of the rules of those particular holidays.

The funny thing about us Jews is that when we want to hear about Judaism, many of us don't *really* want to hear about Judaism. We'd like to hear about a religion or faith that is less demanding, less time-consuming, and less complicated. This makes presenting the material in this chapter something of a challenge. On the one hand, these are some—but certainly not all—of the gateways to traditional concepts of Jewish spirituality and mystical delight. These are the ways by which Jews have made contact with their own spiritual nature and with their belief in a Creator. In most cases, the concepts and practices we are going to examine date back more than 2,000 years.

I'd like to make a deal with you (how Jewish is that?). I'll do my best to present the ideas for your inspection, and all I ask in return is that you lay aside any preconceptions and approach the concepts with an open mind, perhaps as if you were viewing spiritual and mystical Judaism for the very first time.

Keep an Open Mind

There is a wonderful phrase, "contempt prior to investigation." This means being unwill-ing to accept new ideas and not giving them a fair hearing before dismissing them. Surprisingly, most Jews harbor large amounts of contempt prior to investigation when it comes to their own religion. This is because it is very rare for a Jewish person to have absolutely zero feelings or concerns about traditional approaches to Judaism. Unless we are orthodox, the chances are high that we come to the subject not in a neutral position but with some negative attitudes already. For example, many Jews find the masculine ref-erences to God off-putting. Others have had negative attitudes passed down to them through their parents, who were raised in an observant environment that they then rebelled against. Still others question how Jews can pray to a God who could permit such tragedies as the Holocaust.

I understand all of those concerns, and I will do my best to address them along the way. All I ask is that when you view this material, set aside any prejudices you may have in order to give yourself the best opportunity to judge and see just how much of it might be useful in your own life. You must have a serious interest in Jewish mysticism and spiritual-ity to have read this far. Let's examine together some of the key sources and practices that promote a sense of spiritual well-being and mystical connection between the individual Jew and the universe.

Just in Time

The uniqueness of Judaism is that it is a religious system dependent primarily on time and not on place. We do not have holy places to which one is required to travel in one's life-time. Certainly, Jews are encouraged to visit Israel and especially the Old City of Jerusalem. In Biblical days, in fact, there was an obligation to visit Jerusalem three times a year, on the festivals of Passover, Shavuot, and Sukkot. Today, however, there is no require-ment in Jewish law to get on a plane and visit in order to be a "good Jew." Judaism is less a reli-gion that thinks in terms of holy places and instead more of a faith that makes time itself holy.

There are three primary ways by which Jews make time special: through prayer, action, and study. Let's look at each one in turn.

> **Spiritual Citations**
>
> "It is not enough for a man to dwell in the Land of Israel, he must also pray to be free."
> —Shmuel Yosef Agnon

The Importance of Prayer

There are three kinds of prayers in Judaism. The first is the prayer that is spontaneous and entirely original. While organized, communal prayer is an important part of Judaism, as we are about to see, Judaism, from the very beginning, has emphasized the importance of a person simply speaking to God with the words and emotions that are most important and precious to that individual. Traditionally, Jews have thought of God as their constant companion, one who is always present and ready to listen and help. We mentioned earlier the prayer of the Jews in Egypt after the death of the previous pharaoh.

As far as we know, the Jews of that time did not follow a prescribed language for prayer—they said whatever was in their hearts. Speaking from the heart is a timeless Jewish approach to spirituality. Formal prayers were instituted later, in order to help the individual more fully communicate with God, and also to knit the community together. But saying to God anything that is in your heart, whenever and wherever you are, under whatever circumstances you might find yourself, is as authentically Jewish as it gets.

The second kind of prayer is the series of blessings that traditionally minded Jews have pronounced, depending on their circumstances, every day for thousands of years. Many Jews who maintain these blessings find it inspiring that Jews around the world at any given moment are using the very same blessings. Even more exhilarating is the knowledge that if they could be transported back in time to any Jewish community in history, they would hear the exact same words. The Jewish series of blessings has been a common language for the Jewish people as well as a powerful way to remind ourselves of the astonishing nature of life itself.

High Spirits
"A prayer for the Czar? Of course. 'May God bless and keep the Czar … far away from us!'" —*Fiddler on the Roof*

The third form of prayer is traditional, fixed prayer. Traditionally, Jews have offered three prayer services a day: in the morning, afternoon, and evening. On the Sabbath, on the first day of the new month, and on Jewish holidays, the services and prayers are extended and slightly changed.

These three forms of Jewish prayer, for the most part, are not dependent upon location. Almost all are just as valid outside the land of Israel as they are inside. The prayers work whether you are in Guadalajara or standing before Jerusalem's Western Wall; whether you are praying in a train station bathroom or the most resplendent of temples. The key component to Jewish spirituality is time, not place, which is fortunate, since Jews have been dispersed around the world in myriad locations and communities for more than 1,900 years.

Getting into Action

Traditionally minded Jews are busy. They've always got something to do, whether it be planning for the next holiday, shopping for Sabbath meals, or simply headed to the synagogue for morning prayer. Once again, the categories of spirituality-enhancing actions come in three varieties.

The first kind are *mitzvot*, which are commandments—the specific duties and tasks that traditionally minded Jews believe God at Mount Sinai asked us to perform. These commandments are the "613 mitzvot."

The second category consists of the rabbinical laws instituted to allow the Jewish people to fulfill commandments that the Bible does not completely spell out. As a comparison, the U.S. Constitution lays out the framework for the kind of government and society we are supposed to be. The Constitution does not address the question of speed limits, because obviously there were no motor cars in the late eighteenth century. To compensate for these legal gaps, state and local governments have come up with traffic laws which we generally accept (unless we are in a hurry).

So it is with Judaism: The Bible, for example, tells us to "afflict our souls" on Yom Kippur, a *mitzvah* that comes from the Torah. But it doesn't say anything about the rabbinic ordinance to begin the Yom Kippur fast before sunset. This is something that the rabbis devised in order to help the people observe the explicit biblical commandments. We will examine the two categories of mitzvot—those given to the Jewish people directly by God and those created by the rabbis in order to further Jewish communal and religious life.

Devine Devarim

mitzvah   A divine commandment which, when fulfilled, is seen as a privilege. Bar or Bat Mitzvah literally means "Son or Daughter of the Commandment," because 13-year-old boys and 12-year-old girls are considered adults in Jewish law. (Which wisely recognizes that girls become mature sooner than boys do!)

minhagim   Customs that are specific to a particular group of Jews. For example, some Jews have the custom of waiting six hours after they eat meat before they eat any milk products. Others wait three hours and others just one.

A third kind of action that Jews take is called *minhagim*, or customs. While Jewish law basically remains the same from community to community, different customs apply in different parts of the Jewish world. For example, Sephardic Jews come from Spain and

Portugal and live mostly in North Africa and the Middle East. Ashkenazic Jews by and large come from Eastern Europe. Both celebrate Passover, but you are likely to be served rice in a Sephardic home and not in an Ashkenazic home during the Seder. Both communities are obeying their custom. Why do Jews have different rules about the food they can eat on Passover? There is nothing in Jewish law that specifically prohibits rice from being eaten on Passover. The law asks us to refrain from eating food that has leaven or yeast in it. There is no yeast in rice. So why don't Ashkenazic Jews eat it?

One answer (there may be others) goes back many centuries, to a time when yeast was used as a stabilizer in rice. Centuries ago, they did not have the same kind of food preparation and packaging that we take for granted today. The only way to keep rice from going bad, if you wanted to sell it to a customer who would use it over a long period of time, was to put yeast into it. Somehow yeast keeps rice from spoiling. Since Ashkenazic Jews in Eastern Europe centuries ago could not get rice that was not treated with yeast, they developed the minhag of avoiding rice altogether on the holiday of Passover. Sephardic Jews had no such problem with rice, so they never developed that kind of custom. Two equally observant families, one Sephardic and one Ashkenazic, can have some very different practices. Yet remarkably, they would agree on 98 percent of the way they observed Jewish law!

It stands to reason that different practices would evolve over the many centuries of Jewish dispersal across the planet. It would be highly unlikely that every single Jewish community would maintain the same minhagim, especially in eras prior to mass communication.

Keeping It Real Through Study

Jews are called "the people of the book" not just because we read and write so many best-sellers, but because we spend so much time studying our holy scriptures. The practice of study is extremely important in traditional Judaism, mainly due to the belief that learning Torah—delving into the Bible, its commentaries, Jewish law, and the Talmud—provides a glimpse into the mind of God. Just as a carpenter follows a blueprint when building a house, the Torah was the blueprint that God used to create the world. If you want to understand an architect, study the plans she draws up for houses. If you want to understand God, study the plans that God used to get the universe rolling.

> **Spiritual Citations**
>
> "Even when the gates of heaven are closed to prayer, they are open to tears."
>
> —Rabbi Eleazar Ben Padat, third-century Talmudic scholar

Torah study is so important in the Jewish tradition that throughout the centuries a young man was considered a "catch" not because of wealth, social position, or looks—although none of those hurt—but by how much Torah he learned. Today, Torah study is open to men and women. The study of the spiritual architecture of the world is no longer the province solely of men. Jews have traditionally believed that their place in the next world hinges upon the commitment to Torah study they make in their lifetime. The Talmud, the great compendium of Jewish law, makes this statement:

> *Honoring one's father and mother, practicing kindness, getting to the schoolhouse early to learn each morning and evening, hospitality to strangers, visiting the sick, creating a dowry for a bride, attending funerals, concentration and focus in prayer, and making peace between individuals [are extremely important], but the study of Torah is more important than all of these put together.*

This does not mean that if you study Torah you are excused from being a decent person. Quite the opposite: The more one knows, the higher the expectations of that person's character. The Talmud is just saying that you cannot have a healthy society where those practices are not followed. And yet, as important as each is, studying Torah is even more important.

We'll delve further into these topics in subsequent chapters. Jews today struggle with the concept of what it means to be a "good Jew" and fear that if they aren't involved enough they will be considered "bad Jews." I've never seen a reference in Judaism to "bad Jews"— it's probably a term people just apply to themselves when they don't feel right about their level of commitment. So let's explore together how one can experience a more fulfilling level of connection to one's Jewish faith.

The Least You Need to Know

- In Judaism, prayer and practice are not dependent on location.
- There are three kinds of prayer: spontaneous, daily, and traditional.
- There are three kinds of spirituality-enhancing actions: mitzvot, rabbinical laws, and minhagim.
- Torah study is prized more highly than any other trait.

Chapter 12

Like a Prayer

In This Chapter

- ◆ Making contact through prayer
- ◆ The structure of the basic Jewish blessing
- ◆ Prayer examples with eating and drinking
- ◆ The importance of prayer

Let's turn now to the first of our three methods of making contact with the supernatural in Judaism: prayer.

Prayer I: Spontaneous Prayer

Long before there were specified blessings and prayers, Jews naturally turned to God to say whatever was in their hearts. The Bible describes Abraham rising and praying in the morning. Isaac develops the practice of going into the fields late in the afternoon, presumably where he will not be disturbed by others, in order to speak directly to God. And the forefather Jacob prayed at night.

Women pray in the Bible, as well. On Rosh Hashanah, we read the story in Samuel of the prayer of Hannah, who up until this moment has been childless. She comes to the temple, closes her eyes, and speaks silently to God. One of the priests of the temple sees her and thinks that she has been drinking! When he realizes his mistake, he is extremely embarrassed. From Hannah (who subsequently had a son that became one of the leading figures in Jewish history, the prophet Samuel), we derive the practice of silent prayer, whether it is formal or simply whatever words the heart may prompt.

Even the formal prayers in the Jewish tradition that are spoken in temples and synagogues originated in the hearts of individuals who thought that they might be an excellent means of contacting God. The practice of individual, self-directed prayer is alive and well in Judaism and is encouraged in every branch of our faith.

> ### High Spirits
>
> "He hoped and prayed that there wasn't an afterlife. Then he realized there was a contradiction involved here and merely hoped that there wasn't an afterlife."
>
> —Douglas Adams

> ### Spiritual Citations
>
> "I pray every single second of my life; not on my knees, but with my work."
>
> —Susan B. Anthony

How do you practice the art of original prayer? The easiest way is by not thinking about it as an art. I've already mentioned one of the most famous prayers, the avinu malkaynu, spoken on Rosh Hashanah and Yom Kippur. The literal translation of avinu malkaynu is "our father, our king." Today, we might choose to translate that in more gender-neutral terms, as in "our parent, our ruler." The Jewish concept of God is summed up neatly in that phrase. On the one hand, God is the distant ruler of the universe, the Being who brought everything else into existence. This is the God who placed the planets in their paths, created nature, determined the miraculous working of the human brain, and so on. This part of our concept is of God as a ruler on a lofty throne.

But that's not the only way the Jews see God. Jews also understand God as a loving parent. Many of us are familiar with the Lord's Prayer, which begins, "Our father, who art in heaven."

It is not frequently noticed that the first line of the Lord's Prayer is a direct translation of the most common of Hebrew prayers, which begins, "*Avinu shevashamayim.*" You can translate *avinu* as "parent" in order to overcome the gender issue, but it is important to recognize that the belief of God as a loving parent is not originally a Christian belief. They borrowed that concept from the Jews!

Jews trace their lineage back to God. (Not in the sense that our ancestors were godlike. We pretty well established that our ancestors were far too flawed to even pretend to be even partly divine.) Rather, Jews have traditionally believed that God is not only a distant ruler but also a very present parent, one who listens to us and loves us as much as any ideal father or mother would.

When we speak to God, there exists that intriguing combination of God as powerful potentate and God as absolutely present parent. So when we speak to God in our own words, all we have to do is imagine that we are speaking with a loving parent who only wants the best for us and who loves us beyond all imagining.

Sometimes when we pray or talk to God we are actually quite angry about events in the world or our own lives. Tragedy, illness, bereavement—these all tend to alienate us from the concept of God as a loving being. At those moments, we are tempted to speak to God very harshly and angrily. This is entirely acceptable in the Jewish tradition. As the expression goes, "if your God cannot handle your anger, get a bigger God!"

Whether we are approaching God out of a sense of joy or frustration, happiness or dismay, whatever words we choose are perfectly acceptable. The main thing is not so much what we say but the fact that we are reaching out and attempting to make contact, in our own words, to the best of our ability.

Prayer II: Blessings

We all have different strengths. I don't know how to design an automobile. I am really glad other people have figured that out. I don't know how to do anything with my computer other than check my e-mail and use a word processor. I couldn't program for the life of me. I am not too handy, either. When something around the house breaks down, I stare at it and wait, as if by doing so, it might magically fix itself. (Which reminds me of the dishwasher with the blinking red light in my kitchen at this moment.)

We all have different strengths, and some people have a knack for the extraordinary task of composing statements that countless people feel comfortable using to express their spirituality. Such is the case with the individuals who created the series of blessings, or *berachot*, which are at the heart not only of Jewish prayer but of Jewish contact with the supernatural world. The individuals and groups who came up with these blessings did Judaism an enormous service. It's often hard to find the right words to express a deep-felt sentiment. The Jewish berachot provide us with a carefully chosen language of the heart with which to express our deepest senses of gratitude and longing.

Let's examine for a moment the word *beracha*, the Hebrew word for blessing. The root of the word is closely connected in Hebrew to both the word for bending the knee and the word for spring (as in wellspring). The word "blessing" doesn't really capture the meaning of the word beracha. The components of the Hebrew word beracha include the notion of acknowledging and thanking.

Devine Devarim

beracha   blessing; (pl.) berachot.

In addition, because of the connection to the Hebrew word for bending the knee, beracha implies a relationship of humility on our part before the awesome power of the Creator. Many times, people mistake the word humility for the word humiliation. They both come from the Latin word humus, meaning earth or ground. To be humble, to have humility, is to be grounded. By contrast, to be humiliated is to be driven into the ground. The Jewish concept of God is not of a being who goes around bashing people or driving them into the ground. Rather, the Jewish concept of humility indicates that we know who we are: We are limited, mortal, finite people, and we owe everything we have to the Creator of the universe.

In metaphysical terms, we approach God, even when we are standing up or sitting down, on bended knee, the traditional posture of obeisance. Judaism believes that God is in fact the source, or wellspring, of everything good that comes our way in life. A wellspring is something that gives forth water constantly, without surcease, and without being asked. Put all these meanings together and you've got an acknowledgment of the greatness of God while coming from a position of humility, and recognizing that God is the source of all things in life. This is the mystical meaning of the Hebrew word beracha, which the English translation "blessing" simply cannot capture.

> ### Mystical Moments
>
> One of the most profoundly beautiful moments of the traditional Jewish Sabbath is when the parents bless their children. The parent prays that the child will grow up to be like the patriarchs or the matriarchs (depending on the child's gender) and then recites the priestly blessing: "May the Lord bless you and protect you. May the Lord turn His light to you and be gracious to you. May the Lord favor you and give you peace." When kids go to summer camp, some parents send the blessing by fax!

Thus we begin most standard one-line blessings in Hebrew with the word *baruch*, which is the passive form of the Hebrew word for acknowledged or thanked. By starting a blessing in this way, we are saying, "God, you are acknowledged, thanked, approached in humility and recognized as the source of everything. That is the beauty of Hebrew—so many spiritual concepts can be found in a single word.

The typical Hebrew blessing begins. "*Baruch attah, ado-nai elo-hainu, melech ha olam*." We are saying, "You are thanked and acknowledged, God, ruler of the universe."

Why All the Blessing?

Why do we begin blessings this way? One explanation is this: When we think of an important person, be it a politician, a movie star, or even the Godfather, we always want to know how that important person treats the so-called "little people." Are they disdainful of those who have less power and money? Or are they kind? Do they go out of their way to remember names? In the movie *The Godfather*, Don Corleone treated with great kindness the ordinary people who relied upon him for protection. They loved him because he always cared for them and did so with love and not with contempt.

Similarly, traditionally minded Jews remind themselves of the awesomeness of the power of God, who always remembers us powerless, weak individuals with astonishing kindness. How powerless are we? We might run corporations or have six-figure incomes, but let's see how many days we can last without food and water. We are not nearly as powerful as we often make ourselves out to be. You could say that a Jew approaching God is not unlike a supplicant approaching the Godfather on the day of his daughter's wedding.

Spiritual Citations

"Don Corleone, I am honored and grateful that you have invited me to your house on the day of your daughter's wedding."

—Luca Brasi (Lenny Montana), *The Godfather*

After the opening sentence, blessings take an intriguing turn. Let's take a look at a blessing that most Jews recognize, the motzie, or the blessing over bread. It reads, "Baruch attah ado-nai elo-hainu melech ha olam hamotzee lechem min ha'aretz." The first part of the blessing is the traditional introduction ("You are thanked and acknowledged, God, ruler of the universe") and the last part translates as, "the one who brings forth bread from the earth." What happened? In grammatical terms, the first part of the blessing is spoken as if to another human being. Then the grammar shifts from first person to third person. Why the change? The answer is subtle. The rabbis explain that it is so overwhelming to speak directly to God that we can only do it for a moment or two before the whole idea of our actions just blows us away. So halfway through the traditional Jewish blessing, we acknowledge that sense of awesomeness by changing direction and speaking *about* God instead. Virtually every one-line Hebrew blessing follows this same concept: We begin speaking *to* God, realize the incredible thing that we are doing, and back away slightly by speaking instead *about* God.

A Hunger for Spirituality

Let's take a look at some other Jewish blessings. The main reason for saying these blessings is to become more conscious of the simple, day-to-day events and activities that make up our lives. People who are conscious of and grateful for the little things never have to rely on the "big things" in order to make their lives meaningful. Many people believe that this sort of consciousness is strictly the province of Eastern religions; however, its source is in Judaism. As mentioned earlier, a Jew ideally is expected to pronounce 100 of these blessings throughout the day in order to maximize his or her ongoing sense of spirituality.

Devine Devarim

boray p'ree ha'aytz
"who creates the fruits of trees"
boray p'ree ha'adamah   "who creates the fruits of the earth"

Mystical Moments

Although it's an important part of Judaism, meditation is not necessary to achieve an awakening in consciousness. The Talmud relates that the great rabbis would meditate for an hour before religious services and then meditate for *another* hour afterward. Meditation certainly has its place in Judaism, but you can develop your spirituality merely by eating a banana.

Jews love to eat. As such, we have a wide range of blessings specifically for food. All of these blessings in this section, incidentally, begin with the phrase, "blessed, thanked, and acknowledged are you, God, Ruler of the Universe .... " The blessings then continue depending on the type of food. For fruit, for example, you would say either *"boray p'ree ha'aytz"* ("who creates the fruits of trees") or *"boray p'ree ha'adamah"* ("who creates the fruits of the ground"), depending on the food's origination.

Interesting, practicing traditional Judaism requires you to figure out where every food comes from. Bananas, for example, receive the same blessing as fruit from the ground. Because banana trees grow anew each year, they are not considered fixed, ongoing trees like apple trees or pear trees.

Cakes and pastries require a different blessing: *"boray meenay m'zonot"* ("who creates all types of grain"). Everything else (food and drink that are not wine, bread, cake, fruit, or vegetables) receives the blessing *"sheacol neh'yeh bedvaro,"* which translates as "through whose word everything came into being." We remind ourselves prior to, say, drinking a glass of water that everything in the universe came into being through the "speech" or "word" of God.

What does it mean for God to speak? What exactly does it sound like? Only the Prophets and those who were at Mount Sinai know for certain. Did God actually make sounds like we do when we speak? As stated earlier, traditional Judaism posits that the entire world came into being when God "spoke," an event that illustrates the Jewish belief in the power of both God and words. The process of speaking blessings increases our spiritual awareness by simply uttering a few well-chosen words.

Here are some more blessings that Jews say in order to imbue other, apparently ordinary situations with a spiritual component. As before, these all begin with the same *"Baruch attah ado-nai elo-hainu melech ha'olam"* opening.

- Boray m'nay v'samim: Who creates fragrant spices.
- Oseh ma'asay v'raysheet: Who created the world. Spoken on seeing wonders in nature such as the Grand Canyon.

♦ Zochair habrit: Who remembers the Covenant. Spoken on seeing a rainbow (a remembrance of God's promise after the flood in Noah's time never to bring down destruction on the world ever again).

♦ She'asa et hayam hagadol: Who created the great ocean. Spoken on seeing the ocean or a large body of water.

♦ Shenatan mek'vodo l'vasar vadam: Who gave God's glory to "flesh and blood" [that is, human beings]; spoken on seeing a president or king.

♦ Baruch ha-Dayan ha'emet: Blessed is the True Judge. Spoken on hearing bad news.

♦ Hatov v'hamayteev: Who is good and does good. Spoken on hearing good news.

High Spirits
Two Jews spent the whole night debating whether there was a God and decided in the end that there wasn't. One was thirsty after all this talk, so he had a glass of water. He started to say the *bracha,* "shehakol n'heye bidvaro." His friend said, "You're making a blessing? I thought we decided there was no God!" He replied, "There may be no God—but for a Jew not to make a blessing? Are you crazy?"

These are just a few of the blessings that Jews pronounce in day-to-day and extraordinary situations. Blessings also exist for such important events as seeing a great Torah scholar, viewing electrical storms, and attaching a mezuzah to the doorpost. There are even blessings for seeing a person of unusual physical appearance, going to the bathroom, waking up, going to sleep, and acknowledging the existence of our soul.

When we imbue even the simplest acts and moments with an acknowledgment of their spiritual content, we become more grateful, more aware, and more spiritually connected to life and to our Creator. That is what the Jewish system of blessings is all about.

The Least You Need to Know

♦ In prayer, it is not the words that matter, but the attempt.

♦ Blessings exist for nearly every event in our lives.

♦ Traditional Jews are expected to say at least one hundred blessings a day.

♦ Acknowledgment through prayer of even the most mundane events makes us more spiritually connected.

God Loves to Hear from Strangers

In This Chapter

◆ Why Jews pray

◆ How Jews interact with God

◆ The various forms of the amidah

◆ The significance of Sh'ma

Despite Judaism's established framework for regular prayer and blessings, a vast number of Jews do not pray regularly. When I was writing my first book about Judaism, one of my mother's friends said to me, "Michael, you have to remember that most Jews only pray three times a year!"

Although not entirely correct, there is a hint of truth to that statement. The irony is that Judaism, with its complex framework for prayer morning, noon, and night, is a religion where many of its adherents—perhaps even most of them—do not pray on a regular basis. Let's examine traditional, formal Jewish prayer and see what it might offer us today.

I once met a nun who worked with terminally ill individuals in a Boston hospital. When the topic of religion came up, she said, "When Christian patients see me, they want to pray. When Jewish patients see me, they want to tell me jokes." She liked that about the Jews—that we take everything, even our imminent end, with a small dose of humor. And yet, I could tell that it somewhat troubled her that Jews were not as comfortable with prayer.

Certainly, a Jew might feel uncomfortable praying with a Catholic nun. Our belief systems differ in many important ways. Nonetheless, it is fair to say that most Jews are unfamiliar with the order or content of the traditional system of prayers that Jews have employed for several thousand years.

Formal Prayer

On Mount Sinai, the Jews responded to God's deliverance of the Ten Commandments with, "Na'aseh v'nishmah"—"First we will do whatever we are asked to do and then we will wait for explanations later." Jews today are different from that generation. We need to know exactly why we are doing anything before we begin to take it on as a practice for ourselves. I'd like to explain the *why* of Jewish prayer before I delve too deeply into the *how* aspect.

Devine Devarim

tefilah Prayer, in the sense of "attachment."

L'hitpalel Prayer, in the sense of "reminding oneself of what's important in life."

Spiritual Citations

"To pray is to know how to stand still and to dwell upon a word."

—Abraham Joshua Heschel

I mentioned earlier that Jews have about as many words for prayer as Eskimos have for snow. One of the key words for Jewish prayer is *tefilah*. This word, meaning prayer, is closely related to the concept of "attachment."

In other words, the purpose of Jewish prayer is to attach ourselves to a spiritual view of the world, and to come closer to an awareness of the existence of God. Fixed, formal prayers serve two functions. First, they remind us that we are "not alone," that we have a Creator to whom we are obligated for our lives. Just as we have certain responsibilities to our parents, Judaism believes that we have certain responsibilities to our "parent" in heaven as well. When we pray, we attach ourselves to our spiritual side, and we attach ourselves to God.

The second function of formal, fixed prayer is to bring Jewish communities together. Traditionally, Jews gather not only on the Sabbath but also in the mornings and evenings. These prayer services knit the community together. People feel an obligation to attend services not only for religious reasons, but also to find out the latest "news" in the community: births, marriages, deaths—what the rabbis call "hatch, match, and dispatch." They also learn from their rabbi what is happening in the Jewish world.

If prayer were entirely an individual, private matter, the Jewish people probably would not have survived all this time. To begin with, there is something about praying as a group that enhances the spirituality of one's own prayers. Second, if our prayers are entirely a personal, private matter, our own human nature might cause us to become sidetracked. When we have to show up somewhere on a regular basis, we are far more likely to remain committed. That's just the way we're wired. Men and women are designed to form communities as a biological response to threats in nature; we are more likely to survive if we have each other to rely upon. Communal services have brought Jews, as well as other denominations, together for thousands of years.

It's difficult to find as strong a communal glue as prayer. We all have diverse interests, hobbies, and careers. Think about how hard it is just to make dinner plans with a friend—now multiply that by an entire community. Unless there is a compelling reason to get together, it's just not going to happen. Life will get in the way.

Devine Devarim

davening   The traditional approach to Jewish prayer.

Staying in Tune with Prayer

I like to think of the structure of Jewish prayers like this: It's a lot like a pick-up orchestra that gets together and rehearses every week. If you play the violin well, you can pretty much walk into any orchestra in the world, open up the sheet music, and jump right in. So it is in Judaism: If you know the traditional approach to Jewish prayer, or *davening*, you can wander into pretty much any temple or synagogue, grab a prayer book, and know exactly what's going on. If you are a true connoisseur of Jewish prayer, you only need walk into a service and listen for a half a minute, and you will know exactly where they are in the service. Surprisingly, this knowledge level of Jewish prayers is not all that hard to attain.

I think of a typical Sabbath service as a rehearsal of an orchestra. On the one hand, the group is actually performing the entire service, the way an orchestra will perform an entire piece in rehearsal. On the other hand, by keeping our prayer instrument tuned up and well-practiced, we will be ready for that day when we really need to pray—not simply because it's time, but because our life, or the lives of people we love, is on the line. Actually, it's more than just a rehearsal. It's a chance to focus our minds on what is most important, and we get to do it three times a day.

Many Jews feel hypocritical about praying when a loved one is, God forbid, struck seriously ill or otherwise suffering. We feel awkward about turning to God for the first time perhaps in years. We think to ourselves, "Who are we to pray when we haven't been involved in terms of prayer or other spiritual practice for so long?" As a result, people who most feel the need to pray sometimes feel extremely uncomfortable about doing so.

This is a very sad situation, but it can be averted if one is praying on a regular basis, either individually or with a group. I think of regular services as "rehearsals," because as important as they are, they also serve to prepare us for those critical moments when we will *want* to pray. Regular prayer, to change metaphors, is like a hotline to the Divine: Every time we pray, it is as though we are testing the line to make sure that our connection is still strong. Feeling secure with our spiritual connection is one of the most powerful assets that we can possibly enjoy.

> **Spiritual Citations**
>
> "The Sabbath is a reminder of the two worlds—this world and the world to come; it is an example of both worlds. For the Sabbath is joy, holiness, and rest; joy is part of this world; holiness and rest are something of the world to come."
>
> —Menorat Ha–Maor (Candelabra of Light)

Jews pray regularly not just because we are commanded to do so, but also because we want to enhance our own spiritual lives, and that requires a sense of discipline and regularity, much like athletics. Also, by praying regularly, we find common cause with our fellow Jews and help maintain our community and traditions.

Hear, O Israel

Fixed, formal prayer is based on the fulfillment of two sets of obligations. The first is the recital of the *Sh'ma*, the reading form Deuteronomy that reads, "*Sh'ma Yisrael Ado-nai Elo-hainu Ado-nai Echad.*" "Listen, Israel, the Lord our God, the Lord is One." This is a line that is familiar to virtually every Jew who has had even an hour of Hebrew school.

> **Mystical Moments**
>
> Another familiar prayer is the last line of the *aleinu* prayer that concludes most Jewish services: "*Ba-yom ha-hu, yihyeh Ado-nai echad u'shmo echad.*" "And on that day, God will be One and God's name will be one." A kabbalistic interpretation of this line: We pray that we have the ability today to recognize the oneness of God—right now, not just on some distant day in the future."

The second set of obligations is related to remembrance of the services that took part in the great Temple in Jerusalem. Let's explore each of these in turn.

The single most important sentence in all of Judaism is the *Sh'ma*, the one line that summarizes the Jewish concept of spirituality—the monotheistic concept of God. The Sh'ma is the Jew's way of reminding himself or herself that God exists and that God is one. Judaism believes in the existence of a timeless, eternal Creator who predates the universe, who exists with us at all times, and who will exist after the universe has run its course.

Judaism differed from the polytheistic religions that existed when Judaism was revealed. At that time, people tended to assign divinity to many of the different forces that they saw in the world. The sun was a god, as was the Nile, and even the winds and stones. Judaism's everlasting contribution to the world is the notion of monotheism—that one God created and maintains the entire universe, and that all the aspects of nature, while of divine origin, are not gods separate from the one and only God.

Traditionally minded Jews have said the Sh'ma twice a day for thousands of years. They do so in order to remind themselves of the central doctrine of Jewish faith, that there is one God, not zero, and not many. As decreed further on in Deuteronomy, Jews recite the passage twice a day, when lying down and when rising up. The rabbis interpreted this command as a requirement to pronounce the Sh'ma both in the morning and in the evening. An important part of the morning and evening prayer services are given over to the verses of the Sh'ma and the prayers that have been written to precede and follow it.

The entire *Sh'ma* runs 248 words and includes three paragraphs, the aforementioned first line, and the second line: *"Baruch sham kvod maluchuto layolam vaed"* ("Blessed is the name of God's glorious kingdom forever and ever.") The other three paragraphs ask us to love God, to accept the concept of reward and punishment for our actions, to accept the system of mitzvot outlined in the Torah, and finally, to acknowledge our origins in the Exodus. The concepts outlined in the Sh'ma pretty much cover the basics of the entire spiritual component of Judaism. That's why the Sh'ma is a central aspect of the morning and evening prayers.

The Service in the Temple

When Jews speak of the "Temple," they may not be talking about Beth Israel down the block. They are probably referring to either the first or second Temple that once stood in Jerusalem. The first Temple was built by King Solomon in the tenth century B.C.E. and stood until the year 586, when Nebuchadnezzar and the Babylonians destroyed it. Approximately 70 years later, King Cyrus, ruler of the Persian Empire, permitted the Jews to return to the land of Israel and rebuild the Temple. They did so, on the same spot, until the Romans destroyed it in the year 70 C.E. At that time, the Romans expelled the Jews from Israel, an exile that has continued to the present day. While millions of Jews make their home today in the land of Israel, millions more live outside the land, as have the majority of Jews for the past 2,000 years.

As far as we know, nothing remains of the first Temple of King Solomon. I say "as far as we know," because it is possible that some historical or archaeological artifacts may remain, either buried deeply under the Temple Mount in Jerusalem, or perhaps in the hidden chambers in the Vatican, where it has long been rumored that certain implements from the Temple may now reside.

Of the second Temple, all that remains is the Western retaining wall, which Jews call the Western, or Wailing Wall. This is the wall that every Jew who visits Israel makes a special point of seeing. Visitors to the Wall frequently write individual prayers, called *kvitlach*, which they place in the stones of the wall. The kvitlach are yet another example of personal, private prayer that is encouraged in the Jewish faith.

Devine Devarim _____

kvitlach   individual prayers, from the Yiddish word for "short letter."

kohenim   priests.

Beit Ha'mikdosh   proper name of the first Temple.

mikdash ma'at   miniature holy place carried by Jews after the destruction of the second Temple.

amidah   the central part of the Jewish service, during which congregates stand silently as a way of recreating the Temple service in their hearts and minds.

musaf   the additional amidah spoken on special service days (Sabbath, new moon, and festivals) in remembrance of and in recollection of the additional service once held in the Temple.

During the 830 years or so that they stood (410 years for the first Temple and 420 for the second), the Temples were the focal point of Jewish worship. When Judaism was founded, animal sacrifice was prevalent in the religious practices of the day. It probably would have been too much for the first Jews to handle had Judaism *not* contained animal sacrifice. The Bible and the Talmud are quite explicit about the nature of the animals that are offered, the times that they were offered, the reasons, and the uses made of the various parts of the animals. Some animals were completely burnt on the altar, while others could be eaten in whole or in part, by the *kohenim*, or priests. It was believed that the sacrifice of animals was necessary in order to maintain constant contact with God.

After the second temple was destroyed in the year 70 C.E., the rabbis recognized that a different sort of worship would be necessary in order to keep Judaism in existence. Instead of the *Beit Ha'mikdosh*, as the Temple was known, each Jew would now carry in his or her own heart a *mikdash ma'at*, a miniature holy place. We would carry those private, internal sanctuaries with us wherever we went in exile, down to the present day. The rabbis then instituted prayer services that would allow the individual to replicate in his or her own heart the Temple service that had been lost with the destruction of the second Temple at the hands of the Romans.

Amidah Variants

Even today, when you go into services of any of Judaism's branches, the structure of the key part of the service, the *amidah*, is based on this concept of recreating the Temple service in our own hearts and minds. The way it works is this: In the Temple, offerings—animal, oil, grain, and spices—were made on a daily basis in the morning, afternoon, and evening. The rabbis wrote the amidah after the destruction of the Second Temple, in the period between 100 and 500 C.E. This prayer, which Jews would recite three times a day in remembrance of and in replacement of the Temple services that could not take place. On certain days—the Sabbath, the new moon, and festivals—additional offerings were made in the Temple. Even today, on these days a second amidah, called the *musaf*, is spoken in remembrance of and in recollection of that additional service in the Temple.

The traditional morning service, whether weekday, Sabbath, or holiday, begins with morning blessings that acknowledge and thank God both for our physicality and our spirituality. These blessings are followed by a series of prayers and psalms which essentially put us in the mood for the important functions to come—the recital of the sh'ma and its attendant blessings, and the amidah prayers to follow. This is true whether we are talking about a reconstructionist, reform, conservative, or orthodox service. In some branches of Judaism, the amidah is said quietly to oneself and then repeated by the prayer leader, or the *chazzan*. In other branches, the entire prayer community speaks the words together.

You know you are saying the amidah, either to yourself or with the group, if the prayer begins, "Blessed are you Lord our God, King of the Universe, God of Abraham, God of Isaac, and God of Jacob ...." Some branches of Judaism include not just the patriarchs but the matriarchs as well, so they would acknowledge, "God of Abraham and Sarah, the God of Isaac and Rebecca, and the God of Jacob, Leah, and Rachel."

> **Mystical Moments**
>
> During the ten days from Rosh Hashana (the Jewish New Year) to Yom Kippur (the Jewish Day of Atonement), additional short prayers are added to the amidah, such as "And inscribe for a good life the entire Jewish people." Those additions remind the person who's praying that it is a very special and important time of year. Jews traditionally believe that during this special 10-day period, God decides their fates for the next year and records those decisions in the "Book of Life."

The content of the amidah is different depending on the day of the week and, in some blessings, the time of day. On weekdays, the amidah contains specific requests: for wisdom, for health, for the return of the Jewish people to the land of Israel, for the rebuilding of the Temple, and for the restoration of the prayer services in Jerusalem, among other things. On the Sabbath and holidays, most of these requests are omitted. The essential idea surrounding the Sabbath is that instead of working to create more for ourselves, we instead look at our lives with a sense of satisfaction and completeness.

We are saying to ourselves, and to God, "What we have is fantastic, and it's enough. We don't need to ask you for any more than this." People are both material and spiritual in nature. On weekdays we pay somewhat more attention to our material nature, and we work to increase the amount of blessing that we in the world enjoy. On the Sabbath, we try to focus more on the spiritual side of our nature, so we look to appreciate what we have instead of asking for more.

High Spirits
While waiting in line to get his driver's license renewed, a man noticed the woman next to him reading her Bible. He politely began asking a few religious questions, but soon it was obvious that his intent was merely to ridicule. "Take Moses," he said conde-scendingly, "you don't *really* believe he parted an entire sea, do you?" "I don't know," said the woman. "When I get to Heaven, I'll ask him." "And what if he isn't there?" the man sniggered. Without batting an eyelash, the woman replied, "Then *you* can ask him."

The amidah prayer is also slightly different on holidays, Rosh Hashanah (the Jewish New Year), and on Yom Kippur, in order to take into account the special characteristics of those days. It is definitely worthwhile to spend some time comparing the various amidah prayers to see how they vary depending on circumstances. Such study is always well-rewarded in terms of the deepened appreciation of the construction of the prayers and a deepened spiritual connection to the Creator and to one's world.

Spiritual Citations

"Through our soul is our contact with heaven."

—Sholem Asch

So there you have it—the three means by which Jews have traditionally attached themselves to, contacted, and spoken with God: either individually or communally—individual prayer, as prompted by the heart; the series of blessings used to infuse spirituality even into the most mundane of daily events; and communal prayer, focused on the recital of the *sh'ma* and the stating of the *amidah*, to replace the Temple service in Jerusalem.

There is one question we have not touched upon yet with regard to Jewish prayer—and that's the question of how prayer relates to sex! If we say a blessing before we eat bread or when we see the ocean or any of the other ordinary events of our day, is there a specific prayer that is said prior to sex?

The rabbis were a worldly lot, and they definitely instituted prayers that are said prior to the enjoyment of sex. Unfortunately for any of my single readers, those blessings are the seven blessings spoken under the wedding canopy! Sex in Judaism! It has a ring to it!

The Least You Need to Know

- ◆ Prayer brings us closer to spirituality and God.
- ◆ Prayer brings communities together.
- ◆ The one-line Sh'ma summarizes Jewish spirituality.
- ◆ The forms of the amidah vary according to the time of day and time of year.

Chapter 14

Get Busy!

In This Chapter

- ◆ The importance of every action
- ◆ Learning the ropes
- ◆ The many layers of Jewish studies
- ◆ The benefits of studying Jewish texts

The location: Jerusalem. The time: 3:30 P.M., Friday afternoon. The street: *Rehov Malchei Yisrael* (Kings of Israel Street), in the heart of Mea She'arim, one of the city's main orthodox neighborhoods. The Sabbath is coming.

We see a young *Hasid*, an observant Jewish man wearing the traditional long black coat, side curls, and wide-brimmed black hat, rushing across the street, darting through traffic. He is pushing a baby stroller. You look inside the baby stroller, and instead of a baby, you see four dozen eggs.

What does it all mean?

On the Move

This set of facts, which can be seen any Friday afternoon in Jerusalem or in dozens of other observant Jewish communities around the globe, actually contains heaps of useful information about Judaism. The scene tells us that

Judaism is partly a religion of contemplation and mostly a series of actions. Judaism demands from its adherents a continuous series of actions. It's a busy faith!

Take our friend rushing home with the eggs. Why is he rushing home? Because once the Sabbath comes in, he will no longer be able to shop, carry money, or even cook. All these activities need to take place prior to sundown. No wonder he's rushing!

Why does he have so many eggs? Probably because he is obeying the very first commandment of the Torah, "Be fruitful and multiply," the words God spoke to Adam and Eve. Chances are, if he's got four dozen eggs in that stroller, he's got a bunch of kids at home—maybe as many as eight or nine. Orthodox families of that size are not uncommon, especially in religious neighborhoods like Mea She'arim.

Why is he dressed like that? The long coat, broad–rimmed black hat, and side curls identify him as a member of a *Hasidic* sect. This means that he is either a descendant of or a new adherent of one of the many groups that sprung up in the small towns of Eastern Europe in the eighteenth century. These groups centered around charismatic spiritual leaders called *rebbes*, who taught their followers that they did not need to attend the exclusive Talmudic academies of the big cites, which was a good thing since few, if any, of their adherents could have afforded such an education. Then, as now, a Jewish day school education is a serious expense.

Instead, the rebbes taught a Judaism of joy, one that combined varying degrees of intellectual rigor with absolute happiness, faith, singing, dancing, and generally thinking of God as a very dear and trusted friend. The Baal Shem Tov was the first and best known of the early Hasidic rebbes. Many other such individuals formed spiritual communities across what are now Poland, Russia, the Czech Republic, and Slovenia—a broad swath of Eastern Europe and Western Russia.

If a Jew lived in a town without a rebbe, chances are that he or she would travel to the hometown of a rebbe somewhere in the area. The Hasidic communities today take their name from the towns in which they were originally formed. The Lubavitch Hasidim, for example, came from the Russian town of Lubavitch.

Other centers of Hasidic study and worship were Belz, Sanz, Tchortkov, and countless other small towns. The position of rebbe was usually dynastic, meaning that the son, son-in-law, or grandson of a rebbe would usually

Spiritual Citations

"The gravest sin for a Jew is to forget what he represents."
—Abraham Joshua Heschel

Mystical Moments

In Eastern Europe, a Jew who lived in the country-side would travel several times a year to the "court" of his Rebbe to experience the joy of being in his presence. Even today, Hasidic Jews often travel thousands of miles—from South Africa, for example, to Brooklyn—to have that same experience. To see and learn directly from one's Rebbe is a form of recharging one's spiritual batteries.

succeed the older man when he stepped down or passed away. Our friend rushing with the eggs most likely traces his lineage back to Eastern Europe of the eighteenth century, and chances are that his great-great-grandfather considered himself a Hasid or adherent of the great-great-great-grandfather of this young man's own rebbe, 225 years later.

Our young man wears the distinctive black coat and other accoutrements of Hasidism out of respect for the tradition that grew in Eastern Europe to dress in this particular manner. If you examine his coat, you will find that it most likely buttons the opposite way from men's garments in the secular world. The Jews of Eastern Europe actually designed their clothing so that it would button differently; they wanted absolutely every aspect of their life to be different from that of the gentile communities that surrounded them—even down to the buttons on their jackets.

Our friend wears side curls, which bob around his ears as he weaves through traffic with the egg-laden baby carriage. He wears his hair that way because of his understanding of the biblical injunction, "You shall not round the corners of your head." This has been interpreted by many rabbis over the centuries to mean that an individual should not trim a certain spot around the ear or cut it in any way.

Devine Devarim _____

kipa   a knitted head-covering worn by men.

chavurah   a gathering of spiritually committed Jewish friends.

Not all Jews adhere to the notion of side curls; a Hasidic Jew is far more likely to wear them than a mainstream orthodox Jew. Even though he is a young man—probably in his early 30s—he has a longish beard, one that extends a couple of inches below his chin. Once again, this is a combination of Jewish law and Hasidic custom. Jewish law prohibits the use of a straight edge razor against the face, so he certainly would not shave with a straight edge. Were he to shave, he would use an electric razor. Instead, in his group, the men do not shave at all, although they do occasionally trim their beards. Thus his beard is fairly lengthy by the standards of modern secular style.

When he prays tonight, he will most likely welcome the Sabbath in a small, sparse, tightly packed Beit Haknesset, or synagogue. There may be no more than two dozen individuals at the service, mostly men. The synagogue will echo with the singing and dancing of the men as they joyously welcome the Sabbath bride, the symbolic presence of the Sabbath day. The Jewish people, in this metaphor, is compared to a bridegroom and the Sabbath is his bride.

Spiritual Citations _____

"Will and intellect are one and the same."

—Benedict Spinoza

This same scene is likely to be repeated, with certain variation, in every single Jewish community in the world. Instead of a Hasid with nine children, a beard, and side curls, he may be a "modern orthodox" Jew with three or four children, no beard, and a knitted *kipa*, or head-covering. He might also be driving a Lexus SUV instead of pushing a baby carriage. Or perhaps it is a young woman, an adherent of the reconstructionist movement in Judaism, stopping off to buy food for a *chavurah*, a gathering of spiritually committed Jewish friends.

The faces change, the approach to Jewish observance changes, but the bottom line is that Jews are always busy getting ready for the next event on their calendar. This is true from Jerusalem to Johannesburg, from Los Angeles to Latvia. And wherever you go, you will find a warm welcome, whether you are visiting a reform temple in Chicago or our baby carriage–pushing friend's Hasidic minyan in Mea She'arim. If you visit his home on Shabbat, you might even get yourself an omelet. (Not even nine kids can eat 48 eggs in a weekend.)

Learning and Practicing

How do Jews know what to do? How do Jews determine what constitutes the right kind of practice of any given commandment or tradition?

The answer is that we constantly study. The Talmud is quite specific: It tells us that we are not expected to complete the work of studying absolutely every detail in Judaism, but neither do we have the freedom to desist from that study. We are also told to turn in it and turn in it again, because everything in life is contained in the study of Jewish thought.

Jewish scholars go right to the source: The texts themselves. Traditionally, Jewish cultural literacy meant that every child spoke not only the language of his or her country but also *lashon kodesh*, the holy tongue, Hebrew. In the last 20 years, there has been an explosion of translations of every manner of Jewish commentary in English, French, and in other languages of the Diaspora. However, there is nothing like reviewing material in the original Hebrew to get the truest flavor of Jewish thought.

All study starts with the written Torah, the five books of Moses: Genesis, Exodus, Numbers, Leviticus, and Deuteronomy. Traditionally, a Jew is expected to read the weekly parasha (Torah portion) three times over the course of the Sabbath—twice in Hebrew, and once in Aramaic, the common language of Jews 2,000 years ago. In addition, they study the parasha with the commentary of the French Jewish authority Rashi, who lived in Troyes, France, from 1040 to 1105. Rashi takes the reader through each line—and sometimes even each word—and explains the hidden meanings and inner secrets of each verse. For the last 400 years, most traditional Jewish Bibles are printed with Rashi's commentary directly below.

That's still only the beginning of religious study. In addition to the five books of Moses, Jews also study the prophets, such as Isaiah, Jeremiah, and Micah. They review the proverbs and psalms written, according to tradition, by Kings Solomon and David, respectively. They read the Song of Songs, either every Friday night or once a year at Shavuot, the festival of the receiving of the Torah celebrated in late spring. At different times of the year, Jews review various minor books of the Bible, such as the Book of Esther at Purim, the Book of Ruth at Shavuot, and the writings of the historian Josephus on the fast day of Tisha B'av, a dark day in Jewish history.

But wait, there's more! There is also the midrash, an often fanciful but always profound and penetrating series of commentaries on biblical lines and phrases. As mentioned earlier, the story of Abraham destroying his father's work and blaming it on the cheap idol comes from the midrash. And then we come to the largest work of all in the Jewish tradition, the Talmud.

After the second Temple was destroyed in 70 C.E., the Jews found themselves expelled from Israel and headed to all parts of the known world. It was no longer possible to maintain the same type of community discipline that existed in Temple times. Because of this, the rabbis compiled the Mishnah, around the year 200 C.E. According to tradition, when Moses went up on Mount Sinai to receive the Ten Commandments, God also gave him a great deal of laws and traditions that had equal force, even though they were not part of the written Torah. These rules are called the oral Torah (*Torah she baal peh*), in contrast to the written Torah (*Torah she'bech'tav*). All the pieces of the oral law were written down in one place and called the Mishnah, which is Hebrew for "repetition." In other words, the oral laws that the Jews had been following in addition to the written Torah were repeated in one place, so that everyone could have access to those laws, no matter how far they now lived from the land of Israel.

Mystical Moments

Rashi is not the only commentator to whom Jews turn for a better understanding of a specific verse. There are many others: the Kli Yakar, the Sforno, Ibn Ezra, Nachmanides, Maimonides, the Malbim, the Bartenura .... Each reflects the wisdom of their predecessors as well as the exigencies of the time in which they wrote.

High Spirits

A Jew in Czarist Russia, a businessman, was praying the amidah when suddenly he realized he had shortchanged the Czar 500 rubles on a recent business transaction. He asked his Rebbe what to do. "I wouldn't worry about it," said the Rebbe. "Since the Czar doesn't pray the amidah, he probably won't remember the transaction!"

Piecing It Together

Confused? Imagine the Talmud as a set of Russian matrioshka dolls, the carved figures that fit one inside the other. In the Talmud, the smallest doll of all is the Mishnah, which generally lasts about a paragraph. A paragraph of Mishnah will set forth one or two laws, or perhaps several opinions about one law. For example, one Mishnah concerned with the Sabbath states that "on weekdays, one is required to walk carefully in the street so as not to knock other people down, but on Friday afternoons, it is permissible to walk faster because one is getting ready for the Sabbath." This piece of Mishnah provides justification for our Hasid friend racing his baby carriage through the bustling streets of Jerusalem on a Friday afternoon.

The next doll in size, which could be said to hold the entire Mishnah in it, is called the Germara. The Germara was written over the next 300 years and is a compilation of commentaries on each of the laws and traditions contained in the Mishnah. The Germara asks questions, provides arguments, and usually comes to a resolution about the point of discussion of the Mishnah.

Devine Devarim

The following are the groupings of Jewish textual studies, beginning with the smallest.

Mishnah   the smallest division of Jewish textual studies, consisting of a summary of Torah laws given to Moses orally by God on Mount Sinai.

Germara   the compilation of commentaries on each of the laws and traditions contained in the Mishnah.

Rashi's commentaries   further insight into the 20 volumes of the Talmud.

Tosafot   the commentaries written in the twelfth and thirteenth centuries that expounded and further clarified Rashi's original texts.

In this case, the Germara might ask, how fast can you run on Friday afternoons? What happens if two people who are both running to get ready for Sabbath collide into each other? At what point on Friday are you allowed to start running faster? And so on. The rabbis will go back and forth, trying to determine, from Jewish law, practice, philosophy, and history, exactly what the ruling should be. That's the Germara.

The next matrioshka doll is our old friend Rashi, who actually wrote a commentary on virtually all of the 20 large volumes of the Talmud. As Rashi did for the Torah, he now does the same thing for the Talmud. He explains individual words, phrases, and legal terms that may not be familiar to the average reader. Rashi was writing in 1100, again, approximately 600 years after the close of the Germara. Rashi, however, is far from the last word.

You can think of the next matrioshka doll in the sequence as the Tosafot. The word Tosafot comes from the word "addition," or "supplement." The rabbis who lived in the twelfth and thirteenth centuries across Western Europe viewed themselves as supplementing the commentary that Rashi provided. The authors of the Tosafot commentaries did not expound on every single word or line, as did Rashi. Rather, they would pull out certain problems that they believed that Rashi had not fully explained.

But even the Tosafotists, as they are called, are not the last word on the Talmud. For the last 700 years, additional Torah scholars have written their commentaries on everything that went before them, giving us a series of even larger matrioshka dolls encompassing the ones we have already seen.

Even as you read this, Talmud scholars are engaged in grasping how the concepts that first came to us at Mount Sinai, and have since been studied and refined, apply to the world of the twenty-first century. Based on 3,500-year-old principles of study, they seek to determine what does Jewish law and history have to say about cutting edge issues like in vitro fertilization, cloning, partial birth abortion, and the broad range of modern scientific and philosophical endeavors? The answers are contained in the writings of these modern sages. Their work constitutes the biggest matrioshka doll of all. For now ....

High Spirits

If you're going to study in a yeshiva, you better have great concentration skills! Unless you're in class, you're generally in the *beit midrash*—the study hall, a large, long room in which students study in pairs. The difference between a beit midrash and a college library is the volume! Yeshiva students study *out loud*—and sometimes they get *really* loud! First-time visitors are occasionally shocked by the arguing, the table-pounding, the excitement, the noise, and even the singing!

As long as the Jewish people survive, the world will continue to need interpreting in terms of our history, and generations of scholars yet unborn will tackle the issues of their day, creating yet another matrioshka doll to encompass all the rest.

Who's Got the Cliff's Notes?

How do Jews go about studying all this material? *Very slowly*. Many Jews around the world engage in a process called *daf yomi*, which literally means "a double-sided page a day." It takes approximately seven and a half years to read the entire Talmud, one page per day. Such individuals meet for daily hour-long classes. If you take a particular Long Island Railroad train from Far Rockaway into Manhattan on weekday mornings, you'll find yourself smack in the middle of a daf yomi class.

Other Jews study the material in regular classes at their temples and synagogues, or with partners called *chavrusas*.

The Bottom Line

The purpose of all this study is twofold. One benefit is that you get to learn exactly why Jews do what they do. The more you know about Judaism, the more you realize that Jewish practice encompasses a fairly broad range of action and belief on any given commandment, custom, or rule. How do you pick your own way through the minefield of possible choices? One option is to follow in the footsteps of your family, if they were Jewish. The other is to study each individual practice on its own, and learn to make decisions for yourself. Both ways are extremely honored in the Jewish tradition and it is entirely acceptable to practice both forms of Jewish thought.

The other benefit from studying Jewish texts is an insight into the mind of God. As we said earlier, traditional Judaism posits that the Torah is the blueprint that God referred to when creating the universe. The purpose of study is not just to become better equipped to make decisions about practicing Jewish law and religion. The sublime benefit of studying Jewish texts is that they take the reader deeper into the mind of God.

> **Mystical Moments**
>
> The Hebrew language is considered so holy that the decision to make it the "language of the street" in Palestine in the early twentieth century was very controversial. Even today, many Hasidic Jews consider Hebrew so holy that they will speak it only when they pray. They use Yiddish or English for day-to-day conversation. There are even street signs in Yiddish popping up in Israel!

The Least You Need to Know

- Jews are always preparing for the next event on the calendar.
- The best way to study Jewish texts is in the holy tongue, Hebrew, but today there are countless excellent books in English, too.
- There are many layers of Jewish textual study.
- Studying Jewish texts gives insight into the practices of Jews and also into the "mind" of God.

The Mystical Nature of Human Character

In This Chapter

- ◆ The importance of character in Judaism
- ◆ The author of the Tanya
- ◆ The founder of the Mussar movement
- ◆ The Chafetz Chaim
- ◆ The origin of Chabad Houses

A yeshiva student in his early 20s came home one Sabbath afternoon to find his father, a Talmud scholar, sitting in the garden, reading a volume of the Talmud and smoking a cigarette. The young man was shocked. Smoking, of course, is forbidden on the Sabbath. It is contrary to Jewish law to strike a match or create a fire for any other purpose. The young man was stunned by his father's behavior.

The father noticed the look of shock and incredulity on his son's face. The juxtaposition of the open volume of Talmud and the lit cigarette was overwhelming for the young man.

"When you know as much Talmud as I do," the father explained curtly, "you, too, can smoke a cigarette on the Sabbath."

Character Counts

This story, while apocryphal, illustrates a few important points about the danger of devoting yourself entirely to the letter of the law. The story actually illustrates Judaism's concern that people might become self-righteous due to keeping the mitzvot and studying Torah. In fact, the Talmud says, "Don't take credit for studying Torah, because that's what you are created for." The father in our story has developed a certain level of spiritual arrogance, in that he has decided that he has devoted himself so thoroughly over the years to Torah study that the rules no longer apply to him.

There is a second problem that Judaism finds in its adherents who become too devoted to the practice of Judaism without proper character. The father responded in a somewhat rude manner to his son's natural shock. Judaism teaches that it does not matter how high a level one practices the teachings of Judaism if one's behavior toward others is not suffused with a sense of spirituality and kindness.

The concern that somehow religious practice gives people a bye when it came to relating properly, kindly, thoughtfully, and spiritually with others has existed in Judaism for centuries. The problem with practicing religion perfectly is that you can end up feeling—and acting—smug. This is completely contrary to everything that Judaism stands for, yet it is an all-too-human possibility. If we get enough Brownie points, we start to think we are special. Judaism teaches that we should not be sure of ourselves until the day of our death. And yet, if we think we have attained a certain level of religious practice, we are often tempted to believe that the regular laws of human contact somehow no longer apply to us.

> **Spiritual Citations**
>
> "Arrogance is a kingdom without a crown."
> —Talmud

> **Mystical Moments**
>
> Humility and humiliation both come from the same Latin root, *humus*, meaning earth. To be humble means to be grounded; to be humiliated means to be driven into the ground.

In this chapter, I would like to explore with you the lives and character philosophies of 10 of the most influential thinkers and writers in recent Jewish history. Each perceived problems in their generation—either due to overemphasizing practice or lack of proper religious training—or in the general level of character among the Jewish people. Each individual courageously—and often with great criticism both from Jewish and secular authorities—set out new, bold approaches to the question of character. Their illuminating thoughts have much to say about the spirituality of human relations today.

Rabbi Moshe Chaim Luzzato (1705–1747)

Rabbi Moshe Chaim Luzzato was born to a rabbinical family in Padua, Italy, and studied Kabbalah with one of the leading Kabbalists of his generation. By the age of 14, he knew the entire Talmud and midrash by heart—a feat perhaps comparable to memorizing the entire *Encyclopedia Britannica* and all the works of Shakespeare. Rabbi Luzzato is best known for a book entitled *Mesilas Yesharim* (*"The Path of the Just"*), which details just what it means to have awe or fear of God.

Luzzato also wrote about the Zohar and other mystical aspects of Judaism, and was condemned by rabbinical authorities for many of these works. He left Italy altogether in order to avoid public life and worked as a gem cutter in Amsterdam. He longed to travel to Israel, and moved in 1743 to the northern Israel city of Acco. He died the following year, at age 39, in an epidemic of some sort.

Luzzato's teachings echo the Talmudic concepts that animals have souls, although not of the same spiritual plane as that of humans, and that there exists a class of *shedim*, or intermediate beings, between the spiritual and physical worlds. The most common translation of shedim is "demons," but Luzzato does not mean demons in a devilish sort of way. He is saying that there is a kind of being that is neither physical nor spiritual but somewhere in the middle, and that these beings affect the way the world runs.

Devine Devarim

shedim   intermediate beings that exist between the spiritual and physical worlds.

Luzzato also taught that every physical entity and process is under the charge of an angel responsible for maintaining the natural order in the universe as well as carrying out God's decrees. Good and evil on Earth, Luzzato taught, are rooted in good and evil in the spiritual realm. The deeds of individual human beings have the power to cause either spiritual rectification or damage, depending upon how a person uses his or her power.

As for evil, Luzzato taught that God allows for evil but does not create it directly, because without evil there would be no free will. However, he believed that God is still the *indirect* cause of evil, since the actual cause of evil is the absence of good, and it is God's responsibility, as it were, to provide goodness throughout the universe. Luzzato's works are still studied by yeshiva students and traditionally minded Jews more than 200 years after his passing.

Rabbi Levi Yitzhak of Berdichev (c. 1740–1810)

Rabbi Levi Yitzhak of Berdichev was one of the most famous rabbis in the Hasidic movement and is still quoted frequently in Hasidic teachings today. He was known for his tremendous love of Jews, especially those who did not have the economic privilege of accomplishing formal yeshiva training. He founded Hasidism in central Poland and was extremely influential in Lithuania and the Ukraine.

Levi Yitzhak was also known for his sense of humor about Judaism. He would use parables and stories that would bring a smile to people's lips, in contrast with the more serious approach of Rabbi Luzzato. Rabbi Levi Yitzhak emphasized a concept called *dvekut*, which means adhering to God with joy; achieving piety and nobility of spirit through happiness, dancing, great fervor in prayer, and great enjoyment in the simple pleasures of life.

> ### High Spirits
>
> Rabbi Levi Yitzhak of Berdichev once saw a man running. "Why are you running?" he asked. "What makes you so sure," asked the rabbi, "that your living is ahead of you, and you have to run to catch it up? Perhaps it's behind you, and you need to stand still to let it catch up with you!"

> ### Devine Devarim
>
> **dvekut** the concept of adhering to God with joy; achieving piety and nobility of spirit through happiness, dancing, great fervor in prayer, and great enjoyment in the simple pleasures of life.

Martin Buber, in his *Tales of the Hasidim*, tells an emblematic story about Rabbi Levi Yitzhak. One Passover, the rabbi conducted a Passover service that was perfection itself in terms of its spirituality, attention to every single word of the Haggadah, and the revelation of the secret significance of every one of the rituals. The next morning, Rabbi Levi Yitzhak was thinking back on the Seder with great happiness and pride when suddenly he heard the voice of God telling him that the water-carrier in the poor neighborhood on the outskirts of town had created an even more pleasing Seder.

The rabbi and his students went into the poor neighborhood to the home of this individual water-carrier, who was pretty much the lowest rung on the socio-economic ladder. It turned out that the water-carrier had performed the pre-Passover rituals with an absolute purity of heart, unburdened by pride or fear. Rabbi Levi Yitzhak then asked how he celebrated the Seder.

The water-carrier explained that he had heard that it was against Jewish law to drink brandy during the eight days of Passover. So he drank an enormous amount of brandy the night before the beginning of Passover and woke up some time during the evening of Passover. His wife asked him to perform a Seder like the ones in all other Jewish homes. He responded, "I am ignorant and my father was ignorant and I know nothing about these matters. What I do know is that our fathers and mothers were captive in Egypt, and we have a God and he led them to freedom. We are again in captivity, and I know that God will lead us to freedom, too."

In short, one did not have to be a great philosopher, religious scholar, or secular leader to be not just a pious Jew, but one whose spirituality was even greater than that of Rabbi Levi Yitzhak, who loved to tell this story.

Another classic example of the mind of Rabbi Levi Yitzhak was a prayer song he composed in which he brought God as a defendant to a Jewish court on Yom Kippur. The rabbi carefully arrayed the evidence against God, showing that the Creator had permitted far too much suffering in the world, and sought an order from the court demanding that God cease all suffering immediately. The prayer song ends with Rabbi Levi Yitzhak losing the verdict—but not his faith.

I heard the following Rabbi Levi Yitzhak story from Rabbi Yisroel Deren of Chabad of Amherst, Massachusetts. Rabbi Levi Yitzhak once prayed to God, "When a Jew drops his tefillin on the floor, he fasts and weeps for a whole day. *Abishte* [a Hasidic name for God], your tefillin [the Jewish people] has been on the floor for almost 2,000 years! When will you bend down and pick us up?"

> **Spiritual Citations**
>
> "It suddenly occurred to me that there's a very simple meaning in talking about oneself as a Chosen People: If you are chosen, you *cannot choose*. The Jews are a Chosen People because they have no choice."
>
> —Leslie Fiedler, author

Rabbi Shneur Zalman (1745–1813)

Rabbi Shneur Zalman was the founder of Chabad, or Lubavitch Hasidus, perhaps the best-known branch of the Hasidic world known to secular and orthodox Jews. Internationally renowned for his intellect and ability to break down complicated concepts into easily understood terms, Shneur Zalman is best known as the author of the Tanya, the basic text of Chabad Hasidus. Shneur Zalman's great innovation was to turn his focus from the life of the tzaddik, the fully righteous person, to focus instead on the needs of the *benoni*, or average, ordinary Jew. Like Rabbi Levi Yitzhak, Zalman's work was primarily meant for the Jews of Eastern Europe who did not have the exposure to the kind of erudition that their wealthier counterparts in Western Europe enjoyed.

Since its publication in 1796, the Tanya has gone through at least 65 separate editions, and is still studied on a daily basis by Lubavitcher Hasidim throughout the world. The book is profound enough to be the source of endless conversation among great scholars and yet simple and clear enough to be taken to heart by the tens of thousands of adherents of Lubavitch Hasidus.

> **High Spirits**
>
> "Jews are the Chosen People—chosen for tsuris! [troubles and worries]"
>
> —Mrs. Ida Pincus of Brooklyn (and two weeks every winter in Miami Beach)

The idea behind the book was to guide Jews in their religious beliefs. Zalman writes not for people who are perplexed as to the existence of God or other great philosophical issues. His readers were not troubled by doubts about the existence of God or their place in the universe. According to Tanya authority Rabbi Nissan Mindel, Zalman's readers simply wanted to find the right path to God. Shneur Zalman was a tremendous scholar in his own right and certainly knew of the various Jewish philosophy books that had preceded him. He sought to write a book that would be accessible to his Jewish contemporaries.

Shneur Zalman was deeply influenced by kabbalistic thought, the Zohar, and by the ideas of the Baal Shem Tov, the founder of the Chasidic movement. Shneur Zalman's approach was that Jewish law, as found in the Bible and Talmud, provided a basic sense of "law and order" for the universe. The Kabbalah, the secret spiritual doctrines of Judaism, on the other hand, provided an inner dimension—the "soul" of the Torah. The rabbi sought to blend together the Kabbalah and Talmud the same way the body and soul are blended together in every human being.

In the Tanya, Shneur Zalman taught that human consciousness derives from two different types of soul—a divine soul and an animal soul. The conflict between these—the heavenly and earthly, if you will—produces conflicts in human personality, as well as a range of character types from evil all the way to righteous. The ideal, Shneur Zalman writes, is to achieve a unity of the divine and animal souls in order to become that benoni, the person in the middle ground between the truly spiritual and the truly physical.

The purpose of living according to Jewish law and custom, Zalman writes, is not just to attain heaven, but to achieve a taste of heaven on Earth. It is possible, Zalman claims, through perfection of one's character and through proper adherence to Jewish law and custom, to experience a taste of the bliss that awaits us in the afterlife. This is, of course, a rough summation of a complex and weighty book, but my purpose is to give a brief overview of the nature of his philosophy. The Tanya has a ready home in the world of Jewish thought, both in its day and ours, 200 years later.

Rabbi Nachman of Bratslav (1772–1810)

Rabbi Nachman of Bratslav is one of the most intriguing figures in Jewish history. A great grandson of the Bal Shem Tov, Nachman was born in 1772 in the Ukraine. A mystic and kabbalist, he attracted a large number of followers in his lifetime due to his compelling allegories about the relationship between God and the Jewish people.

Nachman cast his parables in the forms of princes and princesses, beggars and kings. Like the Hasidic masters who came before him, he also taught of a Judaism of joy, and was famous for his saying, "It is a great mitzvah to be happy." His Hasidic tales are still studied to the present day, and have been interpreted by no less a contemporary master than Rabbi Adin Steinsaltz (discussed later in this chapter).

The great irony about Rabbi Nachman is that he preached joy but was in fact a highly manic depressive individual. It is possible that his life was cut short due to that condition.

Rabbi Nachman preceded the development of psychology by almost 100 years with his emphasis on the understanding of human nature, a problem that certainly plagued him on a personal level. Nachman was perhaps the first Jewish scholar to recognize that individual Jews did not always operate from a place of absolute faith in the one God. The rabbi is rare among the great Jewish thinkers in that he allowed his adherents to contemplate the possibility that either God did not exist or that God was not all-powerful. He was eventually able to lead them back to the conclusion that the world was created and ruled by one God, but he brought enormous spiritual relief to individual Jews who, without him, most likely could never have found answers to their existential dilemmas.

According to Rabbi David Walk, another unique aspect of Rabbi Nachman's philosophy is that Nachman did not consider it a major difficulty for Jews to devote themselves totally to God and spirituality. Nachman actually suggested that, of course, God had the more difficult job, in that it was a greater compromise for God to become "small enough" in order to make contact with individual human beings. It is in our nature to reach out to God, Rabbi Nachman wrote, but it is actually almost contrary to the infinite nature of God to become "small enough" to reach out to us.

Mystical Moments

"On Yom Kippur, instead of striking your heart, let your heart strike you."
—Chafetz Chaim

After Nachman's untimely death at the age of 38, his followers found it impossible to replace him. Today, the Bratslav Hasidim can be found throughout the Jewish world and are sometimes referred to as the *Toiter*, or "dead" Hasidim, because they are the only group that has never sought to replace their rebbe with another individual.

Rabbi Israel Salanter (1810–1883)

During the nineteenth century, Jews who left traditional Judaism behind would often criticize its adherents as unclean, uncultured, and sometimes downright rude. Rabbi Israel Salanter, a Torah giant of the nineteenth century, responded by founding the *Mussar* movement in Jewish education, which emphasized the development of character and ethics in addition to the usual concentration on Jewish law.

It might sound surprising, but the yeshiva world of his day initially resisted the ideas of Rabbi Salanter. The yeshiva authorities were already facing two very different threats: the challenge of the Reform movement, which for the first time in centuries provided an alternative to orthodox Judaism, and also the *Haskala*, or Enlightenment, which drew many Jews completely out of the orbit of Judaism. Jews no longer had to be totally observant to fit in. They could join the Reform movement, or even walk away from Judaism altogether. Against this backdrop, it would have been difficult to bring about virtually any kind of change in the yeshiva world, which naturally felt threatened by these changes.

> **Spiritual Citations**
>
> "A rabbi whose community does not disagree with him is not really a rabbi. And a rabbi who fears his community is not really a man."
>
> —Rabbi Israel Salanter

Rabbi Salanter explained that his movement did not seek to change Judaism; rather, he sought to change Jews.

In a yeshiva setting, *Mussar shmooze* refers to a lecture by a rabbi, not on a specific Talmudic teaching or biblical story, but on a character trait such as honesty, courtesy, friendliness, or respecting one's fellows. After such a talk, yeshiva students would break off into small groups and discuss, in a constructive and loving way, each other's shortcomings so that they might be able to improve the nature of their character.

The Mussar movement eventually caught on, due in large part to the strength of Rabbi Salanter's own character and the many stories of decency that surrounded him. One story told of the rabbi enjoying a cigar in the smoking car of a train on his return to his home city of Vilna, a great center for Torah learning. A young man in the same car rudely chastised the rabbi, despite the fact that smoking was permitted and that the side effects of secondhand smoke would not be discovered for another 150 years.

Rabbi Salanter extinguished his cigar but continued to find himself berated by the young man. The next day the young man, who had come to Vilna to learn the trade of a *shochet* (ritual slaughterer), discovered exactly who he had been yelling at. Rabbi Salanter went out of his way to help the young man find proper instruction and pass the test. When the young man asked him why he had been so helpful, despite the rudeness that he had endured, Rabbi Salanter gave his explanation: It's easy to tell someone that you forgive him or her, but the only way you can remove any grudge that might remain in your heart is to go out of your way to help that person.

This story can be found on www.torah.org. The works of Rabbi Salanter are still studied to this day, and the Mussar movement has penetrated every corner of the non-Hassidic yeshiva world.

Devine Devarim

Mussar shmooze   a rabbinical lecture on a character trait such as honesty, courtesy, friendliness, or respecting one's fellows.

shochet   a ritual slaughterer.

Mishnah Berurah   the commentary on the Shulchan Aruch, written by the Chafetz Chaim as a guide on behavior and practice, which is even today a staple in practically every observant Jewish home around the world.

Shulchan Aruch   the great code of Jewish law written by Rabbi Joseph Caro; it literally means to set table; in Judaism, the term is used to describe the belief that everyone organizes his or her spiritual life and religious practice as he or she sees fit.

Rabbi Israel Meir HaCohen, the Chafetz Chaim (1838–1933)

Like Rabbi Salanter, Rabbi Israel Meir HaCohen, commonly known in traditional Jewish circles as the *Chafetz Chaim*, was initially motivated to speak out against a form of behavior that was bringing Jews a bad name. That behavior was the speaking of slander and gossip. Rabbi Kagan wrote a short treatise on the importance of "guarding one's tongue" and pointed out that the Torah contained no less then 31 positive and negative commandments with regard to proper and improper speech. The book on avoiding gossip became immensely popular in the Jewish world, and is still studied to this day.

The Chafetz Chaim (Hebrew for the phrase, "Who desires life? Then let him guard his tongue!") is also famous for having written a six-volume commentary on Jewish law, the *Mishnah Berurah*, which is even today a staple in practically every observant Jewish home around the world. The Chafetz Chaim had noted the need for a simple, clearly written guide to Jewish practice and behavior, and he wrote the *Mishnah Berurah* as a commentary on the *Shulchan Aruch*, the great code of Jewish law that had been written centuries earlier by Rabbi Joseph Caro.

Two stories about the Chafetz Chaim illustrate his character. A visitor to his study once noticed that the library of this great Torah scholar was extremely limited. The visitor asked the Chafetz Chaim why he had so few books. The rabbi replies, "Books cost money, and money is time." The Chafetz Chaim never sought or attained great wealth, and he and his wife derived their support from a small grocery store that they owned and ran.

The second story depicts the rabbi as a character witness in a trial. Before he is called, the lawyer asks the judge if he can tell a story about the Chafetz Chaim in order to illustrate what kind of man he is. The judge agrees. The lawyer says, "One Friday night, after Sabbath services, the Chafetz Chaim invited a stranger in the synagogue to come home and have Sabbath dinner with him. In the dining room, the Chafetz Chaim turned his back for a moment, and the visitor took the silver candlesticks and bolted out of the house. Obviously, he was stealing them. The Chafetz Chaim immediately ran to the front door and yelled after him, 'It's a gift! It's a gift!' The reason the Chafetz Chaim shouted this was that he did not want the young man to bear the sin of stealing. By making the candlesticks a gift, the would-be thief would have committed no crime."

The judge turned to the lawyer and said, "Counselor, do you honestly believe that this story happened?"

The lawyer replied, "To be honest, Your Honor, I have no idea whether the story is true or not. But one thing I know for sure is that they don't tell stories like this about you and me."

The Chafetz Chaim zeroed in on the topic of *lashon hara*, or gossip, because he recognized that the primary way by which we reveal our own character and relate to our fellows is through the simple act of speech. If we can be careful in terms of the way we speak to and about others, we can create for ourselves—and for everyone—a peaceful world. Some of the basic rules of lashon hara include that truth is not a defense—even if you speak gossip about someone and it turns out that every word you are saying is true, you have still committed the sin of gossiping. It is lashon hara even if you include yourself in the story, as in, "When Plony and I were younger, we both used to shoplift." There is no marital or best friend exemption; we are just as obligated to avoid speaking lashon hara in the presence of our spouses and partners (and our children) as we are in the presence of anyone else.

According to the Chafetz Chaim, it is even forbidden to *listen* to lashon hara. In the event that you find yourself living in a community where virtually everyone is a constant speaker of lashon hara, you are actually obligated to move.

Rabbi Eliyahu Dessler (1891–1954)

Rabbi Eliyahu Dessler, chief rabbi at the yeshiva at Gateshead, England, is widely considered the heir to the mantle of Rabbi Salanter and the foremost twentieth-century authority on Mussar. Rabbi Dessler wrote a book called *Strive for Truth*, considered the century's most important book on the spirituality of character. *Strive for Truth* is a basic text in Jewish schools worldwide, and is also a frequently studied book in adult education programs in all branches of Judaism.

Devine Devarim

yetzer hara an evil inclination in a person's character.

One of the ideas that Rabbi Dessler's book conveys is that the evil inclination in us, the *yetzer hara*, causes us to forget some of the sins and mistakes we have made.

This is dangerous; if we forget a wrong that we have done, we are not likely to seek forgiveness or change our behavior. So we have to guard against this kind of forgetfulness.

At the same time, Rabbi Dessler writes, human beings frequently act out of mixed motivations. When we perform a mitzvah we may act out of a basically positive motivation, but there still may be some negative aspects to our reason for completing the mitzvah. Perhaps others will honor us, or we might feel an excessive sense of pride in ourselves for what we do.

Rabbi Dessler suggests that we have a responsibility to ferret out the negative motivations that we have, even when we complete a good deed, because otherwise we will be held accountable for those negative aspects of our personality when our lives are judged upon entering the next world. This, he says, is the explanation of the prayer said on Rosh Hashanah: "There is no forgetfulness before Your heavenly throne." The way to overcome God remembering our negative aspects is to concentrate as best we can on the positive nature of God, and then God will render us measure for measure. The more we remember God, the more God will remember us.

Rabbi Menachem Mendel Schneerson, the Lubavitcher Rebbe (1902–1994)

Rabbi Menachem Mendel Schneerson led the Lubavitcher movement of Hasidic Jewry for more than 40 years. Both his parents came from renowned families of Jewish scholars. As a scholar himself, Rabbi Schneerson was a child prodigy, and in 1923, he met the then-Lubavitcher Rebbe, a third cousin, who made him his private secretary. Five years later, Rabbi Schneerson married a daughter of the then-Lubavitcher Rebbe.

The couple, married in Prague, moved to Berlin, where Rabbi Schneerson studied mathematics and science at the University of Berlin. Because of the Nazis, the Schneersons fled Berlin for Paris, where Rabbi Schneerson completed two doctorates in engineering and science at the Sorbonne.

In 1941, the couple fled Europe for New York. Nine years later, the Lubavitcher Rabbi, Rabbi Yosef Yitzhak, passed away. A year later, Rabbi Schneerson ascended to the role of Lubavitcher Rebbe in his own right.

Author Rabbi Herbert Weiner writes in his 1996 book *Conversations with the Rebbe* that Rabbi Schneerson did not willingly take on the role of rebbe, but found that he had no alternative. Weiner asked Schneerson why exactly he decided to become the rebbe. Schneerson's response: "What do you do if there is a library of books and someone puts the key in your pocket

Spiritual Citations

"As if one could know the good a person is capable of, when one doesn't know the bad he might do."
—Elias Canetti

and walks away?" In other words, Rabbi Schneerson recognized that his erudition obligated him to take on the role of leader.

The rebbe was a visionary man, and he recognized the importance of rebuilding Judaism after the devastating loss of six million Jews in the Holocaust. He established schools, social service agencies, a publishing arm of Lubavitch, and perhaps his best known achievement, the sending of emissaries, called *sheluchim*, to virtually every city and town in the world where Jews live. Sheluchim of the rebbe are expected to make contacts in the local community, find donors, create a synagogue, and offer religious services, Sabbath and holiday meals, and classes, emphasizing traditional Judaism and especially the Lubavitch way.

"Chabad Houses," as these outreach centers are called, do not seek to proselytize to non-Jews. Rather, they concentrate on "in-reach," the term used to bring secular Jews closer to traditional Judaism. Chabad Houses became the model for Hillel houses on college campuses, which were established by the Reform movement in following years in order to create a presence among American Jewish college students.

The rebbe was also famous for his *fahrbrengens*, all-night series of talks that he would give at Brooklyn's Lubavitch headquarters before crowds of as many as 8,000 Jews, packed together and on their feet for hours, drinking in the words of their leader. Adherents of the Lubavitch movement would often fly in at a moment's notice from South Africa, Europe, and the West Coast of the United States simply to attend a fahrbrengen.

Seven years after the passing of the Lubavitcher Rebbe, his title remains vacant. It is the belief of many Lubavitchers that the Rebbe is actually the *moshiach*, or Jewish messiah, and that he will reveal himself as such before long.

A typical teaching of the Lubavitcher Rebbe was that the Passover Haggadah speaks of four sons, but there is actually a fifth child—the Jew who is not even attending a Passover Seder at all. Instead of merely "preaching to the converted," the Lubavitcher Rebbe made it his mission—and the mission of Chabad—to seek out Jews and make them aware of their heritage, and thus bring that fifth child to the Passover Seder.

The collected works and speeches of the Rebbe fill dozens of volumes and have also been edited and published by mainstream publishers due to the intense admiration the Rebbe received even from secular Jews.

Rabbi Aryeh Kaplan (1935–1983)

Rabbi Aryeh Kaplan published two dozen books in a writing career that lasted only 12 years. As a Torah scholar and also the holder of a Master's degree in physics, Kaplan had been described in the United States' *Who's Who in Physics* as the most promising young physicist in America. Rabbi Kaplan was drawn to Kabbalah and Jewish mysticism, and is probably the most readable and accessible authority on meditation, Kabbalah, the messiah, immortality, resurrection, and the nature of God in his generation. An excellent introduction to his life and thought can be found in the *Aryeh Kaplan Anthology*, a two-volume series. His sudden death at age 48 shocked the Jewish world and deprived us of a scholar who had "only just begun."

Rabbi Adin Steinsaltz (1937–)

Newsweek magazine once described Rabbi Adin Steinsaltz as possessing the kind of mind that "only comes along every thousand years." A man of astonishing Talmudic knowledge, Steinsaltz is in the process of translating the entire Talmud into both modern Hebrew and English with a revolutionary, "user-friendly"approach, a huge project that only he could possibly carry out. More than 30 volumes of the Steinsaltz edition of the Talmud have already been published. He has also founded schools in Jerusalem and Russia, and in 1988 received the Israel Prize, the nation's highest honor.

Rabbi Steinsaltz is also the author of three popular books on Judaism that explain in the clearest possible terms the Talmud, Hasidic thought, and the tales of Rabbi Nachman. These books, *The Essential Talmud, The Thirteen-Petaled Rose,* and *Rabbi Nachman's Tales,* are excellent introductions for anyone wishing to delve further into these topics.

As yet another highest-level Jewish scholar who is as intrigued by the mystical aspects of Judaism as by the practical, Steinsaltz is practically unique in the Jewish world in that he does not belong to any particular branch of Judaism or mode of Jewish thought. Rather, he is a centrist, and as a result, his teachings are studied not just by the entire Jewish world but also by Christians and Buddhists. He has been invited to meet the Dalai Lama and has spoken at the Vatican; his opinions and theological insights are sought by politicians and ordinary people alike.

Rabbi Steinsaltz's concept of spirituality is that God is far too great to be understood by one particular religious movement or direction. No ideology in the Jewish world is big enough to understand or contain the vastness that is God.

A low-key, lighthearted speaker, Rabbi Steinsaltz teaches a weekly Talmud class in Jerusalem, and anyone is welcome to attend it. His friendliness and comfort with strangers individually and while on the speaker's platform make him perhaps the ideal representative of what spirituality in Judaism can and should be all about.

The Least You Need to Know

◆ The Mussar movement emphasized the development of character and ethics.

◆ Lashon hara, or gossip, should be avoided at all costs.

◆ The Tanya is the basic text of Chabad Chassidus.

◆ According to Rabbi Steinsaltz, no ideology or religion can understand God.

Part 4

Revelations

Buckle up for this section! We're going to delve into Kabbalah and Zohar and get a taste of real, Jewish mysticism. We'll look deeply into the creation of the world—and what Jewish spiritual authorities expect at the end of time.

Then we'll get into two more immediate aspects of Jewish spirituality—the power of human speech, and the presence of the divine in the world (the *shechinah).*

Chapter 16

Kabbalah: Spiritual Life at a Million Miles Per Hour

In This Chapter

♦ The complexity of Kabbalah study

♦ *Sefirot* and *kelipot*

♦ The creation of the universe

♦ A glimpse of the Zohar

♦ The kabbalist Moses de Leon

What is Kabbalah?

If Torah and Talmud are the body and intellect of Judaism, then Kabbalah is its soul. Kabbalah presents the laws of the spiritual world, just as physics addresses the laws of the natural world. Kabbalah, an important aspect of Jewish mysticism that dates back at least 2,000 years, asks the following questions:

1. How can a human being relate to God?

2. How did God create the world?

3. What will happen at the end of time?

The reward of studying Kabbalah is a true, moment-by-moment intimacy with God. It is the same level of closeness that you enjoy on a human level when you are snuggling with someone on a couch: *They're right there.* You can feel each other's presence in the most sublime and wonderful way. Obviously the relationship with God that Jews seek is not in any way a physical one; I just use this as an illustration of the closeness that kabbalists achieve.

There is an expectation about religion—any religion—that its principles must be clear and easy to grasp. After all, religion is not just for heavy-duty intellectuals. Religion is for everyone, no matter what his or her level of intellect or knowledge. If a religion were too complicated, it simply wouldn't be fair to people who don't have the time or freedom to further their education. Religions have to make sense to people.

The Jewish Anomaly

Kabbalah is notoriously complex and difficult to understand. Its adherents claim that it can be compared to the Olympics of Jewish spirituality—not in the sense of competing against someone else for a prize, but in the sense that it is the highest and most difficult level of understanding to attain.

"Kabbalah" is a Hebrew word derived from the root "to receive." Kabbalah, therefore, is a form of teaching that one receives, usually one-on-one, from an expert kabbalist. Traditionally, the study of Kabbalah was not open to everyone, as it is today. Throughout Jewish history, the Kabbalah was a subject available only to married males over 40 years of age with a "full belly" of Torah and Talmud study behind them. The belief was that Kabbalah was simply too powerful to put into the hands of individuals who were not mature enough to handle it.

Spiritual Citations

"The self-explorer, whether he wants to or not, becomes the explorer of everything else. He learns to see himself, but suddenly, provided he was honest, all the rest appears, and it is as rich as he was, and, as a final crowning, richer."

—Elias Canetti

Today, things have changed. The marketplace of ideas has brought many kabbalistic principles to the masses. Women are just as free today to study Kabbalah as men, and there are no longer restrictions on age, marital status, gender, or anything else. Many non-Jews are also extremely fascinated with Kabbalah, including celebrities like Madonna and Rosie O'Donnell. The fact is that this popularized version of the Kabbalah has been simplified and distorted beyond all recognition from the original.

Today, many temples and synagogues offer adult education classes on Kabbalah, and there are some private educational institutions like Metivta in Los Angeles, run by rabbi Jonathan Omer-Man, that offer Kabbalah classes to the general public. Not all Jews believe in the importance of Kabbalah. The irony is that no subject in Judaism draws unaffiliated Jews to a lecture like Kabbalah, yet in many ways Kabbalah is about as extraneous to Jewish practice as a subject could be.

Why is Kabbalah so appealing? Perhaps because it doesn't require you to *do* anything. Traditional Judaism keeps its adherents very busy—from figuring out how to keep the next Sabbath or Jewish holiday to determining what and where to eat next.

High Spirits

I was once in an elevator after a noontime religious service in a New York office building. There were a dozen men in the elevator, all wearing hats or yarmulkes, and one woman. She looked us over and asked, "Why do you cover your heads?"

"Out of respect to God," one of the men said.

"Oh, I thought it was because you're always in a hurry."

To be an observant Jew in a sense *is* always to be in a hurry. There's always something to do or to prepare for. So Kabbalah appeals perhaps because there are no rules attached to it. No rules, no guilt.

This is why Kabbalah is a controversial subject in traditional Jewish circles. The age, marital, and gender requirements of the past were believed to screen all but the most serious of purpose. The rabbis also could assume that a potential Kabbalah student was already in acceptance of the 613 commandments.

The Kabbalah is perhaps the only aspect of traditional Judaism to appeal to Jews who are not orthodox. The problem is that the Kabbalah that is most often offered to secular Jews has nothing to do with the real Kabbalah at all. What purports to be Kabbalah is actually a mishmash of modern, New Age thought. Much of what passes for Kabbalah could have been lifted from any of a dozen popular self-help books written in the last 20 years.

Most forms of Kabbalah that are available to the public today are rather basic compared to the true depths of kabbalistic thinking. Popular Kabbalah is like the front gate of a massive, architecturally unique castle. The front gate itself is beautifully made and worthy of study and admiration, but it barely hints at the glory of the castle concealed behind it.

True Kabbalah is as complex and precise as the science of physics. If you were to walk into a traditional class on Kabbalah, if such a thing existed, you might feel as though you had just walked into the study for advanced physics at Princeton University. The definitions in traditional Kabbalah are just as precise—and just as hard to understand—as some of the definitions in classical physics. What is the difference between a quark and a lepton? How do both of those differ from a nutrino? If you want to understand Kabbalah on a sophisticated level, bring your intellectual A-game. Or as Bette Davis once said, "Buckle your seatbelts. It's going to be a bumpy night."

High Spirits

A newcomer to a synagogue turns to his friend when the rabbi begins his sermon and takes off his watch.

"What does it mean when he takes his watch off?" the newcomer asked.

His friend sighed. "Unfortunately, nothing," he replied sadly.

One of the themes throughout this book is that in Judaism there is no form of spirituality that is separate from the notion of character. The same thing holds true in Kabbalah. Kabbalah is about striving to perfect one's character so that one can become as close to God as that individual snuggling with a loved one on a couch. In Judaism, there are no shortcuts up the mountain, and no tram, either. The only way to reach that spiritual mountaintop is to trudge one step at a time. Kabbalah could therefore be described as the Jewish spiritual equivalent of climbing Mt. Everest.

The Feeling of Kabbalah

What does it feel like to grasp Kabbalah? Let me give some examples of peak experiences, both positive and negative. Let's say you're driving on a treacherous mountain road at night in a fast car, in an electrical storm. Suddenly a bolt of lightning strikes in the distance, and for one brief moment you can see a hundred miles into the distance, the dark valley suddenly illuminated completely. Now imagine living at that lighting bolt level of reality and awareness … *all the time!* That's what it feels like to practice Kabbalah at the highest level. It's a sense that you can touch forever.

Now let's say that you are still on that mountain road, it's still dark, the rain is pouring down, and there are no guardrails on the switchbacks. You cannot see the valley below, but you know that it is a sharp, steep drop from the narrow road to the bottom of the mountain. Suddenly, as you cautiously turn around yet another curve in the mountain road, your car goes into a severe skid. Your steering wheel is useless—you cannot control the movement of the car. The road is just too slick. You skid within inches of the side of the road, but at the last moment you regain control over the direction of the car. Masterfully, you pull out of the skid and continue on, aware that you have cheated death.

While death is considered a soothing experience in most religions, a time of perfect repose, near-death experiences are anything but restful. When you are straddling the border of life and death, you are experiencing the greatest level of terror that human beings can know. I wish I could be clearer about this, but as I've never attained that level of spiritual clarity, I'm essentially describing something I've never lived. My understanding is that a true Kabbalist experiences life at a level of awareness that others (like me) can only guess at.

Shift the scene. You are now walking in a beautiful forest at dawn. You are alone, and you can feel the cool mist against your skin. Every time you step, you can feel the crackle of twigs under your feet, and you can feel the dew on the moss through your shoes. You stop walking and barely breathe, because you don't want to interrupt the sense of perfection that surrounds you. You feel as though time has stopped, and you feel close to all eternity. The loudest sound you hear is that of your heart pounding. It is the only sound that violates the perfection of the forest around you.

In that moment, you are experiencing a profound sense of unity. Imagine living every moment of your day with that same level of awareness. That, too, is living in a peak kabbalistic mode.

Mystical Moments

In the kabbalistic community of Safed in Northern Israel, Jews would actually leave the synagogue on Friday night and go into the streets to welcome the Sabbath.

Spiritual Citations

"Religion consists of God's question and man's answer."
—Abraham Joshua Heschel

Let's change the scene again. You are now in the maternity wing of a hospital, watching someone you love give birth. Suddenly you notice the crown of the newborn's head emerging, and within moments, a perfectly formed baby slides out, taking her first breath in this world, uttering that unmistakable sound of a newborn. You are awestruck by the miracle of this most extraordinary human event. You are aware of a high level of blessing—the amazing privilege of watching life come into existence. Imagine living life at that same level of appreciation for everything that happens around you. Imagine if you could experience all of life, which is an ongoing series of miracles, as much as you appreciate watching a child come into this world. That, too, is what it feels like to truly grasp the nature of Kabbalah.

These four sensations—awareness from the lightning bolt striking and illuminating the valley, justice during the near-death experience, unity in the forest at dawn, and blessing at watching a birth—are but four of the attributes that Jews ascribe to God in the study of Kabbalah. The others are:

Goodness

Truth

Mercy

Forgiveness

Vengeance

Patience

Loving kindness

Now imagine living every single moment of your life at a level of spiritual connection where you are experiencing all of these qualities *at the same time*. That level of engagement is the breathtaking, overwhelming reward that comes from mastering Kabbalah.

A Kabbalah Parable

A rabbi, who was also a Kabbalistic master, sat cutting up and eating an apple, as a long line of people awaited their turn to ask him a question about their lives. One by one, the people in line would sit down next to the rabbi and ask him a question about some vital situation—a health issue, a job concern, a question about marriage, or parenthood. The rabbi would take a bite of his apple and answer the question, and each person went away extremely satisfied with the response that he or she received. Observing the scene, a man who didn't know the rabbi asked, "What is that rabbi doing that I couldn't do? I could sit, eat an apple, and answer questions just as easily as he does."

The rabbi overhears the man and says, "My friend. You see an apple before me. I see the appearance of an apple, not a real apple. I see a hologram of an apple. I see what is both hidden and what is revealed about this apple. I see a whirring mass of electrons inside this apple, giving it hardness and form. But I know that its appearance is not reality; its spiritual essence is reality, and I see that apple. When I walk down the street and see an apple tree, I am aware not just of the visible part of the tree, but also the hidden part—the entire root system that spreads out for many yards underneath the ground.

> **High Spirits**
>
> The first Jew to be offered knighthood by Queen Victoria forgot the Latin phrase he was to recite when she placed the sword on his shoulders. So he blurted out the first foreign phrase that came to his mind: *"Mah nishtanah ha'lilah hazeh mi'col ha'lalote?"*
>
> Queen Victoria turned to her consort and asked, "Why is this knight different from all other knights?"

"When I see the apple still on the tree, I see a round object. The most basic example of perfection in this world is a circle, for it has no beginning or end. A sphere is the next level of perfection. An apple contains aspects of these geometric figures, because it is round and almost spherical in shape. So I am aware of the miraculous nature of the shape of the fruit, which in itself hints at the divine perfection of the world.

"I am aware that as the apple hangs on the tree, it is capable of remaining cold on a hot day. I am aware that the apple, which grows in the shade of the leaves of the tree, essentially comes with its own restaurant. I can pluck the apple and eat it under the tree, and remain cool and comfortable, even on a hot day. Not only that, but the apple speaks to me. It doesn't use words or anything like that. It simply turns the right color to indicate that it is ready to eat. And if I don't notice the change in the color, the apple will take another action in order to indicate its readiness: It will fall off the tree.

"In short, I see the apple as an extraordinary appearance of God in this world. So before I eat it, I will pronounce a blessing over it, which will combine the abstract idea of thanking God with the physicality of breath passing from my lungs through my windpipe where it will be transformed into language, and I will thus be able to create the physical concept of speech out of the combination of my thought and the air that exists in the universe. That is, I have taken upon myself the continual discipline of seeing God in the world, not just to talk about it, but to feel it as well. This has taken years—even decades of effort for me to achieve this level of awareness, so much so that even in eating an apple I am practically overwhelmed with the idea of God and the world.

Mystical Moments

Some Orthodox Jews recite a short prayer before they pray! They state that "Behold, I am about to [pray, perform a commandment, whatever]." The idea is to focus their mind on their actions instead of simply praying or performing the mitzvah by rote.

"When you have achieved this same level of conscious awareness, and when you see not just cut up pieces of apple but the revelation of God's nature, then you will be ready to sit down, take a bite of apple, and help people solve their problems in the intuitive manner that I use."

Did a rabbi ever say such a thing to an individual? Probably not. But I think you get the point: A person who is able to intuitively solve the problems of others is a person who has worked very hard at achieving a powerful level of awareness of the world around us and the underlying spirituality inherent in everything as simple as an apple and as complex as the human soul. This is the reward of the study of true Kabbalah.

When we say that the study of Kabbalah is inseparable from the development of one's own character, we mean that in addition to the years of study of kabbalistic concepts and ideas, one must also be a good member of his or her family and society. It's hard to imagine any of the great kabbalists of the last 20 centuries angrily honking the car horn, flashing the brights, and yelling at another driver. Road rage and Kabbalah study do not mesh well. However, character and Kabbalah study are inseparable.

Devine Devarim

sefirot   a series of 10 emanations, comprised of God's positive traits, that created the universe.

kelipot   the shells of light that held individual sefirot in order to keep the emanations of God from intermingling.

Kabbalah and Creation

The kabbalists derived many theories about how the world came into existence. One of the best-known theories was propounded by the sixteenth-century kabbalist Isaac Luria. This man, who died at the age of 38, had a student named Hayim Vital who wrote down Luria's ideas in a book called *Etz Chayim*, *"The Tree of Life."*

How did God create the world? The first question you'd have to ask is this: If God fills all of space and all of time, how can there even be room for the universe? The answer that Luria gave is that God went into a process of *tzimtzum*, which means "withdrawal" or "shrinking." In other words, God made a space inside of God, withdrawing from a space big enough in which to fit the entire universe, and then placed the attribute of judgment into that empty space. Right now, we have an empty space filled with God's sense of judgment, surrounded completely by God.

God's capacity for judgment, if unlimited, could cause huge amounts of destruction, so God, according to Luria, brought a thin line of divine light into that empty space, where until that moment nothing existed but God's judgment. That divine light was also symbolically a "person" called *adam kedmon*, or original man. If you have ever seen a kabbalistic anatomy chart where each part of the body represents a different emanation from God, you know what I'm talking about. Each of the positive traits of God—wisdom, intelligence, loving kindness, patience, and so on—emanated from adam kedmon into that empty space. The combination of all those traits, called *sefirot*, or emanations of God, came together to create the universe.

Spiritual Citations

"God has put something noble and good into every heart, which His hand created."
—Mark Twain

In order to protect the emanations from intermingling, the pure light of each was wrapped in a shell, itself comprised of a thicker, more resilient form of light. The shells are referred to as *kelipot*. The attributes of God traveled through the kelipot into the formless void that was becoming the universe.

But then ... catastrophe. The kelipot shattered in a moment called *shevirat ha'kelim* (the breaking or shattering of the vessels), scattering the pure light everywhere. Some of it returned to God, and the rest of it lay as if in shards on the ground of the newly formed universe. This is when God stepped in, restoring order and actually creating the world. Humanity would serve as an assistant in the process of collecting and gathering up the divine sparks of light lost at the moment of the breaking of the vessels.

How could Jews restore those lost sparks to their divine source and thereby redeem the world? By observing God's law, by praying, and by practicing acts of loving kindness.

This is a rough description of Lurianic Kabbalah. Jews across the world eagerly embraced this philosophy in the mid-sixteenth century. Its popularity was perhaps due to the Jews suffering the pains of exile from their holy land, and the severe political and religious repression in the lands where they lived. Jews saw themselves as the divine sparks that had been shattered and left on the ground. Just as they now believed they could redeem those individual sparks of divine light, so they hoped and prayed that God would redeem the divine sparks of light that were the Jewish people.

This concept of tzimtzum may be awfully hard to embrace. If you feel that way, you are not alone. Not all kabbalists are comfortable with this approach to the creation of the world. They simply cannot understand how God could, as it were, make a hole in God's self. God is outside time and space, so how could the universe come into existence in a manner requiring the use of space and time, which God is above? This school of thought teaches that it is impossible to understand anything to do with God. Our creator is simply too far beyond human understanding to express even in metaphor. So if you're not entirely comfortable with Lurianic kabbalistic thinking, you are not alone.

According to another school of kabbalistic thought, the creation of the universe, *maasei breishit*, came about when the attributes of God united to create the universe. These kabbalistic rabbis are concerned with the question of moving from abstraction to physicality. They teach that when we look at the world, we often find ourselves caught up in an illusion. For example, when you look at a table, it looks like a solid block of wood. In fact, a table is simply a whirling mass of electrons giving the appearance of solidity and firmness. In a physics sense, there is nothing solid about a table at all—it only *appears* solid.

Devine Devarim

shevirat ha'kelim   the moment during the creation of the universe when the kelipot shattered, scattering pure light everywhere; lit. the breaking of vessels.

maasei breishit   the creation of the universe.

This kind of Kabbalah is about learning how to bridge the gap between appearance and reality in the universe. Since we cannot determine *how* God created the universe—such concepts being outside our realm of understanding—we can focus instead on the intriguing question of *why* God created the universe.

Recognizing Perfection

How do you know that a glass is completely full? You know it's completely full when a little bit of it spills over. Until you see at least a few drops of liquid spilling over, you cannot be absolutely sure. Perfection, similarly, requires a little bit of itself to spill over for it to be recognized.

When Jews hear good news, they often say the following blessing: "Blessed is God, Who is good and does good." The kabbalistic understanding of this blessing is as follows: When we say that God *is* good, we are referring to the perfection of God. When we say that God *does* good, we are saying that God, as it were, "spills over" and creates something in the universe that is at once God and at the same time separate.

According to this approach to creation, it was *necessary* for God to create human beings, who are the "spilled over" perfection. The definition of perfection requires some sort of imperfection to compare it against. So in one sense, the role of human beings is to remind each other that our imperfections stand in contrast to the perfection of God.

Spiritual Citations

The root of the Hebrew word *shalom*, or peace, conveys a notion of perfection. *Shlaymut* in Hebrew means completion. When we feel at peace with ourselves, we feel complete— nothing is missing, nothing is left undone.

Mystical Moments

The goal of creation is to be close to God, to be like Him, even if it means sacrificing physical comfort and pleasure. Physical pleasure is a wonderful by-product of living in this world, but not the goal.

—Rabbi Pinchas Winston, Yeshivat Aish HaTorah, Jerusalem

Kabbalists give the example of a perfectly decorated room: Every piece of furniture is exquisitely crafted, the walls are a beautiful, soothing color, and on the table sits an ornate vase containing a dozen roses. On the table just below the roses lies a single rose petal, all by itself.

The rose petal, in its imperfection, offers a contrast and makes us realize just how perfect everything else in the room is. So it is with God and people. You could say that we are the rose petal on that table which calls to mind the perfection of everything else in the universe.

The problem with metaphors and analogies is that they only go so far. The Kabbalah is *not* saying that people are rose petals, or that God is a room out of *House and Garden*. The Kabbalah is simply trying to find ways to express word pictures that are virtually impossible to grasp without some sort of metaphor or analogy. The leap from limited, faulty analogies to the reality of Kabbalah requires a long trudge up the mountain—with no shortcuts. This book's discussion of Kabbalah is just a small taste of the entire manner of thinking.

The Zohar

Perhaps the best known kabbalistic text is the Zohar, a term derived from the Hebrew word for "illumination." No one is exactly sure of when the Zohar was created, although there are two main theories. The first is that it was written almost 2,000 years ago by a rabbi named Shimon bar-Yochai, who escaped the Romans by living in a cave for a number of years and composed the Zohar while in hiding. The other explanation for the Zohar is that it was the creation of a Spanish Jewish biblical scholar and kabbalist named Moses de Leon (c. 1240–1305). Moses de Leon told the world that he found Rabbi

Shimon bar-Yochai's vast kabbalistic book, but we cannot be sure whether he found it or whether he composed it himself. Some scholars point to Spanish terms—and even Spanish grammatical errors—in the book, which would indicate that Moses de Leon wrote it rather than found it.

The Zohar is virtually impossible for anyone to make any sense of at all without a huge amount of training. It does not present a clear, concise picture of the creation of the world or a description of where the universe is headed. The popular imagination assumes that the Zohar says things like, "God created the world in the following way …." Unfortunately, the Zohar does not contain any such clear statements.

Instead, the Zohar is a commentary on biblical verses that is extremely symbolic in its language and very difficult for people to understand. In terms of lack of clarity, the book could be compared most closely in modern literature to James Joyce's *Finnegan's Wake*, which is virtually impenetrable without years of preparation and study.

> ### High Spirits
>
> "Believe me, the poorest life is better than the nicest death."
>
> —Yiddish proverb

The Zohar was originally written in Aramaic, which is the language Jews spoke 2,000 years ago. Whether Moses de Leon found it or wrote it, the work remains the most important kabbalistic book in the Jewish tradition. It's amazing to think of a 700-year-old work as "cutting edge," but that in fact is the case. Perhaps one day there will be a *Complete Idiot's Guide to the Zohar*, although I'm afraid that this author will never be qualified to write such a book. If someone offers you a course in "Zohar Made Easy," or "Practical, Everyday Zohar," or even, dare I say it, "*The Complete Idiot's Guide to the Zohar*," run the other way!

Mystical Moments

The Kabbalah is perhaps the only aspect of traditional Judaism to appeal to Jews who are not orthodox. The problem is that the Kabbalah that is most often offered to secular Jews has nothing to do with the real Kabbalah at all. What purports to be Kabbalah is actually a mishmash of modern, New Age thought. Much of what passes for Kabbalah could have been lifted from any of a dozen popular self-help books written in the last 20 years.

And as for the Zohar, today people are taught that it is some sort of combination of ideas that can be found in the works of Deepak Chopra, John Bradshaw, and John Grey. You can claim *any* teaching is from the Kabbalah or Zohar, but who would be educated enough in those matters to refute such a claim? Pretty much nobody, which is why popularizations of these books not at all rooted in Jewish tradition are of great interest to so many Jews.

What does the Zohar contain? Guidance about the true meaning of the first sentences of the book of Genesis, describing the creation of the world. The mystical aspects of the Hebrew alphabet. The process of *tzimtzum*, in which God created a space within Himself in which the universe could be created. The journey of the soul after death.

While there are sources that suggest that every Jewish home should be equipped with the Zohar, few observant Jews—even those who study Talmud regularly—spend time studying the Zohar, or any other Kabbalistic writings, for that matter. Judaism is so imbued with practicality that topics of an esoteric nature are of remarkably little interest to traditional practitioners. Perhaps the Zohar is in the category of "things I'll get around to one day" for many Jews. On the other hand, even Jews with a strong background in Torah and Talmud don't really seem to feel as if they're missing anything because they aren't delving into the Zohar.

This lack of time devoted to the Zohar is most likely a form of intellectual or spiritual modesty rather than a lack of interest. Most observant Jews, if queried, would respond that they are really not on a high enough level to absorb the Zohar's inner meanings. So they leave it alone not because it's beneath them, but because they sense that they aren't ready to enter its complex worlds.

It is for this reason that Torah scholars tend to scoff at "popular Zohar" or "popular Kabbalah." Their attitude is this: "If I'm not ready to study it or on a high enough spiritual level to understand it, how could a lay person pick it up and get something out of it?" To be sure, the contempt is directed solely toward those who purport to offer real Zohar or Kabbalistic learning to individuals who are essentially beginners in the study of Judaism. Most scholars tend to view those who popularize (and dumb down) the Kabbalah or the Zohar as snake oil salesmen, out to make a name for themselves, a buck, or both.

The Least You Need to Know

- Kabbalah study requires a solid foundation of Jewish knowledge in order to make sense.
- Kabbalah brings a heightened state of awareness.
- Humans can be understood in kabbalistic terms as God's perfection flowing over into the world.
- Based on the Jewish belief of perfection, it was *necessary* for God to create humans.
- The Zohar requires copious amounts of study to comprehend, and many Jewish scholars consider themselves spiritually unprepared to tackle it.

Chapter 17

The End of Time: The Messiah and the World to Come

In This Chapter

- ◆ Is there a Jewish concept of afterlife?
- ◆ Judgment in the hereafter
- ◆ The coming of the Messiah
- ◆ The Messiah's to-do list

Like most American Jews, my religious education stopped at age 13. As a result, I remained completely ignorant of an entire universe of Jewish concepts that were not taught to children in Sunday school. Many Jews today, whose early educations were as limited as mine, are equally unaware that Judaism believes in life after death, heaven, reincarnation, judgment of our lives after we die, and a savior who will transform the entire world.

The Afterlife

Traditional Judaism believes that there are two worlds: this world, or *ha'olam hazeh*, and the "world to come," or *ha'olam haba*. The first refers to the material, physical world we know so well. The next world is something about which Jewish tradition offers a great deal of guidance. Of course, much of that guidance is conflicting, because we have yet to receive word from anybody who's been there about what exactly it's like. But there are certain concepts in the Jewish understanding of the afterlife upon which all traditional authorities agree.

Devine Devarim

din v'heshbon   a judgment and accounting for our lives before God.

Mystical Moments

"There are halls in heaven that open only to the voice of song."
—the Zohar

After we die, we are obligated to give what is called *a din v'heshbon*, a judgment and accounting for our lives before God. In many ways, the Meryl Streep/Albert Brooks movie *Defending Your Life* comes close to the Jewish concept of judgment in the afterlife. It's as though we watch an entire movie of our lives with God sitting next to us in the screening room. The idea that one day we will be forced to sit through the unedited director's cut helps people want to live their lives in a moral fashion. If we knew that we would have to explain to God why we did every little wrong thing, we would be far more likely to behave, especially if there isn't any popcorn up there.

One of the questions that will come up in that judgment is whether we really enjoyed our lives. Mainstream Judaism is not a religion of self-flagellation. The rabbis teach that God created a beautiful world for us to enjoy and we will be asked why we didn't take full advantage of its beauty and pleasure. This doesn't mean that Judaism condones hedonism. The world is not supposed to be one giant Club Med. Nonetheless, there is an enormous amount of pleasure and enjoyment that we can take that does not come at the expense of causing others pain and suffering.

GOD: How come you never went to any national parks?

YOU: I dunno. There was a *Gilligan's Island* marathon on Nick at Nite.

That's a dialogue I certainly hope to avoid!

GPA in the Afterlife

Traditional Judaism teaches that God weighs all our good deeds against our bad deeds. We do get a handicap, though. Our apologies and annual Yom Kippur atonement help tip the scales more in our favor. These do not count against us. Also, according to Jewish tradition, at the last moment, an angel comes along and knocks out most or all of the bad deeds we committed so that ultimately we will be able to enjoy eternity in God's presence. Judaism does not believe in a concept of eternal damnation.

Instead, Judaism specifies something of a limbo state in which a person is forced to spend at most a year in a holding pattern prior to admission to God's presence. It's not fun: the rabbis speak of burning, searing pain, and embarrassment during that period. Kind of like being stuck in the penalty box.

What exactly happens in ha'olam haba? Of course, no one knows for certain. The rabbis give several intriguing possibilities. The basic idea is that the world to come is a world of 100 percent truth, unlike our falsehood-filled world today. The soul and body are reunited; how this happens, of course, is beyond human understanding in this life.

Other interpretations abound. The world to come may be a large banquet where everyone eats from the leviathan, the huge fish that was created just prior to the end of the sixth day of creation. Other rabbis see the world to come as a great Talmudic academy where all the unanswered questions in the Bible and Talmud are answered, either by God, by his prophet Elijah (who, tradition teaches, will lead the Messiah on his journey into the world), or by a similarly worthy teacher. The Talmud teaches us that all Jews have a share in the world to come, and so do all the righteous, whether or not they are religious. However, we're still uncertain about the seating arrangements.

> ### High Spirits
>
> "The chief problem about death, incidentally, is the fear that there may be no afterlife—a depressing thought, particularly for those who have bothered to shave. Also, there is the fear that there is an afterlife but no one will know where it's being held."
>
> —Woody Allen

> ### Mystical Moments
>
> One of the most beautiful Sabbath songs states, "The whole world is but a narrow bridge, and the main thing is not to fear anything!" A bridge to what? To the world to come!

The rabbis traditionally have believed that we are reunited with our loved ones in the world to come. How exactly this process takes place is unknown and is not described anywhere. The Jewish attitude toward death is that the soul ascends to heaven, where it is first judged and then admitted to ha'olam haba.

The existence of the world to come is a very important part of answering the question, "Why do good things happen to bad people?" If there is an afterlife, that is the place where all scores are settled. That is the place where the wicked are again punished—not with eternal damnation but with a delay, perhaps of millennia, before they are admitted to the joyous presence of God. Suffering in this life is considered a form of purification that prepares us for the joy and beauty that we will encounter in the next world.

Just how wonderful is the world to come? The Talmud teaches that one hour of bliss in the world to come is greater than all the pleasure that can be enjoyed *in this world*. It must be a very wonderful place, indeed.

It Is Written ...?

In the Torah, there are no explicit references to a "world to come," nor are there any statements referring to an individual judging of souls. The few clues of an afterlife given by the Torah are hard to understand. When the great leaders of the Bible such as Moses and Aaron pass away, they are "gathered unto their people." What exactly does that mean? It's hard to know for sure. There are certain crimes in Judaism laid down in the first five books of the Bible that are considered so severe that they rate the punishment of *karait*, which literally means "cutting off from God." Specifically, it means that the soul of that individual is cut off from his or her people. What does *that* mean? Does it mean that such a person does not enter the afterlife at all? The answer is not explicitly revealed in the five books of Moses—the term is nowhere clearly defined. (But it doesn't sound too good!) As Jewish history proceeded into the time of the prophets, more about the afterlife was described. Occasionally, important figures who had passed away would be "consulted," which gives an indication that some sort of afterlife was now believed to exist. Intriguingly, by the time you get to the Talmud, approximately 1,800 years ago, you find that most of the words used to describe the afterlife come from Greek. In the Talmud, this world is described as a *prozdor*, the Greek word for entry hall, while the "main room" is the world to come. Similarly, when the Talmud speaks of the "prosecutor" who lists a person's sins in the judgment of the soul after death, the Talmud uses the Greek word *kategor* (from which we get the word categorize, or to make a list). The "defense attorney" in heaven? That's the *sanegor* in the language of the Talmud. *Sanegor* is also a Greek word.

Most Jews in the United States—almost 85 percent—belong to branches of Judaism which do not accept the idea of any sort of afterlife. As a result, it comes as a surprise to many Jews when they discover that for 3,000 years, Judaism has always believed in the inevitability of some kind of afterlife, even though we are not entirely sure what form it takes.

Devine Devarim

prozdor the Talmudic word for this world, from the Greek for "entry hall."

kategor the "prosecutor" who lists a person's sins in the judgment of the soul after death.

sanegor the "defense attorney" during the judgment of the soul after death.

You could say that Jews have two legacies—one of faith, one of doubt. The legacy of doubt became strong over the last 200 years, when Jews first began to question some of the supernatural tenets of Judaism. Is there an afterlife? Is there a soul? Is there even a God? Such questions were rarely asked during the first 3,000 years of Jewish history. In today's fairly secular world, it is more common for Jews to have doubts about these issues than to believe firmly in the traditional spiritual teachings of Judaism.

While this legacy of doubt is a very important part of Jewish thinking today, it can sometimes overshadow the legacy of faith, the 3,000-year belief in God and an afterlife, and the importance of one's spiritual development. This is not to say that a Jew must believe in God in order to be spiritual—far from it. Rather, we need to recognize that for three millennia, prior to the development of this legacy of doubt, the notion of spirituality and the existence of God were inseparable. My purpose throughout this book has been to illustrate the ways in which Jews have traditionally believed so that you can perhaps make better-informed decisions about what you believe, and about how you will act on those beliefs.

> **Spiritual Citations**
>
> "If you should happen to be holding a sapling in your hand when they tell you that the Messiah has arrived, first plant the sapling and then go out and greet the Messiah."
>
> —Rabbi Yochanan ben Zakkai

The Messiah

One of the most intriguing and complex issues in all of traditional Judaism is the concept of the Messiah, a Jewish leader who will unify the world, bring peace to the nations, and serve as a spiritual guide to individuals everywhere. Jews have traditionally believed in the Messiah and have speculated for centuries about who he will be, when he will arrive, and what he will do.

The word Messiah is the English translation of the Hebrew word *moshiach*, which means "anointed one." In times of ancient Israel, the king was anointed with oil as a means of demonstrating that he had been chosen to rule. The *moshiach*, or Messiah, refers to the individual chosen to lead.

The basic idea behind the concept of the Messiah is that the period of human history in which we now live—one marked by free will, the presence of evil, and suffering and death—is only meant to last for a finite period of time. This world is meant by God as a laboratory or school for people to work on their character and to seek to overcome the baser parts of their nature. At some point, traditional Judaism has always believed, God is going to "blow the whistle" on human history and usher in a new era. That era will be one of peace and tranquility, but it will also be one where people do not enjoy the same level of free will. Free will brings in its train the likelihood that individuals will hurt each other, and so there is no way to have entire peace in the world while people still have the possibility of choosing wrongly and hurting each other.

The Talmud actually speculated as to whether it would have been better for man not to have been created. Ultimately, the rabbis of the Talmud decided that it would have been better had man not been brought into existence! Yet the rabbis continued, "Nevertheless, since people do exist, let them examine their deeds."

Traditional Judaism believes that there are two ways for the Messiah to appear and usher in this era of world peace. The first is through our actions. If the entire Jewish people were to observe Jewish law—if they would even just keep two consecutive Sabbaths in accordance with Jewish law—then the Messiah would appear. By this process, we would *merit* the arrival of the Messiah.

There is a second way by means of which the Messiah will appear, and this is referred to as "the end of day." According to one interpretation, human history is meant to last a total of only 6,000 years. In the Jewish calendar, we are currently midway through the fifty-eighth century, which means that there are only approximately 250 years left of human history. If the Jewish people do not merit the Messiah through the quality of their actions, then the Messiah will simply arrive anyway in the year 6,000 of the Jewish calendar.

According to mystical Jewish teachings, the world will actually "close down for repairs" for 1,000 years, during which time the world will recover from the damage that human beings have caused it. The first 6,000 years, therefore, would be the equivalent of the first six days of creation, and the next 1,000 the equivalent of the first Sabbath day. What exactly this doctrine means, and what would happen for that millennium is very hard to say. Only a truly advanced kabbalist could answer this question. At the end of the 1,000 years, human history would begin again, but on a vastly different basis from the way we know it now. That's a Jewish mystical tradition.

> **High Spirits**
>
> "Life is divided up into the horrible and the miserable."
>
> —Woody Allen

> **Mystical Moments**
>
> The Biblical prophet Ezekiel describes a heavenly chariot that is the source of much advanced kabbalistic speculation and meditation. It may be said that no one alive today completely understands the meaning of Ezekiel's chariot!

The idea of the Messiah waxes and wanes in importance, depending on the position of the Jews in the world. When the Jews are wealthy, secure, and accepted in their community, the concept of the Messiah usually does not get all that much attention. This current period in Jewish history is somewhat unusual in that regard, and that's due to the influence of the Lubavitch Hasidim who strongly emphasize the concept of the desire for the arrival of the Messiah. Generally, however, the worse it is for the Jews, the more they turn their hopes and prayers to a savior who will rescue them from Crusades, pogroms, or the history of European anti-Semitism. In seventeenth-century Europe, when the Jews were constantly in fear for their lives due to the marauding of their non-Jewish neighbors, there appeared several individuals, most notably Shabbetai Tzvi and Jacob Frank, who claimed to be the Messiah. They each eventually turned out to be ordinary men, but not before they had seduced thousands—or even tens of thousands—of Jews into believing that they were the real McCoy. These false Messiahs caused the death of hundreds or even thousands of Jews and had a psychologically devastating effect on those who had their hopes of salvation so brutally dashed.

The Real Messiah

Who will be the real Messiah? We cannot say for certain, but there are a number of clues that the Jewish tradition offers. First, the individual will be a person of extremely high moral character. The individual will be a great political leader as well as a powerful spiritual guide. There is a tradition that states that the Messiah will be born on Tisha B'av, the date in the Hebrew calendar on which Jews fast in memory of the destruction of both the first and second Temples, which were both destroyed on that same date. Another tradition states that at any time in Jewish history, there is always one individual in the world capable of serving as the Messiah; that person's identity is only revealed when conditions are right. Either the world merits the arrival of the Messiah because of the high moral character of the behavior of individuals, or the world desperately needs the Messiah because things have sunk to an all-time inhuman low. Traditional Judaism believes that since the Messiah has not yet arrived, we are somewhere in that middle ground between entirely righteous and entirely evil.

The Messiah has a number of important tasks to perform. One is to bring peace to the world. As if that were not enough, the Messiah is also expected to rebuild the third Temple on the site of the first two. A complicating factor is that there are two great Islamic mosques built on what was the site of the Temple Mount. How the Messiah will handle that question is beyond the scope of this book.

Spiritual Citations

"When the time comes I will go joyfully. Whatever may be there, it will be real, without complication, without ridicule, without deception."

—Isaac Bashevis Singer

The Messiah has yet another important task: the resurrection of the dead. Traditional Judaism has believed for more than 2,500 years that the dead will be reborn when the Messiah comes. The prophet Ezekiel speaks of "dry bones" that will once again become enclosed in flesh. This is said to be an indication that one of the tasks of the Messiah will be to resurrect all the Jewish dead and bring them to live in the land of Israel. Again, how the Messiah will accomplish this feat is completely unknown.

There are differences of opinion in Jewish scholarship as to how the logistical problems will be handled. How will the dead get to the land of Israel, where it is expected that they would be resurrected? Would their souls travel through the air, or would their bodies make their way to Israel via underground passages? What would people do in the time of the resurrection? Would they still have to work? Would physicality be the same? What about the possibility of sin and death—did these notions pertain in the time of the resurrection?

All hard questions for which there are no easy answers. The tenth-century Jewish philosopher, the Rabbi Saadia Gaon, wrote of his conception of life on Earth after the arrival of the Messiah: Faith in God would be universal. The crippled would be healed. People would live for a long time, although not forever. And everyone would have enough living space. Saadia Gaon even predicted the year in which the Messiah would arrive: the year 964. While he had the year wrong, how much of the rest of Saadia's picture of post-Messianic life on Earth is accurate? How on Earth can we know for sure?

According to the Jewish way of thinking, if someone claims he is the Messiah, or others claim that a particular person is the Messiah, there is a very clear test to apply. If the person accomplishes all these things, he (or she?) is in fact the Messiah. If the person does not accomplish all of these things, that person is not the Messiah. This is why traditional Judaism does not accept the idea of Jesus as the Jewish Messiah—the tasks of the Jewish Messiah remain undone, almost 2,000 years after Jesus' death.

The Supreme Irony

The rabbis tell the story of a man who lived in the eighteenth-century Russian-Jewish community of Mozhibosh. One night, the man had a vision from God. In the vision, God told him to go and find the *menorah*—the candelabra—that had been used in the great Temple in Jerusalem more then 1,800 years earlier. At great expense, and with great difficulty, the man traveled all the way to Jerusalem, where he sought the great artifact. The individuals he encountered in Jerusalem all had the same answer for him. "The menorah? It's in Mozhibosh."

The moral of that story is that we think we have to travel great distances, either physically or spiritually, in order to find what we already possessed right where we are. Countless Jews leave Judaism in search of spirituality because their Sunday school education never gave them the slightest clue that spirituality could be found in their own religion. The often surprising fact is that Judaism *does* believe in the afterlife, reincarnation, and the coming of the Messiah—all concepts that most Jews today usually associate with faiths other than their own. Judaism is a surprisingly rich wellspring of spiritual and mystical concepts, the depth and complexity of which are enough to keep any individual studying and growing spiritually for a lifetime.

As the rabbis say, "May you go from strength to strength!"

The Least You Need to Know

- The afterlife is open to all righteous souls, no matter what their faith.
- There is no eternal damnation in Jewish thought, only a temporary limbolike state.
- When the Messiah will come is in question.
- How the Messiah will accomplish the to-do list is also open for debate.

Chapter 18

Guarding Your Tongue: The Spiritual Significance of Speech

In This Chapter

◆ Understanding selective perception

◆ The full range of lashon hara

◆ Exceptions to the rule

◆ Parables of righteous thought

In this chapter, we'll go deeper into the concept of lashon hara, or inappropriate speech. On a spiritual level, speaking gossip, even if the information contained therein is true, is considered one of the most soul-destroying acts in which a person can engage. This is just as true for the speaker as for the listener.

In 1873, the Chafetz Chaim published a book, *Guarding Your Tongue*, about lashon hara, because he saw that rules prohibiting it were so infrequently respected, not just by the man in the street but by supposedly learned people—they were just as guilty of lashon hara as everybody else. So the Chafetz Chaim pulled together all of the positive and negative commandments in the Torah about lashon hara and found that there were 31 specific commandments about the importance of avoiding gossip, tale-bearing, sarcasm, and unnecessary criticism. The basic idea behind these rules is that God wants people to live in peace with their fellows; if we are constantly backstabbing and verbally abusing one another, peace is hard to obtain.

Selective Perception

Come back in time with me several thousand years. It's a beautiful day, and you're sitting outside your well-equipped cave. Your kids are off hunting and gathering with the tribe. The cave is clean and you're sitting on a nice flat rock admiring the beautiful day. Suddenly, off in the distance, you see a cloud of dust, a mastodon. What do you pay attention to? On a survival level, it's not time to notice the beauty of the sky or the cleanliness of your cave. It's time to deal with this oncoming threat. This is known as the phenomenon of selective perception—the ability to focus only on what we consider most important. Selective perception is a survival skill because it allows us to concentrate on the vital and ignore the less significant.

As it is with mastodons two million years ago, so it is with people today: We focus on only those things we consider most important to us. The way we think about other people—the aspects we choose to notice and those we ignore—say a lot about us.

According to the rabbis, this is where the problem of lashon hara begins. We have ideas—subconscious beliefs, opinions, and prejudices—about different kinds and classes of people. Wherever we go, we meet members of groups about which, over time, we have developed opinions. Frequently, these opinions tend toward the negative. Our beliefs may be based in fear, experience (or inexperience), or the background in which we grew up. It's rare for us to meet a person for the first time and have absolutely nothing coloring our expectations or beliefs about that person.

I've never met two people who were the same, whether they were from the same so-called group or not. People are individual. It's said that the difference between God

Mystical Moments

In one Biblical story, Moses' sister Miriam is struck with a case of leprosy for having discussed her brother's marriage. She was concerned that her brother wasn't paying enough attention to his wife, and she made her concerns public. When Moses calls out to God to heal her, Miriam recovers. The Talmud points to this incident as an example of the terrible consequences of lashon hara.

Spiritual Citations

"You dig your grave with your teeth."

—Yiddish proverb

and a mortal king is that when a mortal king makes impressions of himself on a coin, every single one of those coins is identical. God's coins, if you will, are people. Our Creator's image is stamped on each of us, and yet no two of us look alike, sound alike, or think alike.

Devine Devarim

sinat hinam   senseless hatred.

The first phase of lashon hara doesn't even have anything to do with actual speech. It's simply the development of negative attitudes about people over a period of time.

The Jews lost two Temples in Jerusalem, the second to the Romans. Why did they destroy our Temple? Because of one basic sin: *sinat hinam*, senseless hatred. Now, almost 2,000 years later, we still don't have a temple. We have a wall. We're very happy with that wall. But we don't have a Temple in Jerusalem. The problem remains sinat hinam.

After we develop our prejudices, we venture out into the world and witness events that serve to reinforce our negative beliefs. We reinforce our stereotypes through observations that are anything but scientific and methodical.

We then dwell on our experience. We think about it because there's a deep human need to be right. We feel justified in the beliefs that led to us gathering the evidence about our prejudices. Then, as we're pondering these thoughts, somebody comes along and says, "What's new?" You tell them. That's when lashon hara—the inappropriate speech—finally makes its entrance.

How do you weed out inappropriate speech? It's not by just deciding never to talk about others ever again. That's insane. Taking a step backward doesn't do any good, either. Eliminating negative thoughts doesn't work. Since we can't avoid interacting with other people, we'll have to go all the way back to step one: We have to examine the senseless hatred that we have for others. We must question where our feelings come from and why we continue to carry them with us.

Mystical Moments

Pirke Avot, or "Chapters of the Fathers," is a tractate of the Talmud dedicated to teaching judges how to adjudicate. However, the chapter is also intended for the common man in that it teaches us how to behave with other people because, in effect, we're all judges—we're always judging other.

The Gamut of Lashon Hara

There are actually five different kinds of lashon hara. The first is a truth that does not need to be told. For example, suppose you tell a friend that you know a co-worker who cheats on his taxes. You're not lying, but your gossiping doesn't help you or your co-worker. You're spreading information from which no good can come.

Now, suppose you tell the same story, but it's not true. That's a completely different ball-game. *Motzi shem hara* means, in a nutshell, to give someone a bad name. "Slander" is the best way to translate it.

There's a third category: *rechillut*, which literally means "gossiping." It's like somebody who goes around peddling his wares: instead of selling stuff, he's selling ideas or words with negative concepts about other people. I'll give you an example, something that actually happened to me while I was writing this book. I went to a business lunch and saw a guy who had been away for a month in Italy. I asked him how his trip was.

Devine Devarim

rechillut gossiping; headline.

motzi shem hara slander; to give someone a bad name.

"Oh, great," he responded, then quickly changed the subject. "Hey, I heard about that altercation you got into with that other guy."

I thought to myself, "What altercation?" I looked around at the other people at our table and wondered what sort of thoughts were running through their heads. They were all eerily quiet and I could tell that each of them had visions worthy of the *National Enquirer* running through their minds. I asked him, "What are you talking about?"

He said, "You know what I mean." We had become the focus of the entire table.

I said, "Who did I get into a fight with? What are you talking about?"

When he noticed that everybody was paying attention, he shrugged and said, "I'll tell you later." When I pressed him a little further, he finally bit. "If you ask me again I'm going to punch you in the nose."

So I said what I always say in moments like that: "How about those Dodgers?" I figured that if I was being accused of getting into altercations and I don't want people to believe that, then getting into an altercation in front of several eye witnesses over some other guy's rechillut probably wouldn't help my cause.

High Spirits

The best thing for a rabbi to talk about in a Sabbath sermon is lashon hara! That's because even if people think he gave a bad talk, they'll be too embarrassed to criticize him!

Category four is called *avak lashon hara*. Since "avak" is Hebrew for dust, the phrase refers to traces or particles of lashon hara. An example of this would be to imply something negative with an answer.

The rabbis give the following example: Reuben asks Shimon, "Do you think I can get some food over at Levi's house?" To which Shimon replies, "Oh, there's always something cooking at Levi's house."

There's several possible ways to take that. One is that Levi loves to cook. Another is that Levi's a bit of a glutton and just can't control himself. Still another is that there's always some rumor-worthy event happening at Levi's, so why not head on over and be the first to check it out? We just shouldn't imply negative traits about other people.

The fifth and final category is called *onas devarim*, from the Hebrew words for "pain" and, well, "words." As stated before, the word davar can mean either "word" or "thing." You know that old saying about sticks and stones? We don't believe that "Words will never hurt me." Words can cause *a lot* of pain! They can destroy friendships, relationships, and marriages. This is one of the beliefs behind the tradition of breaking a glass at a wedding. Some believe that the act is to remind the couple that saying something cruel is like shattering a glass: it's tough to find all those little pieces and put it back together. Even if you do, it's never as beautiful or as strong as it originally was. That's the power of words in a relationship.

Exceptions to the Rule

Lashon hara differs from the other commandments in Judaism in that Jews are very concerned about how to observe it. With lashon hara, people want to know how to *get away* with it. In most cases, that's the equivalent of asking for a kosher recipe for pork.

However, with lashon hara, there are exceptions to the rule. One involves an engaged couple. Under certain circumstances you have a responsibility to repeat negative information to somebody who can stop the wedding—if you believe the information is bad enough to warrant such action. The other case is in business. If someone is about to make a fatal business decision with an untrustworthy character, it's your duty to warn them.

The problem is this: How often have you ever been privy to such information? It almost never happens. Sure, we often know of some minor, inconsequential details about another person's behavior, but they are usually not detrimental enough to warrant telling anyone else. Usually they are only minor faults, which all of us have.

> **Spiritual Citations**
>
> "All my life I grew up around the sages, and I found that there was nothing more valuable than silence."
>
> —The Talmud, Pirke Avot (Perhaps the rabbis felt this way because of the tendency of our tongue to cause so much trouble!)

When people learn of these exceptions for lashon hara, they often extrapolate a whole lot of others. For example, some people have their own connotation of the phrase "Don't go around being a tale bearer among your people." They understand the words *amisechah* (your people) as meaning they only have to worry about other Jews—everyone else is fair game. However, that's simply a case of interpreting scripture for one's own purpose. The fact that there are other exceptions doesn't mean that we can make exceptions for ourselves.

On closer inspection of this verse, we can find some other interesting information. The verse reads: *Lo telech racheel amitecha,* "Don't go around being a tale bearer among your people." The "don't go around" part correlates to that concept of how we carry about negative conceptions about other people. So God isn't just saying not to speak negatively. The Creator is also saying not to be the kind of person who even *notices* the negative. Rashi says that the word *racheel* from the verse is very much like *rageel,* which can be translated as "busybody." Racheel is very close to rechillut, gossip. In effect, Rashi is saying that just as a peddler goes around peddling his wares, a gossip is somebody who looks for the negative then spreads that information around.

The problem is both the speech itself but the attitude and compulsion behind it. In a lot of ways, it's like uncontrollable eating. When my wife got pregnant, both of us began to put on weight. Yet after the baby arrived, I had only lost 15 of the 30 pounds I gained during her pregnancy. Soon I noticed that when I went to feed the baby at 11 o'clock at night, I would end up bingeing, whether or not I was actually hungry. Once I became conscious of how and what I was eating, what went into my mouth was very different. The cure for lashon hara is to become conscious of what is coming *out* of your mouth and why.

How can we eradicate our negative feelings? If we don't bear grudges, if we don't hate other people in our hearts, if we look at people as individuals and not as members of "groups" we've cooked up in our minds, then chances are we won't look for the worst in them. We won't apply our marvelous ability of selective perception as a means toward character assassination.

Devine Devarim

Ba'al lashon hara a repeat offender of lashon hara.

If you do happen to succumb to lashon hara, you must ask yourself where those words came from and what belief that is rooted in. It's just like my nighttime binges where I learned to ask myself, "Why did I eat that? What was I thinking? Where did that come from?" In fact, with lashon hara, it's not what you're eating, it's what's eating you.

If somebody starts to talk lashon hara, we're obligated to get out of there. If you feel you need an excuse, you can simply say that something came up. What came up? The lashon hara came up. Lashon hara hurts three people: the speaker, the listener, and the subject. In fact, if there's somebody who is a ba'al lashon hara (a continuous lashon hara speaker), we're supposed to *move* away from the neighborhood. Although that might be difficult in the modern world, the fact that the Talmud says this illustrates the importance of avoiding lashon hara.

The Talmud also states that at the judgment after your death, you must spend 70 years outside of being close to God for every word of lashon hara you speak. Not only that, but all the mitzvahs you've done get transferred over to the person you spoke negatively about. That's the strength of lashon hara—it can negate even your most honorable deeds and make them worthless.

Spiritual Citations

"In a place where there are no men, strive to be a man."

—The Talmud, Pirke Avot

The Torah requires that we judge each other favorably—that we give each other the benefit of the doubt. There are, however, exceptions. If a person is known as a habitual offender of some sort, there's no obligation to take a Pollyannaish point of view and assume that he or she has suddenly "straightened out." But if a person has a reputation for being good, we are obligated to ignore negative information we might hear about him or her. Even when we see something that almost certainly indicates culpability, if the person in question is a righteous individual, we have to find ways to make that evidence support the idea that he or she really did something right instead of something wrong. The following are some parables that illustrate this concept.

I'm Outta Here! So Pay Me!

The night before Yom Kippur, a worker tells his wealthy boss that he wants to return to live with his family. "I've worked for you for three years," says the man. "May I have my wages?"

His wealthy boss tells him, "I'm sorry, I have no money."

The man looks around and says, "Well, in that case, you've got a lot of land, I'll take some of that. Or perhaps you'd like to pay me in animals, fruit, or linens?"

The boss just shakes his head. "I'm sorry, I don't have any of those things."

Downtrodden, the worker acquiesces and heads back north to be with his family. Three weeks later, just as the holidays are ending, the wealthy landowner rides up on a camel, leading another camel laden with gifts. He presents both the

High Spirits

When Jews say I'm Jewish in my heart, it's called Cardiac Judaism.

Devine Devarim

maaser in ancient Israel, the act of taking the first fruits of harvest to the Temple as an offering.

hekdesh the act of leaving all property to the temple instead of heirs.

mikva a purifying bath.

camel and the gifts to his old employee. The wealthy landowner then says, "I want to ask you a question. When I said to you I didn't have any money, what did you think?"

"I thought, well, you must have had it invested somewhere."

"That's exactly right. I did. This investment opportunity came along and I couldn't turn it down. What about when I said I didn't have any land, fruit, or linens?"

The man replies, "I figured you'd already rented the land and the animals. I also assumed that you hadn't yet taken maaser on the fruit. As for the linens, I guessed that you must have made all your property hekdesh."

The boss was pleased. "That's exactly right. I didn't have actual legal possession of any of this stuff. And I want you to know that just as you have judged me favorably, so may God judge you favorably as you go through your life."

When in Rome ...

One day in ancient Rome, the rabbis needed to talk to a particular Roman leader. All of the Roman leaders were known to spend time at a certain Roman matron's home, which acted as the salon for all the city's most important people. None of the rabbis wanted to go in there, but one of them bravely said, "I'll go." He walked right inside with all the other rabbis watching. Before the door closed behind him, they spied the woman inside. A while later he came out and headed straight to the mikva.

The rabbi asked them, "When you saw me go straight to the mikva, what did you think?"

They all replied in same. "We figured that something impure —perhaps some food—got on your cloak, so you had to go to the mikva to repurify yourself."

"That's exactly what happened! And just as you have judged me favorably, may God judge you favorably as well!"

Upon Further Review ...

I know what you're thinking. There's no way you would believe your employer if you were told you just couldn't be paid. You wouldn't walk away so easily. Nor would you believe two men locked behind closed doors with tempting women—especially with their suspicious trips to the mikva.

Spiritual Citations

"One who deceives his fellow man deceives his Maker."
—The Talmud, Kallah 10

Although these stories happened over 2,000 years ago, they're retold not because they make sense but because they're incredible. They're worthy of our time because they're really hard to believe.

The world is full of outrageous examples of people judging negatively and acting on prejudice instead of knowledge. That's the fundamental root of sinat hinam. Instead, the Talmud presents these three stories to show us that there's often an explanation. That's the spiritual lesson Judaism comes to teach about living with other people in our crowded world.

The Least You Need to Know

- Lashon hara prevents the world from ever attaining peace.
- There are exceptions to the rules of lashon hara, but that doesn't mean we can make up our own additional exceptions.
- Lashon hara can actually negate the good deeds one has done.
- Try to give everyone the benefit of the doubt—unless it stretches credulity. You don't have to lie to yourself in those situations.

Shechinah: The Presence of God

In This Chapter

- ◆ Grasping the roots of faith
- ◆ The origin of the Tabernacle
- ◆ Defining shechinah
- ◆ Onward to Jerusalem

The key to spirituality is that it cannot be proven. Faith means accepting the existence of something without being able to see it, touch it, or hear it. Even people who do not believe in God are not nonbelievers. Those of us who are not uncertain about the existence of God still believe in other forces that we cannot see. For example, just about everybody believes in the law of averages. We believe that there is some sort of balance to life, and that things tend to even out over time. Some of the phrases we use are quite telling: "Your time will come," or "It had to happen," or "You can't win 'em all."

Who said that? Why can't you win them all? Why is it that we believe in the power of statistics? Even those of us who do not believe in God still believe that there is some sort of order working in the world. Sometimes we call it karma. Sometimes we call it "just desserts." If that's the case, then who's the baker? Where is the logbook that keeps track of every cruller, croissant, and Krispy Kreme donut?

Use the Force

There are other forces in which we all believe. I don't know much about the law of gravity, but I know that we cannot pass a referendum to overturn it. I don't "see" gravity working, but I can't deny it's there.

Similarly, we have never seen the actual source of the forces of nature, but we certainly understand that nature has incredible power at its disposal. Where do winds begin? Canada? If you unplug a lamp, why doesn't electricity leak out of the socket?

Emotions could be placed in the same category as natural phenomena. Like the law of gravity, love can neither be seen nor touched, yet we know when it is present and when it is absent. Like electricity, we cannot touch fear, or hold it in our hands, but we have no difficulty sensing its presence. In short, from the workings of our own human heart to the workings of the universe, we acknowledge that there are two possibilities: Either whatever created the universe is still operating it, or it was created in such a way as to keep trundling on forever, without wisdom or guidance. In short, we need the world a lot more than the world needs us.

Religious or spiritual faith grows out of a sense that some sort of Being or universal mind created the universe—both the part that is visible and the parts that are unseen. An absence of faith assumes that our existence happened by chance, and that the universe continues on to some sort of meaningless conclusion. This is not a very comforting way to look at the world. Only in the last century or so have a large number of people lived without consideration of matters of faith. In previous millennia—whether one was Pagan, Jewish, Christian, Muslim, Zoroastrian, or Mayan—the question was never far from the forefront of people's minds: Who's in charge here? Is someone listening? Does anyone care about me?

> ### Spiritual Citations
>
> "For the truly faithful, no miracle is necessary. For those who doubt, no miracle is sufficient."
> —Nancy Gibbs

> ### High Spirits
>
> Q. Did you hear about the dyslexic, atheist insomniac?
> A. He stayed awake at night pondering the existence of Dog.

Some faiths saw power residing in the wind, the rivers, the mountains, and the animals, and reached the conclusion that each of these types of creatures was, in effect, all-powerful within its domain. The sun ruled the sky, the moon ruled the night, the river god ruled the farm community, and so on. The idea that nothing was in charge was virtually unthinkable through-out human history, until the last few generations.

The primary Jewish gift to the world is the con-cept of monotheism, the idea that one God—not many, and not none—created everything, and is responsible for the continuing miracle that is human life and the ongoing nature of the universe. But how do you take that concept of one God and make it into something that individual people can grasp?

The problem is that the idea is simply too big for a finite, limited human mind. We just cannot wrap our thoughts around the concept of God. No matter how many books we read, no matter how much we study, no matter how many hours we meditate, we can never truly, completely understand the nature of the Creator. So we have to find ways to make God understandable, logical, and somehow credible to a world not always interested in thinking about the divine. The initial Jews wrestled with this question of where can God be found and how can we can understand what God is all about.

Judaism has many different names for God. Some believe that you can identify the source of a given line of the Bible depending on which name of God is employed. Others say that the different names of God do not reflect different source material; rather, they reflect different understandings of different aspects of God. In Jewish thought, God is a gender-less Being. God is neither a man nor a woman, and does not have physical attributes, sex-ual organs, or even emotions. The problem is that Hebrew, like many languages, gives gender to all nouns, even to the name of God. Does this make God a man? No. The whole point of Judaism is that God is not and could never be a man. The Jewish concept of God is not one of a corporeal divinity.

Enter the Shechinah

How do you describe the indescribable? This is no easy task, and yet there has to be some way to put forth a concept of the presence of God that would make sense to everyday people. To describe something is to limit it. The traditional Jewish concept of God is of a limitless Being; to put any sort of descriptive words or phrases on such a Being would automatically leave us with an inaccurate picture. So the Jewish tradition does not try to describe God any more precisely than the definitions given earlier in this book. Instead, traditional Judaism concentrates on trying to understand what it means to have God "dwelling" or "present" in the world.

The key term used in Judaism for this concept is the *shechinah*, which literally translates as "the dwelling place of God." The word comes from the same root as the Hebrew word *shikkun* (neighborhood or location) and also the Hebrew verb *l'shakain* (to establish, place, or locate). Since God is unknowable and not understandable for the minds of mortals, Judaism focuses on this concept of what it means to have God dwelling in our midst.

Devine Devarim

shechinah the concept of trying to understand what it means to have God "dwelling" and "present" in the world; lit. the dwelling place of God."

Spiritual Citations

"I believe Moses was 80 when God first commissioned him for public service."

—Ronald Reagan, on running for the American presidency at age 73

What happens when the presence is not felt? It's said that when people do not believe that a Higher Power is watching, they feel that they can get away with anything. If there is no God, then there is no punishment or retribution for actions we are not caught doing. People feel a greater sense of freedom and licentiousness when they do not sense the presence of God in their midst.

Similarly, when people do not have faith that a Creator or Divine Being is "watching over them," they tend to feel much more fearful. What is the meaning of life? If everything is random, why does anything matter? These questions are infinitely easier to answer if one has faith in the existence of a Creator who is still engaged with the world. In the absence of any sort of absolute bearings, it's much harder to create a philosophy of life that helps people handle fear. Where there is no concept of God, chances are there is a much higher degree of fear.

An example of this can be found, as we saw earlier, in the Book of Exodus, after Moses has gone up the mountain. The Jewish people, only so recently led out of slavery, expect their leader to return on the fortieth day after his departure, whereas Moses knew that he would not be coming down until the following day. There was a misunderstanding as to when to begin counting. When Moses failed to show on the day they expected his return, they grew terrified.

So fearful were the Jews that God had deserted them that they melted down their gold jewelry and created the golden calf. The golden calf was not just a sculpture or a way to pass the time until Moses got back. This became, in the minds of thousands of Jews, the *real* god. To them, the "God" that had theoretically led them out of Egypt had either disappeared or was simply not to be trusted.

The *chet*, or sin, of the golden calf makes sense when you view it against the context of a people who fear that they have no god. There is something in human nature that wants us to worship and admire. It is said that the desire to admire is instinctual in us. The sociobiologist Edward O. Wilson writes in his autobiography, *Naturalist,* that the posture a member of a wolf pack takes toward the alpha wolf is remarkably similar to the physical posture of human beings at prayer. It may be instinctual throughout the animal kingdom to recognize a leader and acknowledge one's fealty toward it. What separates humans from animals, of course, is their ability to acknowledge, worship, and pray to an invisible Deity or leader. When Moses failed to appear on what was assumed to be the appointed day, that instinctual need to worship resulted in the creation of the golden calf.

One of the outcomes of the golden calf episode is that those who were involved forfeited their lives. It became clear that there needed to be some sort of mechanism to keep such an event from happening again. According to one important strand of the Jewish tradition, the result was the command from God to build a prefabricated, portable Tabernacle—the world's first synagogue, if you will—that the Jews would carry with them as they traveled through the desert. The last third or so of the Book of Exodus is given over in extremely precise detail to the description of the Tabernacle— its size, the wood from which it was constructed, the fine materials from which the curtains and wall hangings were made, and in the center, the container in which the two tablets containing the Ten Commandments would rest.

> **Mystical Moments**
>
> Only a small percentage of the Jewish people actually participated in the making of the golden calf, and they paid for that sin with their lives. The majority of the Jews, the Bible relates, had nothing to do with that episode.

The Tabernacle would travel in the middle of the Jewish people as they moved through the desert, and would serve as a physical reminder of the presence of God in the world. The Book of Exodus relates that a cloud traveled ahead of the entire encampment during the day, and a pillar of fire led them at night. The cloud and the fire served to remind the Jewish people of the existence of God in the world.

The Bible relates that the presence of God, the shechinah, rested upon the Tabernacle and could be sensed by the entire Jewish population (Exodus 40: 23–38). According to this school of Jewish thought, the Tabernacle was created as a concession to the Jewish people; because they couldn't experience God without some sort of physical reminder of his presence, they would have this portable synagogue to accompany them wherever they went. (Another approach to the Tabernacle, also considered quite acceptable in Jewish thought, is that there was no connection between the Tabernacle and the sin of the golden calf— there would have been a Tabernacle had there been no golden calf.)

The Hebrew name for the Tabernacle is mishkan. Hebrew words are formed by combining three root letters, generally all consonants, with prefixes, suffixes, and vowels. We saw above the words shechinah, shekun, and mishkan. If you'll notice, each of those three words contains three Hebrew letters: sh, ch, and n (k is interchangeable with ch).

Combine those three letters in that order with vowels, prefixes, and suffixes, and you get the three words above. Now take a look at "mishkan." Once again, we see the sh, ch (or k), and n. The word mishkan is closely related to the word shechinah; it too means "the dwelling-place." In other words, the mishkan was the home to the shechinah. What exactly are we saying here? Are we suggesting that the presence of God only existed in that one building, and nowhere else on the planet? Absolutely not. What we are saying is that the building called the mishkan symbolized the shechinah—the presence of God in the world. It gave a physical form to the intangible idea of God.

> **High Spirits**
>
> **Edifice complex** the psychological drive to have the biggest synagogue in town.

If this is hard to understand, think about the American flag. When you see a piece of cloth with 13 red and white stripes, a blue field and 50 white stars, you immediately think of the idea of the United States of America. The United States, of course, is a nation that rests on a piece of land almost 3,000 miles across (not counting Alaska and Hawaii). It has a population of almost 300 million people, and was founded as a breakaway nation from England in the late eighteenth century. Are all of these facts written somewhere in small print on the face of the flag? Of course not. Yet the flag is a symbol of all of those aspects of America—the land, the people, the history, and so much more.

Did the mishkan represent the only place where God could be said to dwell? Of course not. If anything, it served as a reminder that just as God dwells in the mishkan, so God dwells everywhere in the world. Sometimes we need a physical reminder of an intangible idea, and that is the purpose that the mishkan served.

Settle Down Already!

When the Jews arrived and conquered the land of Israel, they were instructed by the book of Deuteronomy, the fifth book of the Bible, to build a great temple which would become the focal point of national Jewish worship. Could individuals continue to pray on their own, in their own words? The historical response is yes. In the later books of the Bible, we frequently see individuals praying in their own words. But there would be one central, communal, religious site for the entire Jewish people, and that would be in Jerusalem. How did the Jews know that Jerusalem was the spot?

> **Mystical Moments**
>
> One of the many miracles associated with the great Temple in Jerusalem is that its walls mystically expanded to make room for all of the Jews who came to worship there.

The first five books of the Bible—the Torah—never explicitly mention Jerusalem. However, in Deuteronomy, we repeatedly find the phrase, "hamakom l'shakain sh'mo shan." This phrase means "the place where God will cause the name of God to dwell." If you're becoming a Biblical sleuth, you might notice the key word in that Hebrew phrase: l'shakain, which we already know translates as "to cause to dwell." In other words, this is a place where God will next cause shechinah to be experienced. The temple was built, and according to the first Book of Chronicles, chapter seven, the shechinah did in fact take up residence, as it were, in the great Temple in Jerusalem.

Unfortunately, the first Temple only survived 410 years. In 586 B.C.E., Nebuchadnezzar led the Babylonians against the land of Israel, conquered it, destroyed the first Temple, and sent the leadership of the Jewish nation into exile in Babylon. Just 70 years later, King Cyrus of the Persians took Israel for his empire and permitted Jews to return to Jerusalem and rebuild the Temple.

Not all Jews returned, however; for whatever reason, many Jews remained in Babylon. Since Jerusalem had been spurned, as it were, by an accordant percentage of the Jewish people, the level of spirituality was said to have decreased from the times of the first Temple. The shechinah was said not to rest in that second Temple, although it was still the most holy spot in Judaism. But because the Jews had chosen to remain in exile from their land and their God, so the shechinah was exiled or absent from the new Temple.

It is said that the second Temple was destroyed because of the ongoing Jewish practice of senseless hatred, which was discussed in detail in Chapter 18, "Guarding Your Tongue: The Spiritual Significance of Speech." According to Jewish tradition, wherever people are engaging in strife with one another, and are doing so out of a sense of baseless or senseless hatred, that is a place in which the shechinah cannot penetrate. In other words, we have a choice: We can either engage in senseless hatred, or we can enjoy the sense of the presence of God near us, but we cannot do both. The absence of the shechinah from the second Temple represented the lack of spirituality that exists whenever people live in a state of *machloket* (argument) and baseless hatred.

Devine Devarim

machloket   argument

The Shechinah Today

Where can the shechinah be found in today's world? There are two answers to this question. The first place in which the shechinah can be experienced is inside the human heart. The shechinah is often described as Divine Light, light that goes directly from God into the heart of human beings. When we allow Divine Light into our hearts, we are making a place for the shechinah in our world. When we keep our heart closed from spiritual light, the shechinah has no foothold.

The human heart is sometimes referred to as a mikdash ma'at, a miniature sanctuary, one that each of us is obligated to build and tend. As in the time of the second Temple, we have a choice at any given moment of whether we are going to live with resentment and hatred or whether we are going to live with spirituality. We can have the presence of rage or the presence of God in our hearts at any one time, but these two elements cannot co-exist side by side.

The second place where the shechinah is said to dwell in today's world is inside temples and synagogues. The essence of a Jewish house of worship or community center is that everyone contributes to its creation and upkeep. It is a shared enterprise of the local Jewish community. There may be some individuals who are able to write large checks, but chances are that the entire Jewish community plays some role in supporting the ongoing activities of that Jewish institution. When an institution is created with the money—and even the tears—of the entire community, it is said that the shechinah dwells there as well.

> **Spiritual Citations**
>
> "The sins of the angry men will surely outweigh his merits."
> —Rabbi Nachman of Bratslav

Is the Shechinah Feminine?

One of the most intriguing questions about the shechinah is whether it represents a "female" aspect of God. The question arises because the Hebrew word shechinah is a feminine noun. Is God a woman? Is there a belief in traditional Judaism that God has a feminine aspect?

> **Mystical Moments**
>
> Rabbi Y. Haber tells the story of an American businessman who traveled to Europe in the early twentieth century and saw the yeshiva of the Chafetz Chaim. The American visitor was quite shocked to see the simplicity of the school. Immediately, the American offered to write a check to pay for the refurbishing of the entire building. The Chafetz Chaim gratefully acknowledged the generosity of the would-be benefactor, but refused to accept the check. Explained the Chafetz Chaim, "The money—and the tears—of the entire community built this building, and that's why the shechinah dwells here." If he had accepted the check from the American millionaire, that sense of the entire community as the creator of the school would have been lost.
>
> (This is not to say that millionaires are unwelcome during synagogue and temple fund drives.)

In the last few decades, there has been a movement on the part of Jewish feminists to see the term shechinah as indicative of a feminine aspect of God. The shechinah seems like a kinder, gentler form of the Jewish God, who is often described in the Jewish Bible in warlike or violent terms. The God of the Jewish Bible certainly pulls no punches—witness the exile of Adam and Eve, the Flood, the enslavement of the Jews and subsequent plagues and destruction of the Egyptian army at the Red Sea.

As such, it is understandable that in modern times a notion would develop of a more feminine God, one that is not associated with the violence and "keeping score" that goes on in the Jewish Bible. It is certainly understandable to see how such a concept of a feminine God has arisen.

What complicated matters when trying to determine whether there really is a feminine nature of God is the fact that traditional Judaism does in fact speak of male and female aspects of the Jewish concept of God. Rebbitzen Tzipporah Heller writes about this issue, making a distinction between the outward manifestations of God and the inner feeling that we hold in our hearts. The outward manifestations—the God who created the physical universe and keeps the whole thing moving—is described as the "male" side of God. The God that we carry in our hearts, the "inside" aspect of God, is the feminine side. Where things get complicated is that these terms are simply meant as metaphors to help us grasp a concept of God with our limited minds. They are not meant to be actually descriptive of God. In other words, in the Jewish tradition, there really is no maleness or femaleness to God, now or ever.

Sometimes the Bible speaks of the "finger" or "hand" of God. At another important point, Moses is said to watch as God passes by, and all Moses sees is the back of God's head and the *tefillin* that God wears. However, such descriptions are considered symbolic. God doesn't have a head or a hand or fingers, and God doesn't wear tefillin.

> **Devine Devarim**
>
> **tefillin** the system of leather straps and locks that traditionally minded Jewish males (and some women) put on during morning prayers.

It all comes back to the limitations of language. In Hebrew, nouns are either masculine or feminine. Unlike some languages, such as German, there are no neuter nouns. Therefore, whenever the Bible or subsequent Jewish literature speaks of God, it does so in masculine terms. The problem in our generation is that this language that identifies God in male terms is spiritually off-putting and even upsetting to many women, who feel excluded by it. This explains the appeal of the concept of the shechinah, a feminine noun, as a method of understanding God that does not carry all the baggage of male vocabulary and warlike tones. Nevertheless, the shechinah is no more feminine than God is masculine in the Jewish tradition. The problem is simply trying to use the limited tool of language to describe the unlimited nature of God.

The Least You Need to Know

♦ The concept of shechinah allows us to grasp some concept of the Creator.

♦ The Tabernacle acted as a physical symbol of the presence of God.

♦ The shechinah cannot enter where there are ill feelings or arguments.

♦ Modern scholars now debate over possible feminine traits of God.

Part 5

Spiritual Side Notes

We start with gematria, the study of numerical replacement values for letters. You know that twice chai is 36, but how exactly did the rabbis come to that figure? What are the various ways to calculate gematria, and how can they enhance your spiritual well-being?

We then tackle the issue of angels. Although we tend to associate angels with Christianity, Judaic writings point to the evidence of angels practically back to the beginning of time. Who are angels? What do they do? And what messages do they have for you?

We then turn to the issue of Jewish learning and discover why Talmud study is so vital to one's spiritual well-being—and how to engage in same. We delve deeper into the question of why you and I may not have learned these lessons when we were growing up. We finish up with the following intriguing question (if I may say so myself): After reading all the information contained in this book, can we say with certainty that Judaism is spiritual?

Chapter 20

Gematria: The Numbers Never Lie

In This Chapter

◆ The relation of numbers and letters

◆ Getting to the root of gematria

◆ Which gematria to use?

◆ Gematria in action

Gematria is the system of replacing Hebrew letters with their equivalent number based on where the letters fall in the alphabet. The result is that every Hebrew word has a numerical equivalent. Perhaps the best-known gematria is the Hebrew word *chai*, meaning life, which is spelled with the Hebrew letters chet and yod, the eighth and tenth letters of the alphabet, respectively. Add eight and ten and you get 18, the numerical equivalent of chai.

A commonly known expression in Judaism is "to give (or donate) twice chai." To give "twice chai" means to give $36, or $360, or even $3,600, on the occasion of a wedding or bar or bat mitzvah or some other celebration. Many Jews practice the tradition of giving twice chai without realizing that the meaning of the expression derives from gematria, the subject of this chapter.

Gematria is not an originally Jewish idea. The Jews borrowed the concept from other earlier Middle-Eastern peoples. The Mesopotamians are thought to be the first practitioners of gematria. Sargon, the eighth-century B.C.E. ruler of Mesopotamia, built the perimeter of his palace to be 16,283 cubits long. The gematria of the name "Sargon" in the Mesopotamian language comes out to the exact same number. The famous "seer" Nostradamus was also a practitioner of numerology.

It All Adds Up

The Greeks were also said to be fond of gematria, and it is perhaps from the Greek language that the term arises. The only known derivation for the word comes from two Greek words, *geo*, meaning "earth," and *metria*, meaning "measure." In other words, gematria is a way of taking the earth's measure. Many temples in ancient Greece are said to have been built on gematria principles—that is, their design reflects the numerical value of the Greek letters making up the names of the gods to which those temples are dedicated.

Mystical Moments _____

Hebrew is much easier to learn than most people think. There are only 22 letters in the Hebrew alphabet and relatively few irregular verbs. Hebrew words are formed by a combination of a two- or three-letter root, and then prefixes and suffixes to indicate verb tense, number, and gender. If you learned "aleph bait"—the Hebrew alphabet—as a child, you'll be amazed at how easy it can be to read and understand even Biblical Hebrew.

Kabbalists have long believed that we can identify the numerical value of a Hebrew word or phrase and compare it with the identical values of other words and phrases to find intriguing links. For example, after the first Temple in Jerusalem was destroyed in the sixth century B.C.E., the prophet Jeremiah wrote, "from the fowl of the heavens until the beasts are departed." (Jeremiah 9:9) This phrase may not be all that easy to understand at first glance. People who practice Kabbalistic gematria would tell you that the numerical value, 52, of the word beast in Hebrew, *behemah*, alludes to the fact that no visitor passed through the land of Israel after the destruction of the Temple for a period of 52 years.

There is actually more than one way to assign a numerical value to a Hebrew letter. The most common way is

Spiritual Citations

"A human life is like a single letter in the alphabet. It can be meaningless. Or it can be part of a great meaning."

—Jewish Theological Seminary of America, from an advertisement for Rosh Hashanah called the "absolute value." This is the method of gematria that is most familiar to Jews today. Under this method, the first 10 letters in the Hebrew alphabet, alef through yod, have numerical values of one through 10, respectively. The next letter, kaf, has a value of 20. The next letter, lamed, has a numerical value of 30. And so on.

A second approach to gematria is called "ordinal value." Under this system, the first 10 letters have the same values as in the previous system. Kaf and lamed, however, are no longer 20 and 30. Instead, they are 11 and 12, since they are the eleventh and twelfth letters of the Hebrew language. In other words, you simply keep going up one number for each additional letter in the alphabet.

A third approach is called the "reduced value" method. Here, you start counting over every nine letters. Under this method, the Hebrew letters alef through tet, or one through nine, have the same value as in the other systems. Once you get to yod, however, the values return to one. The next letter, kaf, would be two, lamed would be three, and so on.

There is even yet another method of deriving numerical values for Hebrew letters. This system, *atbash*, is so-called because you can transpose the first letter of the Hebrew language, alef, for the final letter, tav. The second letter, beit, can be transposed for the next to last letter, shin. Thus a = t and b = sh, or if you eliminate the equal signs: atbash. Sometimes the transposing of letters reveals an intriguing aspect of kabbalistic philosophy. Let's take a look at some examples of gematria in action.

High Spirits
Speaking of numbers … a man we know stood up at a United Jewish Appeal fundraiser and announced, "I, Morris J. Plotnick, Brooklyn, New York, pledge $25,000—anonymously!"

Putting Two and Two Together

One of the most interesting and intriguing sources of gematria can be found at the website www.jewishpath.org, where Rabbi Akiva G. Belk has established a grid of numbers. Click on a number and you will discover the related gematria. For example, the gematria for the Hebrew word *paro*, the name of Pharaoh, is 22. (If you want to get technical, this is actually *mispar katan* gematria, yet another specialized form of gematria.) The total number for the Hebrew word Moshe, or Moses, is 12. The difference between Pharaoh and Moses, therefore, is 10, which symbolizes the 10 plagues. In other words, Moses believed in the power of God, and Pharaoh did not … until the 10 plagues demonstrated that power to him.

Let's try another simple one. In the desert, the Jews were repeatedly tested by Amalek, a maleficent nation whose name has stood for evil against the Jewish people throughout the generations. The gematria of Amalek is 240. The gematria of the Hebrew word *safek*, which means doubt, also is 240. According to Rabbi Yaakov Asher Sinclair of Ohr Sameach Yeshiva in Jerusalem, this gematria shows how we invite evil into our lives when we doubt the power of our Creator.

> **Devine Devarim**
>
> **atbash** a form of gematria in which the first letter of the Hebrew alphabet is transposed with the last, the second letter is transposed with the second to last, etc.
>
> **Tu B'shuvat** the New Year of the Trees, a holiday that generally occurs in February, the planting season in the Holy Land. Jewish children traditionally mark the occasion by "purchasing" trees in memory of loved ones and also by eating fruits grown in the land of Israel.

> **Mystical Moments**
>
> The Passover Haggadah—the "script" for retelling the Exodus story—speaks of a wicked son. We are instructed (metaphorically, of course) to "break his teeth." Why? Gematria teaches that the sum of the letters of "evildoer" (*rasha* in Hebrew) is 570. Subtract the number for "teeth" (*shinav*)—366—and the result is 204, the gematria of *tzaddik*, a righteous person!
>
> —Rabbi Shraga Simmons, Aish Hatorah Yeshiva, Jerusalem

Here's one involving a longer combination of words. This also comes from Ohr Sameach, specifically from Rabbi Yehuda Samet. Most Jews are familiar with the holiday of Tu B'shuvat, the New Year of the Trees. This holiday generally occurs in February, the planting season in the Holy Land. Jewish children traditionally mark Tu B'shuvat by "purchasing" trees in memory of loved ones. Many of us have memories of receiving certificates indicating the purchase of trees, which we gave to our parents and grandparents.

There is a gematria associated with the holiday. If we take the Hebrew phrase, *"Zeh yom lehodot al kol minei pri ha'etz"* (which translates roughly as "This is the day to give thanks for all types of fruit of the tree"), we get the number 1,234. Intriguingly, if we take the gematria of the phrase "the fifteenth day of the month of Shvat," which is the translation of Tu B'shuvat, we also come out to a gematria of 1,234! Traditionally, Jews have believed that gematria is a powerful insight into the genius of the Author of the Torah.

Just for Fun

On the shulchan aruch, the set table of Jewish life, gematria is not much more than an appetizer or side dish. It's really just for fun, although it can provide us with links between concepts that can give us things to think about or meditate upon. Let's take a look at slightly more complicated gematrias, both from the book of Genesis and the jewishpath.org website of Rabbi Akiva G. Belk.

Rabbi Belk points out that in the Talmud Esau did not "act out" or become involved with the negative behaviors with which Jewish tradition associates him until after the death of his grandfather Abraham. We often see this in modern life: Only when a parent or other relative dies does a person sometimes break out of his or her shell, for better or worse. In this case, gematria links two statements from the book of Genesis.

The first is Abraham "passed away and died in a good old age." (Genesis 25:8) The second phrase comes along later in that same chapter. It reads: "And Esau came in from the field, and he was feeling faint." (Genesis 25:29) Esau is about to demand some of the red soup his brother Jacob is making, and Jacob in turn will demand Esau's birthright in exchange for the soup.

Another gematria suggests that the episode of Jacob taking Esau's birthright in exchange for the red soup happened on the same day that Abraham died. The question is this: How do we know that these two events happened on the same day? The answer comes to us through the fascination of gematria. The phrase relating to Abraham's death equals 799. The phrase regarding Esau's return from the fields yields the same number. Thus, the rabbis of the Talmud are able to conclude, based on the gematria, that the death of Abraham and the incident of the soup took place on the very same day.

Let's take a look at a second example from the book of Genesis. Joseph is now the Secretary of the Treasury for all of Egypt. Ten of his brothers—all except the youngest brother, Benjamin—have come to Egypt to purchase food. Joseph agrees to assist them, but only on the condition that they bring their youngest brother, Benjamin, back to Egypt with them. When their father, Jacob, hears this news, he is extremely distraught. Not only has he apparently lost his favorite son, Joseph, but now it looks as though his son Benjamin will become property of the Egyptian government.

Jacob's bitter comment: If Benjamin is lost, "I will go to the grave in evil." What exactly does that phrase mean? It's hard to say, until we add up the numbers in all the letters of that phrase. Using the rules of substitution, the numerical value of those letters comes out to 613—the traditional number of commandments in the Torah! In other words, Jacob appears to be saying that if Benjamin is lost, there would be nobody to carry on the "613," the commandments that God has given the Jewish people. It's a little bit of a stretch if you actually go into the Hebrew and do the math, but gematria is more for illustration than for serious business.

High Spirits

A Jewish guy from Brooklyn moves to Hollywood and becomes a famous movie star. For Mother's Day, he sends his mother a mynah bird that costs six thousand dollars and speaks six languages. When he calls his mother to ask how she likes the bird, she replies, "It was delicious!"

In consternation, he says, "Mom, you weren't supposed to eat that bird! It cost $6000! It spoke six languages!"

Mom replied, "It spoke six languages? Then maybe it should have said something?"

Let's take a look at one final gematria. This comes from the blessing that traditionally minded Jews pronounce after they go to the bathroom. The blessing actually thanks God for the amazing nature of the human body, with its astonishing array of tubes, passages, and organs. The blessing goes on to say that "It is well known before God's heavenly throne that if one of these passageways should be blocked or if another one that is supposed to be closed should be opened, it would be impossible to stand before God and offer praises." (That's a rough translation.)

Let's focus on four words from this blessing, the Hebrew words used to indicate the system of inner passages and tubes throughout the body. In Hebrew, those words are: *chalulim chalulim nikavin nikavin.* Why are these Hebrew words written twice in the blessing? If you add up the numerical value of *chalulim chalulim,* you get 365, the number of positive commandments in the Torah. And if you add up nikavin nikavin, you get 248, the number of negative commandments, or prohibitions. And to take it a remarkable step further, if you add 365 to 248, you come out with … 613, the number of commandments in the Torah!

On a symbolic level, these words tell us that we are to dedicate our entire physicality to spiritual service, that there is no distinction between the purely physical and the purely spiritual. This also illustrates that each of the commandments corresponds to a particular "limb" of the body, thereby further linking the physical and the spiritual.

> ### Spiritual Citations
>
> "Mankind must remember that peace is not God's gift to his creatures; peace is our gift to each other."
>
> —Elie Wiesel

Not everyone who comes in contact with gematria is deeply moved by it, to say the least. Many traditionally minded Jews look at gematria as little more than a children's game, something that provides occasionally interesting results but in no way affects one's faith or religious practice. If Judaism were a newspaper, gematria would be the crossword puzzle; it's just there to keep your intellect sharp and perhaps to amuse. Is it to be taken seriously? Probably not. You could think of it as Torah with a smile on its lips. In Judaism, character is the main course; gematria is a delightful appetizer.

The Gift

Before we depart from the subject of numerology, let's turn to the fascinating number patterns that occur in, of all places, the book of Numbers. Specifically, when the mishkan is completed, there is a massive dedication ceremony. Princes of each of the 12 tribes of Israel come bearing expensive (and identical) gifts, each carrying its own symbolism. If you're reading the Bible at home, you can follow along in Numbers (8:19) and, if you have it handy, the commentary by the great authority Rashi. This is what each of the princes brought:

- One silver dish, weighing 130 shekels; and one silver bowl, weighing 70 shekels, both of them full of flour mixed with oil for an offering;

- one spoon of gold, 10 shekels in weight, full of incense;

- one young bull, one ram, and one year-old lamb, for a burnt offering;

- one kid of the goats, for a sin offering;

- and for a sacrifice of the feast offerings, two from the herd, five rams, five male goats, and five lambs of one year of age.

Now, you might be saying to yourself, where's the partridge in a pear tree? Allow me to explain. Let's go back to the first gift, a silver dish. The gematria of silver dish (*ke'arat kesef*) is 930, a number that alludes to the lifespan of Adam (of Garden of Eden fame) who lived for 930 years.

Next, the Bible says that the weight of that silver dish was 130 shekels. Shekel, in biblical times, was a measurement of weight; today, it is the financial currency of the state of Israel. The British pound is a similar term, both a measurement of weight and a financial figure. What does 130 shekels symbolize? How about this: According to the Bible, Adam was 130 years old when he and Eve had their first child.

Devine Devarim

shekel   1. in biblical times, a unit of weight. 2. the currency of the modern State of Israel.

The next gift, the silver bowl, weighing 70 shekels, translates as *mizrak echad kesef*. The gematria of that Hebrew phrase, 520, alludes to Noah, who was 500 years old when his children were born. The number 20 refers to the years before his children were born when God made the decree about the flood. The silver bowl itself weighs 70 shekels, which corresponds to the 70 nations that descended from the sons of Noah.

The next gift, the spoon of gold, weighs 10 shekels. In Hebrew, the word for "spoon," *kaf,* also means "hand." On a capitalistic level, this symbolizes the fact that the Torah was given from the hand of God. Why does it weigh 10 shekels? Because the Torah contains the Ten Commandments. Why is the golden spoon full of incense? Because the Hebrew word for incense is *ketoret,* which has an atbash gematria of 613. Just as the golden spoon was full of incense, so is the Torah full of the 613 mitzvahs!

The next gifts: the bull, the ram, and the lamb. The bull, according to Jewish tradition, symbolizes Abraham, who sacrificed a bull to God at the making of a covenant early in Genesis. The ram, of course, alludes to Isaac, because a ram was sacrificed instead of Isaac when Abraham and Isaac went off together in that famous event. And the lamb refers to Jacob, who tended lambs while he was working for his father-in-law-to-be, Laban.

What is meant by "one kid of the goats for a sin offering"? This is an allusion to Joseph, whose coat of many colors was dipped in goat blood after he was sold into slavery by his brothers. That sounds like a pretty serious sin to me.

Next comes the peace offering, which begins with two oxen. This symbolizes Moses and Aaron, who made peace between Israel and God. The three types of animals—rams, goats, and lambs—are said to symbolize the three groupings in the Jewish nation: the priests, or kohanim; the Levites; and the Israelites. Another way to understand those three types of animals is that they symbolize the three sections of the Jewish Bible: the Torah, the Prophets, and the Holy Writings, such as Proverbs and Psalms. And why were there five of each of those animals? To symbolize the five books of Moses.

Spiritual Citations

"In Jewish history there are no coincidences."

—Elie Wiesel

These gifts were important enough that the Bible repeats them 11 more times, once for each of the other princes of the tribes in Israel who were bringing these gifts. We said earlier that the surface meaning of the text is only the beginning of the story. In order to go deeper, in order to get to the levels of remez, drash, and sod, we need to have tools at our disposal in order to dig deeper.

Gematria is a fascinating aspect of Torah study. If you have not yet learned Hebrew, perhaps the idea that you will be able to develop gematrias of your own might spur you on to master the holy tongue.

The Least You Need to Know

- Gematria, like numerology, involves assigning numeric values to letters of the alphabet.
- Gematria can uncover hidden "links" between scripture, concepts, and ideas.
- Gematria has many different forms and methods.
- Gematria is not necessarily a serious practice; rather, it can be considered an amusing pastime that provides fascinating spiritual insights.

21

Do Jews Believe in Angels?

In This Chapter

◆ The origin of angels

◆ Angels in the Bible

◆ Angels in everyday life

◆ The ranks of angels

When we think of angels, we normally think of adorable Renaissance figures with wings and cherubic faces, looking down on humanity with bemused delight. Or we picture celestial beings with halos and human features. In both cases, we are envisioning Christian depictions of angels. However, Judaism also has a place for these heavenly creatures. Angels have been a part of the Jewish religion since its earliest days.

The word angel itself is derived from a Greek word, *angelos*, meaning "messenger." In other words, an angel is a spiritual being with a message, either for an individual or all of humanity. The Greek word *angelos* is most likely derived directly from the Hebrew word *mal'ach*, the Hebrew word for angel, which means "one who is charged with a mission." The word is directly related to the Hebrew word *mal'acha*, which is a spiritual term for work, and *halacha*, the Hebrew word for Jewish law. So in Hebrew, a mal'ach is a being who is charged with a specific spiritual task.

Are Angels Jewish?

The earliest mention of *mal'achim*, or angels, in the Bible comes when Abraham is recuperating from his circumcision. The Bible says that three individuals, who are understood to be mal'achim, come to Abraham. Despite the fact that he is physically inconvenienced, he immediately welcomes them, offers them what they need in order to wash their feet, and runs around his homestead, ordering a festive meal to be prepared in their honor.

Did Abraham recognize that these individuals were not human beings but mal'achim in human form out to accomplish their mission? Hard to say. At any rate, Abraham took them, and their message, very seriously. Sure enough, their prophecy that Abraham and Sarah would be parents within the year, despite their advanced age, came true.

The next mention of angels comes in the life of Jacob, who encounters them twice. At one point, he sends angelic messengers to speak with his estranged brother, Esau. Jacob is no doubt afraid of his brother, and therefore relies on the mal'achim to break the ice in seeking a rapprochement with his estranged sibling. Interestingly, this episode demonstrates that human beings (at least the Patriarchs) have the power to use angels on their behalf.

Jacob's next angelic account occurs in a dream in which he is wrestling with "a man" until daybreak. Was the man really a human being? Or was it an angel in the guise of a human being? The belief is that this so-called man really was an angel. One of the most interesting outgrowths of the wrestling match between Jacob and the angel was that God changed Jacob's name to Israel. Literally, the Hebrew word used for Yisrael, the name by which the Jewish people is known, means "to wrestle with God."

Devine Devarim

mal'ach an angel; lit. one who is charged with a mission.

Spiritual Citations

"Do not forget to entertain strangers, for by so doing some have unwittingly entertained angels."
—Hebrews 13:2

How true it is! Jews, perhaps more than any other people in the history of the world, have had a frequently contentious relationship with God, denying God's existence, denying the validity of divine laws, or simply ignoring responsibilities. No matter what one's affiliation within Judaism, we all tend to wrestle with our concept of what spirituality is, of what God is, or whether God exists, and exactly what is expected of us as members of the Jewish people.

Angels in the Architecture

Angels continue to play a role in traditional Jewish thought. It is said that when a Jew comes home from synagogue on Friday night, two angels—one good, one bad—accompany him or her. If the house to which the

Jew returns is neat and clean, and a beautiful Sabbath table is set, the good angel gets to say, "May it be this way next week!" The bad angel has no choice but to say, "Amen," essentially meaning, "So be it," or "I agree."

If, on the other hand, the house is in disarray, there is no Sabbath table, and the family is in disaccord, the bad angel gets to grin and say, "May it be this way next week!" leaving the good angel no choice but to say, "Amen."

This is why the first song that is sung at the Sabbath table is "Shalom Aleichem." The title literally means "Welcome to You," and it is sung to none other than the ministering angels who accompany the Jew home from the temple.

Another aspect of Jewish faith in which angels appear is on Yom Kippur. If you go into an orthodox synagogue on Yom Kippur, several things are different. First of all, many of the male congregants will be wearing a garment called a *kittel*, a burial shroud. This is a white garment, and it symbolizes the purity to which the soul is restored on that day. It also symbolizes the purity of the angels themselves. Normally, we do not live like angels—we are imperfect beings, and we also have our physical needs for food and drink. On Yom Kippur, since we neither eat nor drink, we are much closer to the angels, so we dress accordingly—all in white.

Moreover, there is one change in the prayers on Yom Kippur that reflects the fact that we are much closer to the angels than on other days. Normally, when we say the first line of the sh'ma, in which we acknowledge the oneness of God, we recite the next line in a whisper or undertone. That line is *"Baruch sham kevod malchuto le'olam va'ed"* ("Blessed is the name of God's glorious kingdom forever and ever"). According to Jewish tradition, this line is actually the primary line of prayer for angels during the course of their day. That's why we only whisper it the rest of the year. On Yom Kippur, when we are so much more like the angels, we actually say the sentence out loud, just like the angels.

Mystical Moments

According to the Talmud, when a baby is in the womb, an angel teaches the baby all of Torah. When the baby is born, the angel gives her a gentle slap, between the mouth and the nose, thus causing the baby to forget everything and have to learn it all anew. This explains that little indentation between the upper lip and the nose!

High Spirits

Rabbi Schwartz answers his phone.
"Hello. Is this Rabbi Schwartz?"
"It is."
"This is the IRS. Can you help us?"
"I can."
"Do you know a Sam Cohen?"
"I do."
"Is he a member of your congregation?"
"He is."
"Did he donate $10,000?"
"He will."
—www.haruth.com

Angels also arise throughout the normal weekday and Sabbath prayer services. For example, on a typical morning, we recite a prayer called the *kedusha*, in which we acknowledge the holiness of God. A key line from the kedusha reads: "*Kedosh, kedosh, kedosh, ado'nai, tz'va'ot, m'lo chal ha'aretz kevodo*" ("Holy holy holy is God, the whole earth is full of God's glory"). This is also a statement that the ranks of angels say to each other every day. Similarly, prayers spoken at the conclusion of the Sabbath also reflect the concept that angels exist and praise God on a regular basis.

Who Exactly Are the Angels?

In the Jewish tradition, there are several different classes of angels. One group simply exists in order to praise God. All angels are incorporeal—they have no body or physical needs. They also lack free will, meaning they have no choice to do anything other than the will of God. In that sense, they are extremely different from human beings, who are said to be "a little lower than the angels" because we act on our capacity to do evil, a capacity that angels lack.

Another kind of angel is created every time we perform a good deed. This angel will ultimately argue on our behalf before God when we are judged for the way we conducted our entire lives. When we perform an act well and out of good intentions, we are said to create the strongest possible sort of angel. Similarly, when we do wrong, we are said to create an accusing sort of being that will testify against us on our personal day of judgment.

> **Devine Devarim**
>
> **sar** a princely angel who looks after a nation's interests and keeps God "informed" of what is happening with that nation.

The Talmud speaks of yet another kind of angel, called a *sar*, the Hebrew word for prince. Each nation in the world is said to have a sar, a princely angel, looking after its interests and keeping God "informed" on what is happening with that nation.

Since angels are discussed in the Torah, traditionally minded Jews accept their existence.

Stories of angels are so prevalent in Jewish history and prayer that they have to be considered a universally acceptable aspect of traditional Judaism, whatever conclusions we as individuals may draw about them. The bottom line: We understand them as agents of Divine will. God channels God's will through angels in order to achieve various tasks in the world.

> **High Spirits**
>
> A father tried to get his son a discount rate for a flight. The airline check-in person said, "How old is he?"
>
> "Four," replied the father.
>
> "Four? He looks like he's twelve!"
>
> The father shrugged. "Can I help it if he worries?"

The Least You Need to Know

- ◆ An angel is a divine messenger.
- ◆ We are the closest to angels on Yom Kippur.
- ◆ The Bible mentions angels in the stories of Jacob and Abraham.
- ◆ Angels exist in different ranks, or orders.

22

Reforming Judaism

In This Chapter

- ◆ Brief history of the Jewish status quo
- ◆ Evolution of reform Judaism
- ◆ The lessons hidden within Bible stories
- ◆ Tales that teach young and old alike

Growing up, I couldn't wait for my Bar Mitzvah. It wasn't because I was anxious to get up and recite 10 lines of a memorized *haftorah* portion, or get an *aliyah* and be called to the Torah for the first time. It certainly wasn't because I was looking forward to the party after the service. All the girls I knew were taller than I was. The photographer took our group picture sitting down to avoid humiliation for me.

I couldn't wait because my Bar Mitzvah meant never having to go to Hebrew School *ever again*. You think the Israelites felt free after Moses guided them across the Red Sea and out of Egypt? That's got nothing on the average Jewish 13-year-old who suddenly finds his Sunday mornings free. No more car pool. No more tedious classes. No more after-school Hebrew sessions that cut into some very serious playtime—or worse, Halloween trick-or-treating. That was the ultimate rip-off.

Why Johnny Can't Daven

For countless adult Jews, their Jewish education ended at age 13—if they even lasted *that* long. Unfortunately, Jewish kids whose education is so severely limited grow into Jewish adults who have no idea of the spiritual richness of their faith. Adults who don't get a solid set of spiritual underpinnings growing up will often spend much of their lives looking for spirituality elsewhere. This offers a partial explanation for the attraction for Jews to Buddhism, various branches of Christianity, and other religions and practices.

The irony is that Jews have a rich supply of spiritual thinking in their own faith. This is the last place that many of us would think to look for it. The last time we checked into Judaism, we were adolescents, and we were being taught an approach to spirituality and religion appropriate to people our age. But now we're adults, and I'm very excited to share with you the fact that Judaism speaks even more powerfully to adults than it does to children.

Devine Devarim _____

daven   to pray. A Yiddish term commonly used by orthodox Jews.

High Spirits

genius   an average student with a Jewish mother.

Devine Devarim _____

ghetto   a city neighborhood in which Jews were required to live. From the Italian *giotto*.

There are many factors that have led to what we could call a decline in Jewish literacy. For one, in previous centuries, secular studies were barely emphasized in a yeshiva education. The main thing was to make a young man literate in Torah and Talmud. (In the old days, educating girls wasn't stressed.) Since the professions and most universities were closed to Jews, secular education wasn't particularly useful. Because a young man was likely to spend his life studying Talmud or pursuing a trade, classes like history, science, and secular literature weren't highly prized.

The orthodox world has changed. First, girls can receive quality education in yeshivot today. Second, secular studies are considered extremely important, although generally the morning is devoted to Hebrew studies and the afternoons to secular classes. Yet, today, unless a child attends a Jewish day school, the majority of Jewish education is limited to those two hours on Sunday mornings and in the Hebrew school that so many of us couldn't wait to escape.

Also, for the past 200 years Jews have been admitted to the mainstream of society in ways unimaginable to previous generations. The term *ghetto* did not originate in low-income neighborhoods in American inner cities. It comes from the Italian word *giotto*, a neighborhood in which all Jews were *required* to live in cities such as Venice and Rome. If you visit those cities today, you can still find the Jewish giottos of old. Jews were actually locked in at night. If caught outside the giotto past curfew without a specific, legitimate reason, they were in trouble!

Jews were practically divorced from much of the European society that surrounded them. They had their own shops, their own schools, and even their own court systems. It was rare for Jews to sue each other in secular courts.

As Europe entered the nineteenth century, ideas of the Enlightenment spread and affected the way Christians viewed Jews. The ghetto walls came down and Jews across the continent were now permitted to live wherever they pleased. A key facet of Jewish practice over the centuries was maintaining the differences between themselves and their non-Jewish neighbors. For example, wines produced by non-Jews were (and are) considered nonkosher—if you observe Jewish law, you won't drink them. The primary reason for this rule: If you don't drink wine with people or celebrate with them, you probably won't end up *marrying* them. A good number of the laws of traditional Judaism exist to maintain a separation between Jews and non-Jews, primarily in order to prevent intermarriage.

> **Spiritual Citations**
>
> "Art is a form of prayer."
> —Franz Kafka

Reforming the Mold

As Jews were admitted to the mainstream of European culture, their status quo changed. As the nineteenth century progressed, Jews were allowed to own land, attend university, and enter professions formerly closed to them. Many Jews wanted a different kind of Judaism, one that allowed them to take part with greater ease in the secular life of the surrounding community. In towns across Germany, in the early part of the nineteenth century, some Jews sought to "re-form" Judaism by removing from it those aspects that made it difficult or impossible to connect with their Christian neighbors. Part of the motivation was the fear that some Jews would leave Judaism altogether if they didn't have an alternative that allowed them to identify as Jews without having to adhere to all of Judaism's laws. The movement we know as reform Judaism was born.

Now that Jews were able to partake of secular society, the emphasis in many Jewish families changed from Jewish subjects to those forms of knowledge most useful in the secular world. Trust me, there wasn't a lot of Hebrew on the 1815 entrance exam to Heidelberg University! Many Jews now devoted much of their educational time to secular subjects. Jewish subjects, while still important, lost some of their value in the eyes of many Jews. Not all Jews, of course, felt this way. The orthodox continued to teach their children the whole range of Jewish subjects, and continue to do so today. But there now existed a sizable group of Jews who did not have the same educational access to Judaism that their parents had enjoyed.

Devine Devarim

reform Judaism   a sect whose ideals and practices are less stringent and more "modernized" than those of traditional or orthodox Judaism. The reform movement arose from the desire to take part in the secular life of the surrounding community.

Not only that, the focus of reform Judaism was different. Some Jews were uncomfortable with aspects of Judaism that were foreign to or conflicted with the beliefs of their non-Jewish (Gentile) neighbors. These included some of the more mystical aspects of Judaism. At a time when rationality was king, if a concept appeared to not make sense, it was deemed old-fashioned and was subsequently jettisoned. Sermons—and choirs, a direct borrowing from the German Christian Church—were now offered not in Hebrew but in the language of the country (German, French, or English).

As for the Bible, Talmud, and Jewish law, the times they were a-changin'. The holy books made sense in their day, but they no longer fully applied to the changed society. Some early members of reform Judaism were actually hostile to the religious practices of traditional Judaism and sought to eliminate them.

Reform Judaism spread to the United States by the late nineteenth century. The "Pittsburgh Platform" of 1885, the first key document produced by American reform rabbis, shared the view that much of traditional Judaism was no longer applicable. They wrote:

> We accept as binding only the moral laws and maintain only such ceremonies as elevate and sanctify our lives, but reject all such as are not adapted to the views and habits of modern civilization.

> We hold that all such Mosaic [meaning derived from Moses] and rabbinical laws as regulate diet, priestly purity and dress originated in ages and under the influence of ideas altogether foreign to our present mental and spiritual state. They fail to impress the modern Jew with a spirit of priestly holiness; their observance in our days is apt rather to obstruct than to further spiritual elevation.

The early reform rabbis were quite radical in their approach to changing Judaism. They sought to eliminate prayer in Hebrew, the concept of the Messiah, the Kol Nidre prayer pronounced on the evening of Yom Kippur, wearing the tallit (prayer shawl), and many other aspects of Jewish learning and practice. Reform Jewish rabbis were even opposed to the idea of a Jewish state! They were considered *so* radical that another group of Jews sought to conserve some of the traditions that early reform Judaism was eliminating. Thus was born *conservative* Judaism, out of a fear that reformers were going too far.

Spiritual Citations

"Anti-Semitism ... is the swollen envy of pygmy minds—meanness, injustice."
—Mark Twain

Today, reform Judaism has changed greatly from those early days. Reform rabbis are finding that reform Jews want more Jewish spirituality, ritual, and practice and are faced with the challenge of "reforming" Judaism once again. Prayer in reform temples is as common in Hebrew as in English, and you would be hard-pressed to find a reform Jewish congregation where people did not wear a *tallit* or prayer shawl or recite the *Kol Nidre* prayer on Yom Kippur. As Americans seek more traditional approaches to spirituality, reform Judaism has been in the lead of bringing traditional Jewish notions and concepts to its adherents.

What About Conservative and Reconstructionist Judaism?

Conservative Judaism was formed as a reaction to the changes that reform Judaism sought. The founders of conservative Judaism sought to "conserve" aspects of Judaism that early reformers wanted to abandon. Conservative Judaism is much more akin to orthodoxy, in that it accepts the importance of following Jewish law. Conservative practice, however, is often more liberal than orthodox practice.

For example, conservative Jews are permitted to drive to religious services on the Sabbath, something their orthodox co-religionists would never do. Conservative rabbis recognized that as Jews moved to the suburbs, only a small percentage of them lived within walking distance of their temples. So they modified the rules prohibiting driving. A religiously observant conservative Jew, therefore, would drive to and from services, but wouldn't stop to run errands. In other words, conservative Judaism seeks to be more in tune with the times.

Orthodoxy is more demanding. An orthodox Jew would not live in a community that does not offer a shule or synagogue within walking distance of his or her home. While orthodoxy does change, its pace of change is far slower than that of conservative Judaism.

Reconstructionist Judaism, the smallest of the major Jewish movements in America, was founded by conservative rabbi Mordecai Kaplan. It emphasizes the cultural aspects of Judaism as opposed to the strictly religious aspects. The website soc.culture.jewish offers this description of reconstructionist Judaism:

> *Reconstructionist Jews are willing to question conventional answers and keep open minds. They believe that a Jew need not and ought not sacrifice intellectual integrity for the sake of his/her Jewish identity. Reconstructionists are Jews who take the Jewish traditions seriously and live Jewish lives even though they don't believe in the divine supernatural origin of the Torah.*

While spirituality is by no means the exclusive domain of the orthodox, few would argue the point that orthodox Jews are more likely than adherents to the other movements to organize their entire lives around their practice of Judaism. The practice of traditional, halachic Judaism (that is, Judaism that requires adherence to Jewish law) simply takes more time and energy than those forms of Judaism that do not demand quite as much commitment in terms of time, behavior, and belief.

As we said at the outset of this book, every Jew sets his or her own shulchan aruch—every Jew must decide where on the spectrum of Jewish practice and spirituality he or she fits in. Perhaps the greatest tragedy of modern Jewish life is that the high level of information available to Jews today is matched only by the extraordinary degree of apathy so many Jews feel toward their religion. Part of this is due to the times: religion simply doesn't have the same power in society that it enjoyed even half a century ago. It's one thing to *decide* not to participate in Jewish communal life; it's another thing, and a far sadder one, to ignore the possibility of learning what Judaism offers.

The Least You Need to Know

- ◆ The adherence to traditional Jewish values has evolved over the last 200 years.
- ◆ Reform Judaism came about due to the desire to adapt Judaism to the modern world.
- ◆ Conservative and reconstructionist Judaism offer alternatives to the opposite poles of orthodoxy and reform Judaism.

23

Hitting the Books

In This Chapter

◆ Sources for further study

◆ Beginning to set your own shulchan aruch

◆ A year in Israel

◆ Main topics of further study

Congratulations! The mere fact that you have read this far in the book—almost to the end—means that you have been engaged in one of the primary forms of Jewish spiritual observance, the study of Torah. Learning is such a vital part of Judaism that it would be difficult, if not impossible, to be a knowledgeable Jew without lifelong study of its precepts. Judaism, quite frankly, is immense.

As I've noted earlier, Judaism is a commentary on the basic concept of "do unto others." But the fact is that human life is complex; if you want to have a society that runs on spiritual principles, we need something a little more definite than that essential piece of Jewish philosophy. Life is indeed complicated. We are born, we must be educated, we must work, we marry, we raise children, we age, and we die. In order to have social cohesion among a people spread out across the planet—and a people who have survived for thousands of years—some specifics about how to handle each of the aspects of life becomes necessary. If we are to endure as a people and bring out the best in ourselves, our families, and our fellows, we need some structure.

Give Yourself a Mitzvah

The essential belief in Judaism is that the Torah is the blueprint God used when creating the universe. When Jews study Torah, we are studying the very plans by which the universe came into existence.

We have seen elsewhere in this book that the words of the Bible can be understood on many levels; that there is far more than the simple surface level for us to examine. We have also seen that the Talmud and later commentaries offer analysis and debate as to the nature of that blueprint: What exactly did God intend? How are we to be godly ourselves? What does God want from us? These are matters that the patriarchs, the prophets, the rabbis, and Jewish philosophers have considered across the millennia.

> ### High Spirits
>
> "I've got good news and bad news. The good news is that I got Him down from 15 to 10. The bad news is that adultery's still in there."
>
> —Moses

The result of all that intellectual ferment is the Judaism we have today, which is no doubt extremely different in many ways from the Judaism that Moses knew. In fact, there is a story in the Talmud that Moses stood in the Beit Midrash, or study hall, of the great authors of the Talmud—and wept! He wept because he didn't understand a single thing they were saying. The moral of that story is that Judaism changes to fit the times. What might have been unthinkable even a hundred years ago is today considered common practice and completely Jewish in every way.

For example, until a thousand years ago, it was legitimate for Jewish men to have more than one wife. That practice was outlawed because it no longer fit the times. As we said at the very beginning of this book, the rules of kashrut, the dietary laws, are probably much more complex today than they were, say, 800 years ago. This presents us with a paradox of individuals who study the great commentators like Rashi and Maimonides, yet could not even eat in those great authorities' kitchens. The debate in Judaism is mainly over how fast Judaism should change, and who has the power to make those changes.

For example, there are virtually no ordained Orthodox women rabbis. I say "virtually" because there are a small handful of women who say that they have been ordained in secret by respected Orthodox authorities. And yet, the other branches of Judaism—reconstructionist, reform, and conservative—all have an open process by which women are ordained.

The question also arises with regard to converts to Judaism. The orthodox requirements are far more strict than those of the reform, conservative, or reconstructionist movements. As a result, while orthodox conversion is universally accepted throughout every branch of Judaism as legitimate proof of Jewishness, a conservative or reform conversion carries little to no weight in orthodox circles. We all have the same texts before us; it's just that different branches of Judaism come to different conclusions about the meaning and even the validity of those texts.

Set Your Own Table

In the beginning of the book, we described Judaism with the phrase "everyone sets her or his own shulchan aruch." In other words, every Jew has to decide for himself or herself exactly how to approach Judaism. The beauty of the religion is that there is a certain amount of freedom to choose—not just the degree of observance in one's life but also the pace at which one moves toward observance. There is no central authority in Judaism (thank goodness!) with the power to declare that one person is "not Jewish enough" while another person is "too Jewish." We all have to set our own table.

As we all know, the best way to make decisions is to become as informed as possible. This book truly is only a beginning. We have touched lightly on a wide variety of subjects related to the spiritual and mystical essence of Judaism, but this is just the tip of a vast body of knowledge that awaits you. To make truly informed decisions, you must become well versed in Judaism's various arenas. How else can you possibly evaluate the conflicting claims of the various movements and rabbis? How can you decide whether to keep kosher, what level of kashrut to observe, or what *hechsherim* to accept if you are not informed as to what *kashrut* is all about?

> **Devine Devarim**
>
> **hechsherim** the symbols on food packages indicating a particular item has been produced in accordance with Jewish dietary law. The most common *hechsher* is a U in a circle, which is the sign of approval of the Orthodox Union, a leading body of orthodox rabbis. Other rabbis have different symbols to represent their own imprimatur, so a person who is careful about *kashrut* may accept some hechsherim but not others.

And that's just food. We have said earlier that Judaism is not just a religion, but a legal system and method for approaching all of the great events of life. The rabbis call those great events "hatch, match, and dispatch"—birth, marriage, and death. Judaism speaks to all of these issues. For example, when a baby is born, there are rules regarding the time and place of the naming of the baby. If the baby is a boy, a *brit*, or ritual circumcision, is in order, with the appropriate accompanying rules. If the boy is firstborn and was delivered vaginally, a separate ceremony is involved in which the baby boy is "redeemed" from his obligation to the priesthood.

Then there is the matter of Jewish education. As a friend of mine once put it, "We still haven't decided how much Judaism to inflict on our daughter." For those who consider that it's actually a *positive* thing to give children a Jewish education, many questions arise. At what age should Jewish education begin? Should the child go to public school and then get religious education in the late afternoon and on Sunday mornings? Or should the child go to Jewish day school? If Jewish day school, what kind? Reform? Conservative? Orthodox? Something different altogether?

> **Spiritual Citations**
>
> "Do not do unto your neighbor that which is disagreeable to you."
> —The Talmud

What should happen at age 13? What kind of *Bar* or *Bat Mitzvah* is appropriate? What form should it take? When the young person turns 18 and is ready for college, how much should Jewish experience be weighed in the decision about which college to attend? What about going to Israel for a year of study? If so, where?

And then there's work. Although there's a stereotype that Jewish life begins upon one's "graduation from medical school," there are in fact many Jews who are not doctors. How they make a living, we're not quite sure, but Judaism definitely speaks to the question of morality and ethics in the workplace. It also speaks about what sort of careers a person should choose. (According to the Talmud, anything involving great smells, like tanning, for example, are not considered ideal careers, simply because the smell might be overpowering to that person's wife.)

And then there's the question of marriage itself. How do you get married? Who do you marry? What should go on at the ceremony? What should go on at the reception? Where should Aunt Sadie sit, since she isn't speaking to Uncle Lou? While the Talmud does not specifically address the question of Aunt Sadie and Uncle Lou, it has an enormous amount to say about marriage … and divorce.

Judaism also has much to say about the question of death and bereavement. The Jewish concepts of mourning are fascinating and extremely humane. The basic idea is that a person should not be alone for the initial period of time after the loss. Our concepts of burial, sitting *shiva* (the seven-day mourning period during which guests come to the house of the mourner), the 30-day period of mourning following the death, and the reciting of *kaddish* (the mourner's prayer) for the 11 months after the death of the loved one, all derived from various events and episodes in the Bible. (See Appendix A, "For Further Reading," for suggested reading in this area.)

> **Devine Devarim**
>
> **shiva** the seven-day mourning period during which guests come to the house of the mourner.

In short, from birth through death, Judaism has an enormous amount of wisdom to offer. It's also understood that the Torah and all its commentaries are so voluminous that no person could hope to master all of them in a lifetime. Nonetheless, Judaism firmly believes that we do not have the right to ignore our obligation to study as best we can.

As a Jew, in other words, you have the obligation— not just the right, but the obligation—to educate yourself about Judaism. Otherwise you are simply missing out. King Solomon wrote 3,000 years ago, "There is nothing new under the sun." Judaism is the repository of almost 4,000 years of wisdom about handling the events of life. Sometimes you hear people say, "I sure wish life came with an owner's manual." The good news is that it does, and it is yours for the asking.

> **Mystical Moments**
>
> As the Talmudic rabbi Ben Bag-Bag said, "Study the Torah constantly, because everything is found in it. Constantly examine it and grow old and gray while studying it, and never turn away from it, because there is nothing greater than it for you."

Where Do I Go from Here?

The best method of accomplishing such a daunting task is to go to Israel for a full year, enroll in a baal teshuva yeshiva, and immerse yourself in the literature, history, language, philosophy, spirituality, and mysticism of your Jewish heritage. I did this; it's one of the greatest experiences I've ever had in my whole life and I recommend it wholeheartedly.

It was during my year in Israel at the baal teshuva that I acquired the foundation for the knowledge about Judaism that has served me well in the past 20 years and which I have sought to present over the course of this book.

Today Israel boasts a wide variety of yeshivot for Jews with little or no Jewish background. I urge you to do what I did: Get a one-year ticket with an open date, fly to Israel, and then visit each of the schools until you find one where you feel comfortable. The process of registering for enrollment is fairly fluid; essentially, if you have a pulse and you're Jewish, you're in. This experience of "total immersion" into Jewish literature, law, history, philosophy, and everything else, is truly a life-changing event. Living in Israel is amazing in itself. It's quite remarkable to walk the streets and climb the hills where the history that you study in yeshiva actually took place.

> **Spiritual Citations**
>
> "On everything you need to hear other people's opinions. It's the only way to do things. You ask a friend's advice and then between the two of you things somehow get clearer."
> —Shmuel Yosef Agnon

Closer to Home

When I visited that baal teshuva yeshiva in 1979, they made this point: "You know all about the American side of your personality. You've been immersed in it for your whole life. But you have a Jewish side as well that you may not know nearly as well. Unless you take time to study it, the unbroken 300-generation chain dating back to Abraham and Sarah is likely to break off at your feet." That argument strikes as relevant a chord in me today as it did then.

However, not everyone is in a position to pick up and move to Israel for a year. Fortunately, there are opportunities for learning in practically every city in the United States.

> **Mystical Moments**
>
> Lionel Nathan Rothschild, of the famous banking family, holds the distinction of being the first Jew to hold a seat in the British House of Commons. However, Rothschild did not assume his position until Parliament presented him with a swearing-in oath suitable to his Jewish faith. The event came to pass some 11 years after Rothschild initially held claim to the seat.

Virtually every temple and synagogue offers adult education classes, and some of the programs are vast in scope. One night a week is surely not too much to devote to the study of your culture and history.

The Internet also provides unbelievable resources for Jewish study. You can sign up for daily e-mail deliveries of discussions or lectures on virtually any topic in Judaism. (Appendix B, "Twenty Top Websites," lists some great options on the Web.) No matter what level of observance you currently maintain or might be interested in reaching, there's information waiting for you either in your hometown or on the Web. Judaism is a text-heavy religion, which in many ways makes it perfect for the Internet. The information that you seek is more accessible than ever.

People of the Books

In the last 20 years, there has been an explosion of books about every aspect of Judaism written in English for the lay reader. Only a generation ago, you needed to know Hebrew to study Judaism with any depth. In the last several decades, countless authors have written English translations of most of Judaism's important texts, and certainly all of the ones that have been mentioned in this book. Every major city in the country has at least one good Jewish bookstore, which more often than not employs far more knowledgeable clerks than any chain bookstore. You might find it useful to talk with an individual behind the counter in a Jewish bookstore, and explain where you are in Judaism and where your interests lie. That person will be able to recommend books that will take you deep into any subject area that you desire.

Why all the emphasis on book learning if spirituality is primarily something you feel? That's a great question—I'm glad I asked it. You could say that Judaism comes down to a kind of educated simplicity. All the learning that you do about God, mankind, and everything else—all of it prepares us for those moments when we seek to experience our deepest spiritual selves. Then, in the moment of deep spiritual contact between ourselves and God, all that knowledge somehow falls away and we experience what it means to know before Whom we stand.

While it's true that every Jew sets his or her own shulchan aruch, the fact is that without some sort of common ground, we would no longer have a uniting faith or means of remaining a people. You can make a case that Judaism is a cultural phenomenon, but the fact is that Jewish culture in the United States is radically different from Jewish culture in, say, Morocco or Yemen. Except for religious belief, American Jews have more in common with American Christians than we do with Jews in Syria. (Yes, there are still Jews living there.) So culture is really not the ultimate common ground in Judaism.

The same can be said of cuisine. Or dress. Or nonreligious literature. Or even music. The only true common bond uniting all Jews is the spiritual aspect of their faith. Even Jews who are atheistic (certain that there is no God) or agnostic (uncertain about the existence of God) are in some sense coming from the same place as Jews who are absolutely convinced of God's existence. Jews across the broad spectrum of religious observance and belief pretty much all agree that there's some indefinable, ineluctable core of their being which connects to the whole idea of being Jewish. I'd like to suggest that the basic core we're discussing is the spiritual nature of Judaism.

Devine Devarim

parasha a selection from the Torah; pl. parashiyot.

Whaddaya Know?

So how do you reach that sense of educated simplicity? What specific topics or subjects are most useful if you want to become spiritually educated so as to maximize an appreciation and awareness of the spiritual core in Judaism? Let's take a look at some of the topics that are worth exploring in greater detail.

Torah

There are two ways to study the Torah: in-depth and in-breadth. A simple way to acquaint yourself with the entire contents of the Bible is to read it, a few pages a day. I did this, and I found it to be an exhilarating way to see the broad scope of Jewish biblical experience, from Adam and Eve all the way to the Promised Land of Israel. If you're going to do this, don't try to understand every single word or expression. Just go for the general flow of it, and see how the Bible feels to you when you read for "the big picture."

The Torah is divided into 52 weekly *parashiyot*, or portions, and one portion a week (and sometimes two) is read at most temples and synagogues. You can subscribe to many weekly email services that will provide you with an overview of the parasha, along with a commentary on that portion. You can also get a "linear" translation of the Bible, in which the text is translated into English on a phrase-by-phrase basis. This way you can see exactly what's happening in the text at any given point. Most linear translations also contain translations of the commentary by Rashi, widely considered throughout Jewish circles to be the most important commentary on the Bible in Jewish history.

> **High Spirits**
>
> "One mitzvah can change the world. Two will just make you feel tired."
>
> —Yiddish proverb

You can also find English translations of commentaries on the Torah by such leading Jewish scholars over the centuries as the Bartenura, the Kli Yakar, Maimonides, Nachmonides, Ibn Ezra, the Sforno, and in more recent times, Rabbi Elie Munk and Nachama Liebowitz. If you were to dip into any of these commentaries, you would find a wealth of ideas about the Torah presented by these individuals, who span the last thousand years of Jewish thought.

Nach

Nach is the Hebrew acronym meaning *nivi'im* and *ketuvim*, the Prophets and the Writings. The acronym is formed by taking the N from Nivi'im and the K from Ketuvim; in Hebrew the letter CH and the letter K are very closely related. The Prophets include Jeremiah and Isaiah, and the Writings include books such as Proverbs, Ecclasiastes, and the Psalms.

To read the way the Prophets continually upbraid the Jewish people for their failure to adhere to God's law, you'd think nothing has changed in the last 2,500 years! It is extremely interesting to think about the courage it must have taken for these individuals to stand out from the crowd and criticize the practices of everyone from the king on down to the common people. The history of the relationship between God and the Jewish people is a surprisingly stormy one, and no one captures the flavor of that drama like the biblical prophets.

> **Spiritual Citations**
>
> "There is no doubt: the study of man is just beginning, at the same time that his end is in sight."
>
> —Elias Canetti

The Writings include the Psalms, said to have been written by King David; the Proverbs, said to be written by King Solomon; and many other books. Here you will find the Purim story in the Book of Esther, the stories of Ruth, Jonah, Job, Daniel in the lion's den, and so many of the other tales that you may perhaps vaguely remember from childhood. The basic difference between reading these events as an adult and reading them as a child is that when you are a child, they took out all the sex! The stories are a lot more compelling now, and they shed fascinating light on human nature, which appears not to have changed much over these past 4,000 years.

Talmud

The Talmud, as we have discussed, is a massive, 20-volume compendium of Jewish law and lore composed between the first and sixth centuries B.C.E. Actually, there are two Talmuds, the best-known having been composed in Babylon, where the Jews were exiled after the Romans destroyed the second Temple in 70 C.E.

There's also the lesser-known Jerusalem Talmud, which was composed in its namesake city at the same time. Because it is written in a terse combination of Aramaic and Hebrew, the Talmud is very difficult to read without commentaries or teachers. There are all sorts of place names and legal concepts that are referred to only by abbreviations, and the text itself contains almost no punctuation.

Mystical Moments

One of the stories of the Talmud tells the story, most likely apocryphal, of a wealthy nineteenth-century Jewish businessman traveling to a distant city to find an appropriate son for his beautiful daughter. He and his party were staying at an inn and entered into a deep argument about where a period should be placed in a particular line of Talmud. The wealthy man and his friends fell asleep in the course of their debate, and while they were sleeping, the lowly innkeeper, a pious and learned Jew, inserted the period in their text. When the wealthy man and his friends awoke and saw the period exactly where it should be placed, they realized that the poor but honest young innkeeper was a true *talmud chachim*, or Talmud scholar. Naturally, he became the groom of the wealthy man's daughter.

Fortunately, Talmud teachers and English translations abound today. We discussed earlier the English translation of the Talmud by Rabbi Adin Steinsaltz. This series of books, along with his work *The Essential Talmud*, offers an outstanding way to enter the mesmerizing world of the Talmud, in which awaits a thorough discussion of every aspect of human nature, character, and Jewish law. In short, it is the adventure of a lifetime.

Jewish Law

The Hebrew word *halachah* means Jewish law, and it is derived from the verb to walk or to go. In other words, Jewish law simply means "the way to go." Jewish law exists to serve a number of purposes. First, it binds its people close to God. Traditionally, God is considered to be the source of much of Jewish law. The rabbis of the Talmud, acting with a deep understanding of the nature of God, created many of the rest of the Jewish laws.

Devine Devarim

taharat hamishpacha

the laws governing family purity.

The second function of Jewish law is to bind the Jewish people to one another. Many aspects of Jewish law exist simply to keep the Jewish people together, somewhat segregated from the mainstream of society, so as to avoid intermarriage and assimilation. Today, most American Jews have little knowledge of Jewish law, and this is something of a tragedy.

Granted, it is in many ways quite inconvenient to observe many aspects of Jewish law. The laws of the Sabbath certainly interfere with going to movies or ball games on weekend nights. The laws of kashrut restrict the types of restaurants to which one can go. The laws of *taharat hamishpacha*—family purity—actually restrict the times of the month when a married couple can make love. It's impossible, however, to see the upside of this entire system of individual and community behavior unless you take the time to study it, and maybe even to experience it as well. For the most part, most Jews in our society are more familiar with the downside of Jewish practice than they are with any benefits.

Observant Jews will tell you that they find that the laws of kashrut, for example, infuse even the mundane act of eating with spirituality. The laws regarding the Sabbath provide a weekly "vacation" from the cares and strife of the work world and financial responsibilities, and allow a chance for families and friends to spend not just quality but quantity time together.

As for the laws of family purity, it's easy to see the downside. Most people don't want any sort of restrictions on their sex lives (that is, if they're lucky enough to have one). And yet, countless married couples who observe this practice, in which sexual contact is avoided during and after menstruation, maintain that their sex lives are even more exciting and fulfilling than those of people who, in theory, can have sex whenever they want.

Many couples who observe taharat hamishpacha claim that the first night they are free to make love again is as romantic as the wedding night itself. This stands in sharp contrast to the major problem that confronts sex lives of married people or couples in committed relationships: boredom.

The bottom line is that it's very hard to make a decision about whether to become involved with any level of Jewish practice unless you have the specific information that you need. That's why it is so useful to study Jewish law and then make those decisions for yourself.

High Spirits

A friend of mine, who describes himself as "not the handsomest man in the world," likes to tell this story about himself. One Friday night, he was waiting for his wife to emerge from the mikva, the community ritual bath that women enjoy prior to the commencement of relations every month. He was standing outside the mikva waiting for her, and every time a woman emerged, she would look at him with a look of horror on her face. That night at the Sabbath table, the man asked his father-in-law, a very learned rabbi, why the women were dong this.

The rabbi looked embarrassed. "There's a belief," the rabbi explained, "that if you conceive a child on the first night after your visit to the mikva, the child will look like the first man you see when you come out of the mikva!"

Spirituality and Mysticism

But wait! There's more! This book covers only a tiny fraction of what Jewish mysticism and spirituality are all about. Lectures on virtually any aspect of Jewish life and religion tend to draw small crowds for the most part—unless the lecture includes an incredibly "in" topic such as Kabbalah, Zohar, or anything mystical. There are many outstanding books, tape series, and sources on the Internet that can take you deeper into the mystical side of Judaism that we have only touched upon in this book.

Jewish History

Most American Jews know more about Abraham Lincoln than about Abraham. We know more about crossing the Delaware than crossing the Red Sea. We know more about landing on the moon than entering the land of Israel. And we know more about the destruction of the Twin Towers than we do about the destruction of the two temples in Jerusalem. It all comes back to the argument that the rabbis made at the baal teshuva yeshiva I attended 20 years ago: We know so well the American side of our nature, but how much do we really know about the Jewish side? In Appendix A of this book, you will find a number of excellent, highly readable histories of Judaism. The net effect of reading these books is to understand where you come from as a Jew and where you fit into Jewish history.

There you have it: the six key areas worthy of further study. Please let this book be only a beginning. As hard as I've tried to present everything interesting and exciting, Judaism is just too big to fit in a publication like this. Turn with me now to the last chapter of the book, in which we will explore, after all this time, the basic question: "Is Judaism spiritual?"

Chapter 24

About the Sabbath

In This Chapter

- ◆ The many phases of the Sabbath
- ◆ Why Jews rest on the seventh day
- ◆ What work violates the Sabbath rules
- ◆ The joys of the Sabbath

One of the central mysteries surrounding Judaism is the question of its survival. The other religions and practices that existed thousands of years ago, when Judaism was first conceived, are pretty much relegated to the history books, while Judaism continues to the present day. How could this be? How could a people survive the destruction of its central place of worship—not once but twice—within a 700-year period? How could those people then go on to survive and thrive despite almost 2,000 years of dispersal?

Perhaps the main reason for Jewish survival is the concept of holiness in time as opposed to holiness in place. If a religion derives its sense of holiness, or apartness, from a particular location or structure, once that location or structure is destroyed, falls into enemy hands, or otherwise ceases to be meaningful to the lives of its practitioners, that religion is going to have a very hard time surviving. Judaism in large part survives because it is not dependent on a place for its practice. Virtually all of Judaism can be practiced anyplace on the globe, because Jews sense a holiness in time in their religion, not just a holiness of location.

Six Days Shalt Thou Work

In the Bible, God commands the Jews to work six days and rest on the seventh. This, according to the book of Genesis, is the pattern that God followed when creating the world. God created light, land, animals, trees, and finally people during the six-day period. Then on the seventh day, God rested. One of the keys to Jewish worship is the idea of the imitation of God, a concept in many religions.

Devine Devarim

Sabbath   the day of rest observed by Jews on Saturday, the seventh day of the week, as a reminder of how God rested on the seventh day after creating the world.

In Judaism, part of the idea of trying to imitate God involves character; just as God is loving, giving, sharing, creative, and forgiving, we are expected to be the same way. In Judaism, imitating God takes on an additional twist: We are expected to work for six days and take that seventh day off. That seventh day is the Sabbath, a word that derives from the Hebrew word for "seventh."

High Spirits

A neighborhood bar had a running bet based on the belief that one of the locals was the strongest man in town. The bartender offered $500 to anyone who could prove otherwise. One day a rather lanky man with wiry glasses walked in and wanted to take up the bartender on the bet. After he stopped laughing, the bartender called over the local strongman and handed him a lemon. The strongman squeezed the lemon until nothing was left but the twisted rind. "Now," said the bartender, "all you need to do is ring out one more drop and the $500 is yours." The lanky man took the lemon and—much to everyone's surprise—managed to squeeze out five more drops. As he handed the lanky man his winnings, the bartender said with wonder, "What are you? A weightlifter or something?"

"Nope," replied the man, grinning ear to ear. "Just the accountant for the yeshiva down the block."

The idea of holiness in time makes Judaism portable. You can keep the Sabbath in New York City, and you can keep it on Greenland. You can even keep it in the desert or at the polar icecap.

The Rhythm of Sabbath

In Judaism, Sabbath observance lends a special rhythm to the week. Everything is always building toward the next Sabbath or moving away from the previous one. In Hebrew, words like "Monday" and "Tuesday" do not exist. After all, these words are contractions of names of Norse gods or Roman emperors, and Judaism celebrates neither pagan gods like Thor, from which we get "Thursday," or the planet Saturn, from which we get "Saturday." In Hebrew, Sunday is simply known as *yom rishom*, or "first day" (of another new week). Monday is *yom sheni* ("second day"), Tuesday is *yom shlishi* ("third day"), and so on. The weekly Jewish calendar is always building toward the Jewish Sabbath, *yom ha-sh'vi'I*, the seventh day.

The Jewish Sabbath begins prior to sundown on Friday night with the lighting of candles. Traditionally, Jewish women, and unmarried Jewish men, light two candles to inaugurate the Sabbath, and some Jewish women light an additional candle for each child or grandchild they have. By the time the candles are lit, the house has been transformed. The Jewish home is cleaned, pretty much from top to bottom, as if anticipating a special guest. Indeed, the "Sabbath Queen" is the ultimate special guest who could possibly enter a Jewish home, according to tradition.

Enough food has been brought in so that it won't be necessary to go grocery shopping during the Sabbath. Among that food are the twisted loaves, or *challah* bread, and wine or grape juice. (We'll get into why those particular items are necessary for the Jewish Sabbath momentarily.) In some religiously observant Jewish homes, the lights have all been set on timers or they are simply left on throughout the holiday. This is because the Torah enjoins the practice of lighting (and by extension putting out) fires. Rabbis today have deduced that turning on a light creates an electric spark that is the equivalent of fire in biblical times. So whatever lights you want on during the Sabbath go on and stay on (unless they are on a timer) prior to candle lighting time.

> **Mystical Moments**
>
> In Medieval times, some Jews began hiring Gentiles to perform forbidden Sabbath tasks such as lighting fires. This practice became a subject of much debate. Some rabbis declared that the practice of hiring a Gentile was permissible, while others declared it was forbidden except in cases of extreme emergency. However, even the strictest of rabbis concede that it is a Talmudic, rather than Biblical, code that prohibits the practice.

> **Spiritual Citations**
>
> "Things are the saddle and ride us. Getting and spending, we lose our powers. Little that we own is ours."
>
> —William Wordsworth

In addition to the house being cleaned, everybody else gets clean as well. There is often a mad rush for a hot shower in the hour prior to the welcoming of the Sabbath. Everyone wants to be clean and dressed in his or her nicest clothing to welcome the Sabbath bride. That extra level of busyness prior to sunset adds to the sense of anticipation and excitement that comes every Friday afternoon in observant Jewish homes.

Taking Time for Spirit and Family

Why all this? Why the bread and wine, and all the cleaning up? We work hard. We work hard at school (at least we do at finals time). We work hard at our jobs. We work hard at just about anything we undertake. Today's world exists in an era of hard work, competition, and getting and spending. As a result, many of us have a very hard time taking any time off.

Many people who can afford vacations simply do not take them. They are too afraid to get away from the office for any length of time, lest others realize that they are not indispensable. We are so used to working that it is often hard to make ourselves stop, even for a short period of time.

The thing about life is that work is only one part of it, and perhaps a highly overrated part at that. As it's been said before, none of us lie on our deathbeds and say, "I sure wish I had spent more time at the office." Indeed, if we have any regrets, they often center around the fact that we spent so much time working that we missed out on the important stuff: watching our children grow up, taking time to smell the flowers, visiting national parks, and so on.

High Spirits
I used to be a lawyer, and not a very good one. I worked for a firm in Boston that had offices on five floors of an office tower. The firm library was located on a different floor from my office. The practice in that firm was not to leave work before seven thirty or eight at night. I found the work so dull that I would frequently leave at six. There's nothing worse than standing waiting for an elevator at six o'clock when one of the partners walks by and gives you a dirty look that says, "How come you're going home? Everybody else is staying."
I came up with a way to avoid the dirty looks, though. I started leaving my suit jacket and overcoat on another floor in the office of a friend, so when six o'clock rolled around, and I was either too tired or too bored to keep on working, I would grab a yellow pad and stand in the elevator bank, looking for all the world as if I were heading to another floor, perhaps to do research at the firm library or speak with one of the other lawyers at the firm. In actuality, I was going to pick up my suit jacket and coat on another floor and sneak out of the building.

This is where Judaism steps in and says, go ahead and work for six days—but on day seven, take the day off. Smell the roses. Hug your children. Look around the table at your family. Don't let the house go to hell, regardless of what it looks like the rest of the week. Make it beautiful. Make it clean.

We live our lives in such small increments of time. If you are an attorney, accountant, or other professional, it is entirely likely that you have to account for your professional time in increments of as small as five minutes. The concept of "face time" is familiar to countless people who work in offices. It's the idea that even if you aren't productive, you at least have to look busy, especially whenever the boss happens to walk by.

It's very rare in America to enjoy the kind of long, languorous meals that the Italians, French, and Spanish are famous for. Stateside, however, we hunch over desks, barely noticing the food we eat, in our desire to remain as productive as possible.

Taking Time Away from Things

It's so true—we spend so much time either working or shopping that our lives are ruled by things. Either we are earning money to pay for things, or we are out in the stores, buying things. Most people find their work is a means of earning a living and paying for a lifestyle. Few of us could honestly say, however, that they find much, if any, spiritual content in their work. So we have a problem of a society where people devote enormous amounts of time to something that, by and large, is not spiritually fulfilling.

Enter the Sabbath. No matter how important we think we are, no matter how important our work seems to be to us or to society, on Friday afternoon, Judaism asks us to quit. Stop thinking about it, talking about it. Stop checking our messages, reading our e-mail. Many observant Jews will not even read the newspaper—or at least the business section of a newspaper—on the Sabbath. The idea is to get away as completely as possible from everything to do with thoughts of the workweek. If we do stop thinking about work, what's left?

The answer: Ourselves. Our families. Our lives. Our purpose on Earth. Our relationship to God. These are the main themes of the Jewish Sabbath, and they can only come to the fore when we actively refrain from work.

> **Spiritual Citations**
>
> "The biblical concept of melacha applies to work involving the production, creation, or transformation of an object. One may spend the entire Sabbath opening and closing books until one drops with exhaustion and yet not violate the Sabbath. On the other hand, the mere striking of a match, just once, is a desecration of the Sabbath because it involves creation."
>
> —Rabbi Abraham Chill

Work Is a Four-Letter Word

In the time of the Bible, there was no e-mail, of course. There were no cars. There were no elevators. So how exactly do we get from the Torah a system of rules about work that can be applied to modern time?

You can compare the Torah to the U.S. Constitution. Back when the Constitution was written, more than two centuries ago, the fastest vehicle available didn't have 350 horsepower, as today. It had one horsepower, because it was ... a horse. And yet, from the U.S. Constitution are derived virtually all the principles that regulate modern life, from stoplights and speed limits to securities and criminal law.

Similarly, the Torah offers certain principles that define the nature of work, and for the past 3,000 years, these principles have guided Jews in their celebration of the Sabbath, no matter where on the globe they were, no matter how mechanized or rural their society might have been.

When you don't have the obligation of work hanging over your head, life is very different. You can relax, breathe deeply, and truly take time to be with the people you love. The human spirit, so often deadened by work that pays for our lives but doesn't add much to our joy of living, awakens. You can think of the Jewish Sabbath as a weekly, 25-hour (sunset Friday to sundown Saturday) vacation from all that is worldly, stultifying, and repetitive. Instead, we are given a day when the true focus is not on our work but on our souls.

Devine Devarim

neshamah yeterah the traditional belief that the soul magnifies on the Sabbath so as to maximize enjoyment and recognition of the spirituality inherent in the day. (lit.) "doubling of the soul."

In fact, on the Jewish Sabbath, we receive a *neshamah yeterah*, which can be translated as a "doubling of the soul." According to tradition, our soul actually magnifies on the Sabbath so as to maximize our enjoyment and recognition of the spirituality inherent in the day.

We've said in this chapter that traditional-minded Jews refrain from "work" on the Sabbath day. But what exactly do we mean by work and how do the rabbis decide what is work and what is not? Most of the restrictions about what a person can do on the Sabbath come from the Book of Exodus and the time when the Jews had just entered the desert.

Shortly after Mount Sinai, a tabernacle—or portable, prefab temple—was constructed. One third of the Book of Exodus describes in great detail exactly what materials were used and exactly how it was constructed. At each of the stops along the way in the desert, individuals would assemble and later disassemble this portable sanctuary, which would stand at the head of the camp. Whatever kind of work went into the building of the tabernacle is forbidden on the Sabbath day.

For example, the Jews had to write in order to create the plans for the tabernacle, as well as for other purposes. Thus religious Jews who observe the Sabbath do not do any writing on the Sabbath. Similarly, material was needed to be washed and sewn together in order to form some of the components of the tabernacle. Therefore, washing or bleaching a garment, sewing, tearing, knotting, and even untying knots are all forbidden on the Sabbath. Cooking is another category of forbidden Sabbath activities. Generally, hot food is served on the Sabbath, but it is prepared in advance and kept warm in an oven that has been turned on prior to the entrance of the Sabbath. One of the traditional Sabbath dishes among Jews of Eastern European descent is called *cholent*, which consists of beans, vegetables, and meat stewed together in a crock-pot for about 18 hours (or more) prior to enjoying it on Sabbath afternoon. Indeed, cholent is famous for inducing serious naps on the part of those who partake of it.

Another type of forbidden work is carrying from the inside to the outside, or from the outside to the inside. In theory, you could carry a table from the basement to the third floor of your house up and down all day long without ever violating the rules of Sabbath. (However, it certainly wouldn't be restful, so it would tend to violate the spirit of it.) Yet, if you took that same table and brought it from outside the house into your house, or vice versa, you would have violated the prohibition against carrying.

What is this all about?

In the desert, the Jews were concerned about how exactly they were going to eat. (I'd be concerned about the same thing—a couple of million people wandering around would surely get hungry from time to time!) The Torah tells of the *man* (usually pronounced "manna" when spoken of in English), delicious food that would descend from Heaven every day. According to the Torah, on Fridays, a double portion of manna would descend from Heaven, so Jews had no need to gather food on that seventh day. They had a double portion on Friday that would last them through the Sabbath.

The symbolism here is quite intense. By refraining from work—the equivalent of gathering money so that we can go buy food on the Sabbath, we are indicating our faith that God will take care of us if we just work those other six days. This is a cornerstone of Jewish belief: Just as God was able to create the universe in six days and rest on the seventh, so we need only work six days in order to provide for ourselves and our families.

How can we be sure that our needs will be taken care of even on that Sabbath day when we do not work? According to tradition, if we are willing to work those other six days (or five, whatever our schedule requires), God will take care of us the rest of the time. When we do not carry and follow all of the other Sabbath restrictions, we are actually demonstrating our great faith in God's ability to provide for us.

> **High Spirits**
>
> There is a Talmudic joke (yes, the rabbis make jokes in the Talmud!) that the mere fact that you can eat cholent on the Sabbath afternoon and still wake up from your nap is proof positive that God will be able to awaken the dead.

> **Spiritual Citations**
>
> "There is no great religious leader—from the Buddha to Moses to Jesus to Mohammed to Luther—who offered people what they want. Only what they need."
>
> —Neil Postman, *Shuffle Off to Bethlehem*

There are many ramifications of the decision not to carry. For example, among the things we're not carrying is money. Since we are not carrying money, we are not in stores. We are not at the movies. We are not at the ball game. Instead, we are with our loved ones, appreciating what we have instead of focusing on what we lack and think we need. I keep coming back to this point because everything in Sabbath observance comes back to this same key tenet of faith.

There are actually 39 different categories of *melacha*, or work prohibited on the Sabbath. All of these categories reflect the kind of work that was required in the construction and deconstruction of the tabernacle in the desert.

In our society, our wallets and purses seem to contain our entire identity (thus American Express's highly successful slogan "Don't leave home without it.") It feels very odd to go an entire 25 hours without even touching credit cards, a driver's license, library card, and one's AAA card, let alone money. It is a remarkable adjustment to go from carrying all these items the other six days and then putting them aside in a drawer and not even thinking about them or using them. On the Sabbath, the only thing we "spend" is a day away from the identity built around consumerism that occupies so much of our mental space during the rest of the week.

Devine Devarim

melacha work prohibited on the Sabbath; there are 39 categories of melacha.

Enjoying the Sabbath

Normally, when secular Jews think about the Sabbath, they see it in terms of restrictions that don't sound like a lot of fun. Religiously observant Jews do not drive on the Sabbath. They don't watch TV. They don't go to the movies. In today's world, they don't use their computers or go online. What fun is that? The answer is that these restrictions actually provide, paradoxically, a tremendous sense of freedom, even liberation.

In today's society, virtually everything that is open on Saturday is open on Sunday, so we're not missing out on that much. Granted, there are certain sporting events that take place on Saturdays, like college football, that cannot be replicated on a Sunday, but even college football games could be taped by a VCR and replayed on Saturday night.

But it's not entirely accurate to the concept of Sabbath to look at it simply in terms of restrictions. Paradoxically enough, the reward for accepting these limitations is a profound sense of freedom. Many people who become observant report that it is liberating not to have to answer the telephone, return e-mail, fight the weekend traffic to return videotapes or pick up groceries. They find that it is very gratifying to spend a day during which they can truly commune with their loved ones and with their souls as well.

High Spirits

During his days as a freshman Senator, Joseph Lieberman, the first Orthodox Jewish Senator in the United States, found himself in danger of violating the Sabbath. After working late in his office one Friday, he retired to the office gym to sleep on one of the mattresses. A short while later, in walked Senator Al Gore. After Lieberman explained his predicament, Gore offered the use of his parents' apartment, which was just across the street. He accompanied his fellow Congressman so that Lieberman would not have to turn on the lights.

Years later, Lieberman joked that he knew of no other Jew who could claim they'd had the privilege of having the Vice President of the United States as their Sabbath goy.

A Typical Sabbath Day

Let's take a look at how an actual Sabbath day is observed in today's world. As we said earlier, Friday afternoon is a time of preparation for the Sabbath. If it's in wintertime, people will make arrangements to leave their jobs early so that they can be home in order to prepare for the entrance of the Sabbath. The house is sparkling clean, the kids are clean, everybody's clothing is clean—and with that cleanliness comes a sense of anticipation and excitement.

On Friday evening, members of the family are likely to go to synagogue, where prayers welcoming the Sabbath Queen are offered. The theme of the prayers is enjoyment of rest. The prayers express gratitude to God, not just for creating the world and everything in it, but for specifically creating the Sabbath day itself, so that we have a chance to rest and reflect about who we are and want to be. Those prayers remind us that while the material side of life is important, the spiritual side is even more important.

After the service, people walk back to their homes, often with friends who are coming to join them for the Sabbath meal, or even with strangers they have met who need a place for the Friday night Sabbath dinner. It is a long-standing tradition in Jewish communities to match up visitors who need a place for Sabbath with families who have extra places at their table. Indeed, in many Jewish homes, families deliberately prepare more food than they will need, just in case they can have the privilege of a guest in their home for the Sabbath. It is such a great honor to have guests for the Sabbath that Jews often compete for the honor of bringing home guests.

Mystical Moments

The challah bread eaten on the Sabbath is symbolic of the loaves of bread that were brought in the Sanctuary in the times of the First and Second Temples. The salt that is placed on the challah prior to eating it is a reminder of the salt that was placed on the offerings that were brought on the altars of the Temples 2,000–3,000 years ago.

The family, guests perhaps in tow, return home to find a beautifully cooked meal awaiting them. Traditionally, the Sabbath meals are the biggest and best of the week. First of all, there is simply more time in order to enjoy them, but it is also a mitzvah to experience *oneg Shabbat*, the joy of the Sabbath. Frequently, people save the foods they like the best to be eaten on the Sabbath, and some religious Jews even speak the phrase, *"l'kaved Shabbat kodesh"*—"for the honor of the holy Sabbath"—just before they begin a new special dish.

The Sabbath meal commences with singing the song *Shalom Aleichem* (Hebrew for "Welcome"), which is sung to the angels that are said to accompany Jews home from shul on Friday night (see Chapter 21, "Do Jews Believe in Angels"). Parents give lessons to their children at this point in the festivities, and then husbands frequently sing a portion of the Book of Proverbs to their wives, a song that has become known as *Ayshet Chail*, "A Woman of Valor." I cannot describe how beautiful and moving it is for children to see a father sing a love song to their mother every Friday night of their lives. It gives children a sense of expectations about what marriage should be: that a couple should value, appreciate, and recognize each other's fine qualities on a constant basis.

That song sets the stage for an acknowledgment of the love that Jews have for their creator, which is enunciated in the Friday night *kiddush*, or blessing, that is spoken over the wine or grape juice. It should be noted that the wine or grape juice itself is not being blessed. Rather, the blessing indicates the gratitude that Jews have toward their creator for taking them out of Egypt, giving them the Torah, and, in this case, creating the Sabbath day and giving it to us as an extra special gift.

Devine Devarim

oneg Shabbat the joy of the Sabbath.

After everyone has had a sip or two of wine or grape juice, the next event is the *motzi*, the blessing that is spoken over bread. In Jewish law, the presence of bread indicates that we are actually sitting down to a real meal, as opposed to a snack. Traditional-minded Jews say a blessing any time during the week they eat bread. On the Sabbath, there is always a wonderful moment of anticipation when the entire table is silent except for the person making the blessing, and then cutting and distributing the delicious *challah*. Truly, this taste lets us know that "it's that very special time of the week again." It's not much of an exaggeration to say that participants in this ritual find themselves carried off to a spiritual place where thoughts of work, stress, money worries, and other such unpleasant real-world matters somehow completely disappear.

And then comes the meal itself. The courses, for it is generally a multi-course meal, are interspersed with songs that are sung in the Jewish tradition only on Friday night. In addition, one or more members of the table are likely to deliver a short discourse on the parsha, or Torah portion of the week. Children are deeply involved in this process as well. In most religious Jewish schools, children study the weekly Torah portion and come home with a *d'var Torah*, a short commentary on the portion, that they present to a hushed table.

Even children as young as four and five years old come home from school with comments to offer at the Sabbath table about the Torah portion. There is always respectful silence at the table and the child gets to command the attention of the entire family—as well as the guests—when delivering this brief explanation of that parsha. Children love this, because it gives them a sense of power and self-respect. It is a heady experience for a child of four to command the attention of so many grownups, and there is invariably applause and smiles for the child who offers a d'vat Torah. It's also a joyous experience for the parents, because they get to witness the continuity of Judaism extend into the next generation.

One of the main differences between religious Judaism and the secular world is that in Judaism children and adults share the same culture. In secular society, children and adolescents have their own music, television shows, movies—in short, they live in their own world. Chances are that if you are over 25, you have absolutely no idea of any top singers under the age of 25, unless one happens to appear in a Pepsi ad. Children have the greatest amount of disposable income of any age group in society. Therefore it is to the advantage of advertisers to create a separate "youth culture" on which young people can spend their allowances.

Mystical Moments

The prohibition against carrying applies even to such ordinary items as house keys. In order to get back in their homes, Jews often *wear* their keys (there is no rule against wearing) in order not to disobey the Sabbath law. The law also extends to carrying children, so many women are often stranded in their homes on the Sabbath because they are unable to carry their children outside of the home.

In recent years, local Jewish communities have come up with a further way to circumvent this law. *Eruvim* are areas set up as "private domains," in which Jewish law allows items to be carried (carried within, but not outside of). An eruv is often delineated by posts with wire across the top, enclosing a certain area of a neighborhood. In this way, more members of the local Jewish population are able to partake in the mitzvot of the Sabbath.

While children brought up in religious Jewish homes are aware of the youth culture, they're not quite so consumed by it. You might say that they are in it but not *of* it. Instead, because they have so much to share with adults—the Sabbath, other Jewish holidays, Torah study—there is much more of a sense of unity in families and much less of a sense of isolation. Also, respect for parents is much more prevalent in traditional Jewish circles than in American society, so many first-time visitors at Sabbath time are struck by how well-behaved the children are.

In the world of observant Judaism, parents and children share a common mission: the practice of halacha or Jewish law. This includes the celebration of the Sabbath, which brings families together with a shared purpose every week. This is one of the reasons why observant families do not suffer the sense of isolation and alienation that many children in secular society experience.

After all the words of Torah have been spoken, after the last dishes have been cleared away, after the last songs have been sung, there remains the grace after meals, which is recited or sung at the conclusion of the evening. On the Sabbath, there are several additions to the grace after meals, which is commonly known by the Yiddish term *benching* (actually a Yiddish variant of the Latin phrase *benedictus*, or blessing). The additions on the Sabbath day thank God for the relief and freedom that come along with the rest that one enjoys on the Sabbath, and also looks forward to the day that is "entirely Sabbath" that is, the time of the messiah and the new world the messiah will usher in.

> **High Spirits**
>
> The rabbi was telling his congregation about the next week's parsha, assigning "all 66 verses on the story of Lavon in Genesis chapter 33."
>
> The following week, he asked all in the congregation who had read all 66 verses. Virtually every hand went up. The rabbi smiled. "Genesis chapter 33 only has 53 verses. Now, this week's drash will be on the subject of lying ...."

What happens after the meal? It all depends on whether you are married! Sex, which is considered a healthy part of life in the Jewish tradition, is actually a commandment on the Sabbath for married couples! Judaism has never viewed sexuality as a shortcoming or failing, but rather a beautiful part of life to be enjoyed, within certain limits. In traditional Judaism, that limit is marriage. Judaism understands the enormous power of sex to bind people together, and in traditional Judaism there is little tolerance, if any, for sex outside of the marital relationship. The Jewish concept of sex could perhaps best be compared to fire: A controlled burn is one thing, but when it's out of control, a lot of damage can take place!

Sex notwithstanding, another obligation that traditional Jews undertake on the Sabbath is to review the Torah portion. Many Jews read the entire parsha along with the commentary of Rashi (see Chapter 1, "Defining Jewish Mysticism and Spirituality), the eleventh-century French commentator who, almost 1,000 years later, is still considered the most important expositor of the Torah. The act of reading the Torah portion—either with Rashi or, according to another tradition, twice in Hebrew and once in Aramaic—every Sabbath prepares the individual for the Torah reading that will take place on Saturday morning at the synagogue.

It's All Greek to Me

This is as good a time as any to make a pitch for learning Hebrew. Many Jews learned the Hebrew alphabet when they were children, but still look at Hebrew as a very difficult language to learn. That's really not true. Once you get past the alphabet barrier, you will discover Hebrew to be governed by a fairly small number of rules, which makes the language, if not easy to learn, then at least considerably easier than it may appear at first.

The benefits of learning Hebrew are numerous. The first is that you can truly understand what's going on during a synagogue or temple service. Before long, if you do study Hebrew, you will become so adept that all you will have to do is listen for a few moments to know exactly where they are in the service. Second, and more importantly, you'll understand exactly what they are talking about. It's a cliché that things get lost in the translation, but this is certainly true when it comes to biblical Hebrew and the Hebrew of prayers—simply no English translation can possibly do justice to its beauty, simplicity, and poetry. Until they come out with *The Complete Idiot's Guide to Biblical Hebrew*, you're going to have to take my word for it! Or better yet, find a class, either in your community or on the web, and add Hebrew to your skills. It's not as hard as it seems!

Spiritual Citations

"Anybody can observe the Sabbath, but making it holy surely takes the rest of the week."

Okay, you've been to services on Sabbath morning. You've heard the Torah read, and you've recited the prayers that relate specifically to the Sabbath day. One of those is the *mussaf amidha*, the "additional silent prayer." One of the paragraphs in that prayer is written with each word starting with a different letter of the Hebrew alphabet—going from the end of the alphabet to the front. That is, the first word begins with the Hebrew letter taf, the last letter of the Hebrew alphabet; the next word begins with shin, the next to last letter; and so on through the alphabet to aleph. The prayer is written in this manner because on the Sabbath we take an entirely backward look at our lives. The usual way we look at our lives is in terms of what we don't have, what we want, what we think we need. On the Sabbath, we look back at where we have come from and where we are. Instead of thinking about all the things that we don't have and might like, we focus instead on what we do have, and what we might not fully appreciate. When you think about it, there are very few ads on television that are trying to sell you on loving your child. There are plenty of ads that want to sell you stuff you can buy your child, but nobody makes any money when you give your child a hug and a kiss.

Because we don't watch TV on the Sabbath, we are removed from the world of advertisements, and therefore, we are removed from the sense of lack that advertisements seek to trigger in us. This said, now we are focusing on the joys of our life as it is right now. We are focused on our loved ones, our family, our home, our community, our religion, and our God. This is a reverse of the way we usually think; normally we think in terms of what we don't have. That prayer that comes along with the letters of the Hebrew alphabet in backward fashion reminds us of that reverse way of looking at the world that the Sabbath portends.

We come home from synagogue to another family meal, once again inaugurated with kiddush and motzi. Then comes the meal, with more singing, more *divrui Torah* (words of Torah spoken by everyone from little children to grandparents) and then comes the benching, or grace after meals. At this point comes a well-earned Sabbath nap for many people. Others choose to take a walk around the neighborhood, in a park, or some other scenic locale conducive to quiet thought and contemplation. The rabbis suggested that one visit a place of beauty on the Sabbath in order to remind oneself of the majesty of nature. Consider their forethought: The rabbis wrote this several thousand years before the advent of Dogbert-like cubicles and ergonomically threatening workstations.

Again, if it were not for the Sabbath, few of us would spend any part of Saturday walking around. This is especially true where I live, in Los Angeles, where it is practically against the law to be out walking. If it weren't for the Sabbath, we would mostly find ourselves back at the dry cleaners or the mall, getting and spending, instead of concentrating not on what we own but who we are.

There is a third brief synagogue service on the Sabbath (as on every day in the Jewish calendar); many Jews return to synagogue in the late afternoon for this service. It is usually preceded or followed by a talk from the rabbi, and then also a third meal. At this meal, once again, we have two twisted loaves of challah, but no wine or grape juice to start the meal. That's because we have already acknowledged the holiness of the day at the meal we enjoyed after morning synagogue services. In Jewish tradition, the great leader Moses was said to have died on a Sabbath afternoon. So as the Sabbath begins to wind down, there is a slightly more somber tone to it. The songs are slower, in a minor key, and without the raucous joyousness that marks many of the Friday night and Saturday afternoon songs. The sun is beginning to set, and there is a sense of loss as the lovely Sabbath bride prepares to make her departure.

Devine Devarim

havdalah   the "separation" ceremony performed to mark the passing of the Sabbath day.

Reentering the Weekday World

The Sabbath officially ends when three medium-sized stars are visible in the night sky. Since many of us live in cities where it is impossible to see all but the absolute brightest stars, we rely on astronomical charts written by rabbis who are competent in astrophysics. Those charts tell us when three medium-sized stars could be expected to be seen in the night sky over a given city. You can invariably find these times either on the Internet or in your local Jewish newspaper. After those stars appear and we are back in the weekday world, the synagogues and families alike make a brief and very lovely service called *havdalah*, or separation, in order to mark the passing of the Sabbath day.

In order to make havdalah, one needs a braided candle, by which we can see our hands to remind us of the fact that we are going back to work, if not tomorrow then the next day; some spices, in order to revive us, now that the *neshama yetaira* (that extra Sabbath soul) is leaving us; and a glass of wine or grape juice to commemorate the fact that the Sabbath is departing.

The last act of the havdalah ceremony, which lasts only a minute or two, consists of snuffing out the flame of the havdalah candle into the wine, signifying the end of the Sabbath. Some Jews have the custom of dipping their pinkie fingers into the wine and then rubbing a tiny bit of wine under their eyes, symbolic of tears for the end of the Sabbath and also for the fall of Jerusalem. Some Jews take that tradition a step further and put a tiny bit of wine on their pinkies and rub the inside of their front pockets, as a symbolic prayer for *parnassah* (income) for the weak.

While it is perfectly acceptable to go out to dinner on Saturday night—or to the movies, a ball game, or any other activity—sometimes the Sabbath experience is continued in the form of an after-Sabbath party called the *melave malke*, Hebrew for "escorting the Queen." The Sabbath Queen is on her way out of town and she won't be returning until next Friday night. So as to give her a proper send-off, Jews gather to have an additional celebration, perhaps with singing or Torah study. When a baby is born, it is a fairly common custom to have a melave malke in honor of the new child. Similarly, if an engagement is announced, a melave malke is a great way for the community to get together to celebrate. And so to bed, with the new week beginning the next morning, yom rishon, of the seven-day period culminating in the following Sabbath.

High Spirits
"Stand by your mensch." —Tammy Wynetsky

One of the most amazing aspects of the Sabbath is the way it levels all members of the community, rich and poor. For example, I remember visiting a synagogue for a Sabbath about 20 years ago. As is the case in many communities, there were several poor individuals who attended the afternoon service prior to the inauguration of the Sabbath, seeking a few coins from the rest of the service attendees. A few hours later, these same individuals were rather magically transformed—they had on their finest clothes and did not look at all like beggars. If you looked very closely at their suits, you might notice that they were a bit shiny or threadbare, but they looked *menschlich*—proper, well-groomed. (In Yiddish, a *mensch* is a "standup guy.") After the conclusion of the Sabbath, those individuals must have put their nice Sabbath clothing away, and were back in their ordinary clothing, seeking coins from the other synagogue-goers.

For six days a week they may have been beggars, but on the Sabbath, they were kings.

The Least You Need to Know

- ◆ Observing the Sabbath is part of emulating God in that you rest on the seventh day.
- ◆ In spite of its "restrictions," the Sabbath is a day or rejoicing, a weekly festive family occasion.
- ◆ Forbidden activities are defined as those that went into building the tabernacle used during the Exodus.
- ◆ Sabbath activities vary between Jewish sects, but all share the same joy and belief in love of family.

Chapter 25

Holiday In's and Out's

In This Chapter

- ◆ The origins of various Jewish holidays
- ◆ The most sacred holidays
- ◆ The most joyous days ... and the saddest
- ◆ Why holiday lengths may vary according to location

It's often said, only partially in jest, that the two most important American Jewish holidays are Passover and Thanksgiving. This is because most Jews in America celebrate the holidays that are "family affairs"—the events when entire families travel, often from great distances, to be together and celebrate. Passover and Thanksgiving fall about six months apart, so they offer a kind of punctuation to the calendar and ensure that families, however widely far-flung, are never separated for more than 26 weeks or so at a time.

The fact is that Judaism has a range of holidays that many Jews may have only vague childhood memories of, but not a great deal of specific information about what the holiday commemorates. In this chapter, we will explore the cycle of the Jewish year and see exactly what Jews celebrate, why, and how.

America's Holy Days?

In the United States, after Passover and Thanksgiving, the next two most important Jewish holidays are probably New Year's Eve and Halloween. This is not because either of these holidays has any Jewish content; but probably in terms of sheer numbers, no Jewish holiday attracts the same number of Jewish participants as do New Year's Eve and Halloween.

The origins of each of these two holidays is instructive. New Year's Eve has origins in Roman times. Two thousand years ago, in the days of ancient Rome, the calendar was not as advanced as it is today. At the end of every year, there were always a few days that somehow did not quite fit into the cycle. If something wasn't done to rectify the situation on a yearly basis, holidays would end up occurring at the wrong time of the year. Harvest holidays might migrate down the calendar into winter, winter solstice celebrations might take place in early spring, and so on. So each year, a certain number of days were added to the calendar, and during this time, no work was done. In fact, it was the equivalent of an ancient form of Mardi Gras—everybody got as blitzed as they could and stayed that way throughout those extra intercalative days.

The idea was that time itself emerged from a state of chaos. Romans would seek to recreate that chaos during those magical extra calendar days. They would party hard enough to create a sense of total disorder, and from that sense of disorder, the new year would emerge. This holiday, called *colendria* (the word from which we take the word calendar), is actually the origin of why people get drunk on New Year's Eve. When we get toasted on December 31, we are reenacting the creation of chaos that the Romans used in order to inaugurate their new year. So next New Year's Eve, don't forget to drink a toast to Caesar, Nero, and Claudius, because without them, we might all be sipping orange juice as the ball descends in Times Square.

Spiritual Citations

"I was thrown out of NYU my freshman year … for cheating on my metaphysics final. You know, I looked within the soul of the boy sitting next to me."
—Woody Allen

Devine Devarim

colendria the ancient Roman holiday that celebrates the days added to the year to maintain order in the calendar.

The origins of Halloween are similarly ancient, and also subject to considerable dispute. One school of thought has it that Halloween began as Samhain, a Druid or Celtic holiday that took place at the end of the fall planting season. This time of year, when the rhythms of life changed from the farming season into the winter season, was considered a time when the "wall" that separated this life from the world of the departed was at its thinnest. The ghosts of the dead were said to roam the countryside on Samhain, and could only be placated with gifts of food.

Practical jokes became a part of the holiday as well, and these are the origins of our tricking and treating on Halloween. During the Middle Ages, the Catholic Church sought to eliminate pagan influences, and so created a holiday called All Saints' Day on the first of November. The evening before All Saints' Day was called All Hallows Eve, or, simply put, Halloween. Thus the controversial nature of Halloween in certain Christian quarters today.

I mention these holidays simply to indicate that there is often a long and fascinating story behind why we do the things we do on a given holiday—things that we often take for granted as practices or behaviors related to that holiday. Jews, with their great respect for and fascination with history, are far more likely to guard, study, and teach the traditions related to Jewish holidays than are most secular individuals. In fact, today, in secular America, virtually every holiday, whether it marks a military event, such as Memorial Day or Veteran's Day, or whether it celebrates a president's birthday, is simply an excuse for not going to work and having a sale. In other words, much of the meaning and joy has been drained from America's holidays and they have become trivialized by the commercial nature of our society. In Judaism, that hasn't happened, and it most likely never will. Why is that? Let's turn to the calendar of Jewish holidays and discover why and how they are celebrated—and why they are not likely to be watered down as have so many of the holidays on the secular calendar.

> **Spiritual Citations**
>
> A clubwoman once said proudly to a visiting rabbi, "One of my relatives signed the Declaration of Independence." The rabbi coolly replied, "And one of my relatives signed the Ten Commandments."
>
> —Catherine Ponder, The Millionaire Moses

The Month of Elul

In many ways, the cycle of the Jewish year can be said to commence in the Hebrew month Elul, which usually corresponds with late August and early to mid-September. During this period, Jews begin the process of reflection about their lives, character, and families as a prelude to the high holidays of Rosh Hashanah, the Jewish New Year, and Yom Kippur, the Day of Atonement.

The Hebrew letters that make up the word Elul form an acronym that is said to stand for *ani l'dodi v'dodi li*—"I am my beloved's." Elul is seen as a time when God is closest to us. This is certainly a metaphorical understanding, as God is just as close to us throughout the rest of the year. Yet there is a special sense of awareness of our spiritual side during this time, when Jews are enjoined to reflect upon their deeds and think about what sort of person they want to be in the coming year.

New Year's resolutions are actually a Jewish thing! During the month of Elul, Jews resolve to make changes in their behaviors and attitudes and improve as a person during the coming year. The resolutions we make during the month of Elul come into play with great importance during the high holidays, when we reflect on them and decide how best to implement those changes.

Devine Devarim

shofar the ram's horn that is blown during religious services.

Mystical Moments

Many lives were saved during the September 11, 2001, attack on the World Trade Center due to when it occurred. Jews who ordinarily would have been at their desks early that morning were detained for an hour or two due to their attendance at selichot services.

Every weekday morning during the month of Elul, the *shofar*, or ram's horn, is blown during religious services. It is just blown once, and the effect is like an alarm clock for the soul: It awakens us to the great moral responsibilities we carry as members of the Jewish people.

Another feature of the month of Elul are the late-night services called *selichot*, or prayers for forgiveness. In modern Hebrew, the word for "Excuse me!" is selicha. *Selichot*, the plural of that term, is, in effect, our opportunity to ask God to excuse us for the sins, errors, and shortcomings of the previous year. When I say late night, I mean late night—selichot services generally take place after midnight. They serve a secondary function of offering a social opportunity to the community. It's kind of fun to see all your friends that late on the weekend.

Selichot services intensify in the days prior to Rosh Hashanah. They take place in the morning at the conclusion of regular morning services and, in some synagogues, can last an extra hour or two.

Rosh Hashanah

The Jewish New Year takes place on the first two days of the Hebrew month of Tishrei. The occasion is a solemn one. According to Jewish tradition, God decides the fate for the coming year for every individual on the first night of Rosh Hashanah. The holiday is famous for the many blowings of the shofar. The different lengths of the shofar blasts all have deep symbolic meanings. For example, one of the types of blasts is said to sound like a mother crying for her lost children. The order and number of shofar blasts on Rosh Hashanah is prescribed in the Torah, and the gematria for the number of blasts spells out the Hebrew words meaning, "Uproot Satan!"

The dinner table for Rosh Hashanah meals is famous for a wide variety of symbolic foods. The challahs are round, to indicate the cycle of the year. Instead of salt, we traditionally dip the challah, as well as apples, in honey, that we may have a sweet year. Some traditions include placing a fish head on the table, so that we should be the head and not the tail.

Also, the fish is said to symbolize God, who never sleeps, just as a fish never sleeps. At Rosh Hashanah, we do not serve nuts, because the Hebrew word for nuts has the gematria for "sin."

The key theme of Rosh Hashanah is the idea of God as king or ruler. According to one opinion in the Talmud, Rosh Hashanah is the day on which the world was created, and the Rosh Hashanah prayers frequently say, "Today is the birthday of the world." In other words, Rosh Hashanah is considered God's "inauguration day." The two-day festival is in large part to remind Jews that God is the ultimate ruler.

There is a special greeting on the first night of Rosh Hashanah, which is familiar even to many secular Jews: *Leshana tova tikatevu tech atmu*, "May you be inscribed and sealed for a good year!" Technically, we only wish each other this greeting on the first night of Rosh Hashanah. It is said that the judgments for the righteous are inscribed on Rosh Hashanah night, while those people who are average or even wicked have to wait until the next day in order to receive their judgment. As such, greeting someone in this way after the first night of Rosh Hashanah would imply that he or she is either average or evil and not totally righteous.

Devine Devarim

teshuva   repentance.
(lit. "turning")
tefilah   prayer.
tzedekah   charitable donations.

The Talmud suggests that we are not be sure of ourselves—even until the day of our death. Therefore, we never assume on Rosh Hashanah that we have been judged entirely favorably. Instead, we like to prepare ourselves for less pleasant possibilities as we take stock of the year we have just concluded. Where were we lax? Where did we fall down in our commitments to Judaism, our families, our work, and each other? What shortcomings of ours evidenced themselves in the preceding 12 months? Since we have the humility to recognize that we were not perfect, we try not to assume that we are automatically judged for a completely successful year right off the bat.

Instead, Jews undertake three specific tools in order to ensure a positive inscription in the Book of Life for the coming year. These are *teshuva*, or repentance; *tefilah*, or prayer; and *tzedekah*, for charitable donations.

Teshuva: Turning Toward the Light

Teshuva is at the heart of Judaism. It literally means "turning." The idea is that we are able to turn from activities and behaviors that are not wholesome and instead turn toward the light—toward God and a spiritual way of life. In Judaism, a person who changes his or her ways is known as a *baal teshuva*, an individual who has forsaken evil and error in order to live in keeping with God's path.

There is no sense in Judaism that a person is eternally banned because of wrong choices that he or she has made (with the exception of truly heavy sins such as idolatry or heinous crimes). Even in many such cases, according to even the strictest interpretation of Jewish law, there is still a place in *gan eden*—the world to come—for such wrongdoers. But God is patient and waits even until the day of a person's death to determine what kind of person he or she has been. According to the Talmud, "everything depends on the conclusion." In other words, it is understood that human beings are works in progress, and that until our lives are complete, we cannot truly be judged.

Mystical Moments _____

Yes, there is a Satan in Judaism, but he is not a devil with a pitchfork. Instead, the word "Satan" comes from the Greek word meaning "accuser." When it comes time for each of us to be judged, according to Jewish tradition, a Satan will stand at one side, listing all our evil deeds, while a good angel stands at the other side, enumerating everything that we did right. Our hope is that on Rosh Hashanah Satan will be uprooted and we will be blessed with a good and healthy new year.

So, on Rosh Hashanah, we receive what could be called an interim report card on our lives, and we do our best, if we think that we may not be getting the grades we want, to return to God's ways in order to improve the judgment that we have merited.

Tefilah: Talking to God

The second avenue open to improve our inscription for the new year is tefilah, or prayer. To put it as simply as possible, prayer means talking to God. The Hebrew word tefilah, as we have said elsewhere, is related to the verb meaning "to attach." So prayer is, in some sense, attaching one's self to God. Another word for prayer, *l'hitpalel*, implies the idea of memory. So when we pray, we are reminding ourselves of what is most important in life. It is said that whatever we think most about is our God. So Rosh Hashanah is a time when we can return our thoughts to the real God, and not the false gods of materialism, money, and whatnot that we chase during the rest of the year.

Spiritual Citations ____

"I once wanted to become an atheist but I gave up. They have no holidays."

—Henny Youngman

Tzedakah: Charity and Righteousness

The third option during the high holidays is tzedakah, or charitable giving. Jews are taught from a very early age that tzedakah does not mean charity; rather it means righteousness. We give because it is simply the right thing to do. As such, Jews tend to up their charitable giving during the high holidays. This often leads to discomfort on the part of Jews who attend synagogue only during this time of the year because the high holidays are also the high fund-raising days. It's very expensive to run a synagogue, and the only chance that rabbis and temple presidents have to address the entire congregation is this one time of the year. This leads to the sometimes-unpleasant phenomenon of people coming in to pray only to find that they have to sit through an appeal. Yes, it's true—money and spirituality sometimes co-exist uneasily. And yet there is certainly a place for money within the realm of the spirit.

God created the world; God therefore knows that life is very expensive. According to Judaism, God wants us to be happy, and God knows that this sometimes requires a buck or two. Although it's true that "when we're happy within, we can be happy without," life is a lot happier when we are able to meet our obligations and perform some kind deeds for both our loved ones and ourselves. The idea exists strongly in Judaism that the more we give—financially and of ourselves—to God, the religious institutions that serve us, and other charitable organizations, the more that will flow back to us.

Yom Kippur

The most powerful day of the Jewish calendar is Yom Kippur. Although technically the weekly Sabbath is in some sense more powerful and important in Jewish life, there really is no day like Yom Kippur, the day of prayer par excellence on the Jewish calendar.

High Spirits

One Yom Kippur, a rabbi decided that he couldn't take missing his regular golf game and so sneaked off to play a round. An angel happened to spot the rabbi and went back to inform his superiors of the sin being committed. On the fifth hole, God took a deep breath and blew the rabbi's ball straight into the cup for a nearly impossible hole in one.

"You call that punishment?" the angel asked.

God shrugged. "Sure. Who can he tell?"

On Yom Kippur, we live the way the angels live: We refrain from eating, drinking, marital relations—we even refrain from wearing leather shoes. The written Torah tells us that we are to "afflict our souls" on Yom Kippur and the Oral Torah, as encapsulated in the Talmud, explains exactly how to do that: Just as the angels neither eat nor drink nor make love, neither do we. And although Elvis Costello might have sung that the angels want to wear his red shoes, in Judaism, angels go barefoot. Wearing leather shoes and even sleeping with a pillow are signs of comfort. On Yom Kippur, we eschew physical comforts in order to bring home to ourselves the power and importance of the day.

Yom Kippur is important in the Jewish calendar because it is the last chance to affect the decree that has been brought down in our names on Rosh Hashanah. Yom Kippur is, spiritually, the "last house on the block" for the Jew. On Yom Kippur, we spend the entire day in synagogue praying, learning, and above all, reflecting on the kind of lives we have led and the kind of lives we want to lead.

One of the most spiritually powerful aspects of Yom Kippur is that all the sins that are enumerated in the prayers are written in the plural. The idea behind this is that, as a community, we are responsible for each other's actions; as such, we share on a communal level the rewards and punishments for the way we live. According to the Talmud, if we live in unspiritual times, evil is dispersed almost randomly, and bad things happen to good people. Conversely, if a generation is righteous, then the entire world benefits from that higher level of righteousness. On Yom Kippur, we even wear white to symbolize the purity that we aspire to.

The day itself is one where we can completely give ourselves over to the spiritual, without any thought of material concerns. As on the Sabbath, we do not use money. We are not in the kitchen. We are not at work. We are not even at the gym. Instead, we are communing with our spirit and with God, striving to remind ourselves of the specialness of our responsibilities as human beings and deciding how best to fulfill those obligations in the coming year.

The final prayer service on Yom Kippur is called a *ne'ilah*. During this service, we typically remain standing for the entire hour or so that it takes to present it. The Hebrew word ne'ilah implies the closing of the gates, our last chance to get in a few words with God before the decree is finalized. Somehow, Jews who have been fasting all day long get a second wind right here, and try to end the fast on a very high note.

Devine Devarim

ne'ilah   the final prayer service on Yom Kippur.

The great rabbi Chafetz Chaim taught that instead of striking our hearts at the mention of each sin, as is the practice on Yom Kippur, our hearts instead should strike us.

Sukkot

Five days after the conclusion of Yom Kippur comes the joyous festival of Sukkot, a word that literally means "tabernacles" or "booths." It is likely that Sukkot was a harvest holiday that was combined with a concept of rejoicing over the fact that our prayers had been accepted and that we had been granted a good decree for the coming year. Some of the symbols of Sukkot that are well-known to Jews include, of course, the booth itself in which Jews are commanded by the Torah to dwell in the seven or eight days of the festival. These pre-fabricated small booths are set up in the backyards of homes, on the roofs of apartment buildings, and behind restaurants so that Jews may eat, drink, be merry, and even sleep in them during the holiday. The booths are typically decorated with leafy material, such as palm fronds or other greenery, on the roof. The Talmud requires that we be able to see through the roof to the stars above during the nights of Sukkot, so the booth cannot be completely covered over.

The spiritual significance of the booth is twofold. First, it reminds us that the Jews traveled in tents or booths while they were wandering in the desert during the 40 years after their escape from Egypt. Second, the very flimsiness of the booths reminds us of our reliance on God. When we are sitting in our houses or apartments, which are solidly built (or so we hope), we don't think quite so much about relying on God for our safety and security. Instead, we have deadbolt locks, alarm systems, perhaps a superintendent or elevator man to let us know who is coming up to see us. But when we eat in the *sukkah*, we are reminded of the fact that we are protected in life not by four walls but by our Creator.

The other most commonly known symbol of Sukkot is called the *arba minim*, the four species that are held in the hands each day of the festival (except, of course, for the Sabbath, when carrying is forbidden). The commandment for these four species comes from the Book of Leviticus, chapter 23: "And you shall take for yourself on the first day [of Sukkot] the fruit of the hadar tree and branches of palm trees, and the boa of the tree 'avot' and willows of the book, and you shall rejoice before the Lord your God for seven days."

Devine Devarim

sukkah the booth in which Jews are commanded by the Torah to dwell in during the seven or eight days of the festival of Sukkot.

While we are not entirely sure what is meant by the *hadar* or *avot* trees, we interpret this commandment to mean that we hold a citrus fruit called the *etrog*, which looks like a large lemon, along with three types of greens, and we shake them in all directions—east, west, north, south, up, and down. We are thus spiritually symbolizing the dominion of God over the entire world, all the directions, as well as heaven above and the earth below. It is a mitzvah to buy the nicest etrog that one can afford, and in the days prior to Sukkot you can find Jews poring over displays of etrogin, trying to find the perfect one for their Sukkot experience.

Another fascinating aspect of Sukkot is the *ushpizin*, the royal guests. It is a belief that Abraham, Isaac, Jacob, Moses, the brother of Aaron (Moses' brother), Joseph, and David all come to visit the Sukkot on a specific night of the holiday. Many Jews place simple pictures of the ushpizin in the Sukkot, and say special statements of welcome to them on their given night. This is the equivalent of the visit of Elijah, which is far better known, to the Passover Seder table.

Sukkot is one of three festivals called in Hebrew the *regalin*. This word for festival is related to the Hebrew word for—of all things—"foot." That's because at each of these festivals—Sukkot, Passover, and Shavuot (described below)—all Jews in the land of Israel while the temple stood were expected to travel to Jerusalem, by foot, most likely, to celebrate as an entire nation. It is said that the roads to Jerusalem were never marked with signs indicating "Welcome to Jerusalem." The purpose of omitting such signs was to cause people to actually speak to each other and ask, "Is this the way to Jerusalem?" This way, Jews from all over the nation got to know each other on the way to the greater festivities.

> **Spiritual Citations**
>
> "In the history of old Jewish literature there was never any basic difference between the poet and the prophet. Our ancient poetry often became law and a way of life."
>
> —Isaac Bashevis Singer

At the Simchat Torah

Simchat Torah literally means the "rejoicing of the law." At the conclusion of the Sukkot festival comes this joyous holiday, which is marked by parading around the temple or synagogue, and even outside in the street, with Torah scrolls, getting drunk, and reading the last few lines from the Book of Deuteronomy and the first lines from the Book of Genesis. This is the time of year when the annual cyclical reading of the Torah is completed, and then immediately begun anew.

Yes, getting drunk really is a part of this festivity. This is one of the times in the year (Purim is the other) when you will actually see alcohol carts pushed through the synagogue. Simchat Torah is a chance for the rabbis to cut loose, dance on the table, and shed some of their inhibitions. The holiday is also a wonderful tradition for families, as parents join with children dancing with the Torah, celebrating the continuity of the Jewish faith.

Hanukah

One of the most popular of the Jewish holidays, the eight-day festival of Hanukah celebrates the rededication of the Temple by the priestly Jewish family of the Hasmoneans, who took the temple back from the Greeks.

The Hanukah story is a favorite with Jewish children. When the Greeks took over the Temple, they defiled all of the oil except for one container. When the Maccabees, led by the famous Judah Maccabee, came and retook the Temple, only that one vial of pure oil could be found. Miraculously, that one vial of oil lasted not for just one night but for eight nights, until more purified oil could be created by pressing olives.

Hanukah, despite its prevalence in American culture, is actually a relatively minor holiday in the Jewish experience. There was never a tradition of gift giving—until a generation or two ago, children would receive only a few coins. Its proximity to Christmas naturally led Hanukah to become a time of gift exchange. Lighting the menorah, or Hanukah candelabra, is a special mitzvah to publicize the miracle of Hanukah by lighting our candles in such a way that they can be seen from the street.

High Spirits

An aerospace engineer was having a hard time with his latest design. Each time he thought he had a final product, the wings would fall off the plane. Frustrated beyond belief, he went to his rabbi to vent his frustration. To his surprise, the rabbi not only offered consolation, he offered design advice. "Just put a bunch of holes right there above the wing," he told the engineer.

At wit's end, the engineer did as the rabbi told him. Sure enough, the plane held together and flew better than expected. The engineer returned to the rabbi and asked how he knew the solution.

"Ah, was simple!" replied the rabbi. "All those Passover suppers and never once has the matzoh broken on the perforation!"

Purim

Another favorite with children, the holiday of Purim celebrates the survival of Jewish people during the time of Haman the Wicked, who sought our destruction. Children and adults alike love to obliterate the name of Haman with noisemakers whenever his name is read.

There are four main commandments tied to the observance of Purim. The first is the reading of the *Megillah*, the Hebrew Book of Esther. Megillah literally means "rolled-up document," because in ancient times a notice from the king or any other important document was not bound in a book but instead was rolled into a scroll. The Hebrew root of the word Megillah is *gal*, meaning "wave." Just as the waves roll down to the beach, so similarly a scroll consists of a long rolled-up sheet of papyrus.

The second main component of Purim is a festive family meal, during which the children often dress in Purim-related costumes. The third aspect of Purim is the sending of gifts, usually different kinds of foods, to friends. The fourth aspect is giving gifts to the poor.

Devine Devarim

Megillah the Hebrew Book of Esther, read during the holiday of Purim. (lit.) "rolled-up document."

Mystical Moments

Jews celebrated happy events in ancient times by bringing each other gifts and also giving gifts to the poor. That's a very good model for the way that we should celebrate happy events today.

Passover

Perhaps the Jewish holiday that needs the least introduction and yet commands the most explanation, is Passover, or *Pesach* in Hebrew. This most well-known of holidays celebrates the freedom of the Jews from Egypt and the beginning of our peoplehood in the desert. The main focus of Passover, of course, is the Seder meal, at which the entire family gathers and retells the story of the exodus from Egypt. Many people will be surprised to learn that the name of Moses nowhere appears in the Haggadah, the traditional script from which the Passover story is told at the Seder table. The idea in Judaism is that we do not idolize individuals—we give credit to God, who works through individuals in order to accomplish desired ends.

In the haste to leave Egypt, Moses and the Jewish people did not have enough time to complete the baking of bread, so the thin, unleavened matzoh is used instead. According to Jewish law, one is not to eat matzoh during the 30 days prior to Passover, in order that it should have a special taste when it is eaten during the holiday. The dietary laws of Passover are the most stringent throughout the year, as observant Jews seek to avoid eating any type of food that might have had any contact with a leavening agent.

Ashkenazim, Jews of Eastern European origins, also avoid *kitniyot* (legumes), which were traditionally packed in starch as a preservative. Ashkenazim will not eat peanuts or beans, while Sephardic Jews—those of Spanish, Middle Eastern, or North African backgrounds—have no such dietary restrictions on those foods.

On the Seder table we set three matzot, which are used during the ceremony. We also display a Seder plate with special Passover foods. These include a roasted shankbone, memorializing the paschal lamb that was offered at the great Temple in Jerusalem; bitter herbs, which symbolize the tears the Jews shed at their forced labor in Egypt; and charoset, a mixture of nuts and wine that symbolizes the bricks the Jews made with which to build the storehouses of Pharoah.

Traditionally, Jews recline on pillows during the Passover Seder, as did royalty in ancient days. The four cups of wine are an important aspect of the Passover Seder. They symbolize the four moments in the Bible in which God promised to redeem the Jews from bondage in Egypt. It is also a tradition in many families that people pour each other's wine or grape juice prior to the drinking of the four glasses. Just as free people have servants to serve them, so we serve each other as a symbol of our own individual freedom.

Devine Devarim

Seder the traditional Passover dinner and customs surrounding it. (lit.) "order."

Haggadah the traditional script from which the Passover story is told at the Seder table.

One of the favorite traditions of children at Passover time is the hiding and finding of the *afikomen*, half of the middle piece of matzoh that is broken at the outset of the Seder. Children always marvel at the ability of adults to sneak the afikomen away from the table, and parents always delight in watching the children try to find that piece of matzoh, which the children ransom for a specific sum of cash to be paid after the holiday.

There are at least two possible derivations, both Greek, for the word afikomen. One possibility is *epikomos*, which is ancient Greek for "after the meal" or "dessert." Another possible explanation is that afikomen is the ancient Greek word for "I have found it!" Perhaps when Jews lived in areas dominated by Greeks, a child would yell out, "Afikomen!" or "I have found the matzoh!" upon discovering the hiding place of that highly coveted piece of unleavened bread.

Sefirat Haomer

The 49 days between the festivals of Passover and Shavuot (to be described below) are called the Sefirat Haomer, Sefirat meaning, "counting" and Omer being a measure of wheat. Wheat was certainly a primary agricultural product in the time of ancient Israel, and the agrarian-based Jews would count seven weeks, or 49 days, before the first fruit of their growing season were usable. This 49-day period between the two holidays is pregnant with spiritual meaning. Each night, Jews count out loud what number of the Omer it is: "Today is the tenth day, which is one week and three days of the Omer." During this time, Jews are symbolically counting the days between the exodus from Egypt (celebrated at Passover) and the giving of the Torah, which is said to have happened on Mount Sinai at Shavuot time. Just as we count the days toward a vacation or other exciting upcoming experience, so Jews count the days toward the giving of the Torah out of a sense of mounting excitement.

According to the Kabbalah, each of the 49 days has a separate spiritual significance, and different divine emanations reach the world on each of those 49 days. Any traditional Jewish prayer book will list the special spiritual significance for each day of the Omer. The rules of counting them are quite strict—one is allowed to make a blessing prior to counting the Omer. However, if one forgets to make the blessing (and does not make it up by counting the Omer without a date during daytime the next day), one can no longer recite the blessing prior to counting. Because of this, Jews actually keep special counting devices in their homes to remind them to count the Omer each day.

The first 34 days of the counting of the Omer have additional and quite sad significance. According to

> **Spiritual Citations**
>
> "One of life's gifts is that each of us, no matter how tired and downtrodden, finds reasons for thankfulness: for the crops carried in from the fields and the grapes from the vineyard."
>
> —J. Robert Moskin

the Talmud, literally thousands of pairs of Jewish scholars died during this time. As a result, the first 34 days of the Omer are considered in some ways a period of mourning. Weddings do not take place during this time in traditional Jewish communities. Many male Jews will not even get haircuts or shave their beards. These restrictions are lifted on the thirty-fifth day of the Omer, known as *Lag Ba'Omer* (*lag* is the Hebrew equivalent of the number 35). On this day, weddings take place, people get their hair cut, and children go to the park to shoot bows and arrows, weapons that symbolize the time in the first century C.E. when Jews were not allowed to study Torah.

During this time, the rabbis would take children into the forest, away from the watchful eye of the Roman government then occupying the land of Israel. The rabbis would teach Torah to the children, and if Roman troops came into the area, the children would pick up their bows and arrows and pretend to be simply out for an afternoon of fun in the woods.

Devine Devarim

Lag Ba'omer the thirty-fifth day of the Omer, on which mourning and other restrictions are lifted.

For some Jews, the restrictions about weddings, haircuts, and other nonmourning related events conclude on Lag Ba'Omer; for others, those restrictions resume on the day after Lag Ba'Omer and continue until the festival of Shavuot.

Shavuot

Shavuot, Hebrew for "weeks," takes place on the sixth and seventh days of the Hebrew month of Nisan, seven weeks to the day after Passover. Shavuot may have been initially a harvest holiday; it is married in Jewish tradition to the anniversary of the giving of the Torah by God at Mount Sinai. On Shavuot, many Jews stay up all night studying Torah, attending lectures, and preparing themselves spiritually so as to reenact the receiving of the Torah the next morning. For those Jews who stay up all night, morning prayer services take place (and at a brisk pace) at dawn, culminating in the reading of the Ten Commandments and the related material from the Book of Exodus in the Torah. Shavuot lasts for two days in the Diaspora—that is to say, in countries outside the land of Israel, where it is a one-day holiday.

Jews often wonder why some holidays last longer outside of Israel than they do within. The reason for this has to do with the calendar. In ancient times, the only way a new month could be declared would be upon the testimony of witnesses that they had seen a new moon in the sky. Once that testimony had been given and verified at the court in Jerusalem, signal fires would go out at the tops of hills across the land of Israel to let everyone know that a new month had been declared. Outside the land of Israel, it would be impossible to get news of when those signal fires had been lit or seen.

So for that reason, just to be safe, certain holidays were celebrated over two days instead of one so as to cover all the bases. If a new moon had been declared at the earliest possible time, then the actual holiday would take place on the first of the two days celebrated in the Diaspora. If the new moon did not appear, then the holiday would begin a day later. Even after the great Rabbi Hillel II set the entire Jewish calendar centuries ago, Jews outside the land of Israel continued to keep the custom of celebrating multiple days of certain holidays (Passover, Shavuot, and Sukkot, in particular) so as to keep alive a tradition of the ancestors. Reform and Conservative Judaism, in the land of Israel and everywhere else, celebrate one day at the beginning of each of these holidays, not two.

Sometimes people ask why, if these other holidays are kept over two days, Yom Kippur is only kept over one day. Well, it's just too hard to fast for two straight days.

Spiritual Citations

"It's so simple to be wise. Just think of something stupid to say and then don't say it."

The Fast of the Seventeenth of Tammuz

This sunup-to-sundown fast usually falls in early to mid-July. It commemorates the day upon which the Romans began their siege of Jerusalem in the year 70 C.E., which culminated in the destruction of the Second Temple on the ninth day of the Hebrew month of Ohg. The seventeenth day of Tammuz begins a somber period in the Jewish calendar called the "Three Weeks." During this time, many Jews refrain from activities that are joyous in nature. Many refrain from listening to music, attending movies or concerts, or swimming.

During the last nine days of the three-week period, the restrictions become even more stringent, as the Jewish people begin a period of mourning for the destruction of the Temple that took place more than 1,900 years ago. Weddings do not take place during the nine days, and just as in a house of mourning, traditional-minded Jews even refrain from doing the wash during this period. It is truly a time of sad reflection on the loss of the Second Temple, and of all the other tragedies that have befallen the Jewish people on the ninth of Ohg.

Tisha B'Av

Tisha B'av, Hebrew for "the ninth day of the Hebrew month of Av," is, at this point in history, the saddest day of the Jewish year. On the ninth of Av, according to tradition, both the First and Second Temples were destroyed. Many other horrors and disasters have befallen the Jewish people on that day, including the expulsion of Jews from Spain in

1492, and many other anti-Jewish decrees, massacres, and pogroms. The ninth of Av is marked by a Yom Kippur-like 25-hour fast, from shortly before sundown until almost an hour after sunset the following night.

At services during this holiday, Jews sit on the floor or on low chairs, as they would in a house of mourning, and listen to the doleful melody of the recitation of the Book of Lamentations. The prophet Jeremiah wrote Lamentations to describe the horror and sadness that he experienced upon witnessing the Babylonians' destruction of Jerusalem and the First Temple 2,500 years ago. In addition, many other *piyyutim*—poems of sadness written over the last thousand or more years—are read in synagogue, both on the evening of Tisha B'Av and the following morning of the holiday as well. Those who can avoid it do not go to work that day; those who must go to work do so after they have been to morning services where they hear the Book of Lamentations and piyyutim for the second time. This is also a day for recollecting losses the Jews have suffered during the Holocaust and at other tragic moments in our history.

According to tradition, the Messiah will be born on the ninth of Av, thus transforming it from a day of mourning to a day of the greatest possible joy.

Devine Devarim

piyyutim poems of sadness written over the last thousand or more years

High Spirits

An Israeli Jew was driving through Israel when he came to a red light. He sat patiently and waited, but the Jewish driver behind him kept honking impatiently until finally he drove around him and straight through the light. The first Jew shook his head. "Two thousand years he's been waiting for the Messiah and he can't even wait for a red light!"

Tu B'Av

Tu is the Hebrew way of expressing the number 15; thus Tu B'Av is the fifteenth day of the month Av. To counterbalance all the sadness we have just experienced from the seventeenth day of Tammuz through the three weeks and Tisha B'av itself, we now have the joyous holiday of the fifteenth day of Av.

The focus of this holiday is on women and marriage, and it is said that unmarried Jewish women would traditionally all go out to the vineyard, wearing borrowed white clothing. The white symbolized purity, and the clothing was borrowed so that poor young women would not be ashamed of the fact that they did not come from families of great means. Everyone dressed equally beautifully on that day. Unmarried men would go to the vineyards to choose a wife. They would be advised to choose wisely, not looking only at physical beauty but also looking at inner beauty so as to choose the best possible spouse with whom to "go the distance." It is said that anyone who has not seen the celebration of the fifteenth of Av does not know what true joy is all about.

Rosh Chodesh Elul

In Hebrew, *Rosh Chodesh* literally means "the head of the month," or the first day of the month. We have now come full circle, and we have reached the beginning of the month of Elul, the time of preparation when God is said to be nearest and when we look inside ourselves to examine our own levels of spirituality. The Rosh Chodesh, or new month, holiday is traditionally associated, like Tu B'Av, with women, because of the monthly cycle that affects female lives. Even today, women will join together for special Torah classes and services on the first day of the new month. Rosh Chodesh Elul is a special time for Jewish men and women, because once again we see Rosh Hashanah and Yom Kippur just around the corner, and so we all contemplate our lives as we hear the shofar blown for the first time in 11 months.

So there it is—some of the inner meanings of the cycle of the Jewish year. Certainly there are some other minor holidays or fasts, but it was my desire to bring you some of the most important and meaningful days on the Jewish calendar and offer you some of the mystical and spiritual components thereof. I hope these brief descriptions inspire you to go out and see what kind of celebrations are taking place in your community.

Hag samayach—Happy holidays!

The Least You Need to Know

◆ The cycle of holidays begins in the Hebrew month of Elul, which occurs anywhere from late August to mid-September.

◆ The most powerful day of the Hebrew year is Yom Kippur, the day we all strive to live like angels.

◆ Holiday celebrations outside of Israel may last longer than those within Israel.

◆ Due to the solemnity of certain holidays, weddings, and other joyous events may be forbidden.

Chapter 26

In the Land of Israel

In This Chapter

- ◆ The top 20 spiritual sites in Israel
- ◆ A brief history of each site
- ◆ Reasons to visit Israel
- ◆ Safety concerns when traveling to Israel

Throughout this book, we have been discussing ideas, concepts, symbolism, literature, and commentaries. Now it's time to take a virtual tour of spiritual sights in the land of Israel. The purpose of this chapter is to acquaint you with a personal, subjective list of 20 of the top spiritual sights in Israel, which you can use either for an armchair expedition or as a planning tool for an actual trip.

A Word About Violence

Given the proclivity of the media to focus on the sensational and the frightening, it makes sense that Israel looks a lot more dangerous on American television or in American newspapers than it does when you are actually there. This is almost always the case—you feel a lot safer when you're traveling in Israel than when you're in the United States thinking about Israel.

Since the "Yom Kippur Intifada" began in September 2000, the level of terrorism within the land of Israel has grown exponentially. Whether it is a safe time to visit Israel really is a question that you have to answer for yourself. Today, journeying to Israel is a demonstration of solidarity with the Israelis, whose tourist industry has virtually collapsed in the wake of the various bombings and killings. It's a very tough sell for many people to want to visit the country right now, although perhaps this will have changed by the time this book is published. One can only hope.

So whether you choose to visit these sites from the safety of your armchair, or whether you actually choose to get on a plane, I hope that you find these descriptions useful as you contemplate the spiritual sites within the land of Israel.

Devine Devarim _____

intifada a term used to describe the milestones of various struggles between Palestine and Israel.

Jerusalem, the Golden

The first 10 of our 20 spiritual landmarks are located within the city of Jerusalem. "Ten measures of beauty descended upon the world, and Jerusalem received nine of them." So said the Talmud when speaking about the extreme beauty of the city of Jerusalem.

High Spirits
Israel proudly boasted the world's fastest slalom skier, and so had high hopes of bringing home a gold medal in the approaching Olympics. As the scores came in, the citizens of Israel were ecstatic. Switzerland had the fastest time so far at 38 seconds, but that was still well behind the Israeli skier's trial time of 35 seconds.
When it came time for the Israeli skier to compete, the attending Israelis held their breath. Soon a minute passed, then two, then three. Finally, five minutes later, their would-be champion crossed the finish line.
His coach couldn't believe it. "What happened?" he asked.
Exasperated, the skier blurted, "Who fixed a mezuzah to each of the gates?"

Jerusalem truly is a beautiful place, nestled in the hills approximately 45 minutes to an hour from Tel Aviv (depending on the relative insanity of your taxi driver). Jerusalem has inspired devotees of the world's three major faiths—Christianity, Islam, and Judaism—for millennia. Jerusalem is never referred to by name in the Torah, although in Deuteronomy Moses speaks frequently of a place to which God will direct the wandering Jewish people, and it is understood that this city to which he refers is Jerusalem. These 10 sites will give you a strong sense of the spirituality of Jerusalem, and in many ways will bring the ideas and concepts discussed throughout the rest of this book to life.

The Western Wall

The holiest site in Judaism, the Wall has attracted the faithful for 2,000 years. The Western Wall, also known as the Wailing Wall because of the degree of mournful prayer that has taken place over the centuries, was not actually part of the First or Second Temple. Instead, it is believed to be the retaining wall for the Second Temple. It was built by King Herod approximately 2,000 years ago, and was the only piece of the entire structure remaining after the Romans destroyed the Temple in the year 70 C.E.

Until 1948, the Wall was the possession of various nations, most recently the Turks and then the British. Arabs would frequently rain down garbage on Jews who sought to pray at the Wall in those pre-1948 times. During the war for independence, East Jerusalem, including the Old City of Jerusalem where the Western Wall is located, fell into the hands of the Jordanians. The Jordanians refused access to Jews and no Jew was able to visit the Wall until General Moshe Dayan led the Israeli defense forces to retake it during the Six Day War of 1967.

When you visit the Wall today, you will pass through several security checkpoints before finding yourself on a large, attractive plaza built in the early '70s. The Wall itself actually descends for approximately 15 stories beneath the level of the plaza—the part of the Western Wall we see is actually the very top of it. Jews come to the Wall to kiss it, insert small prayers in its cracks, meditate, and contemplate the broad sweep of Jewish history. It is one of the most awe-inspiring sights in the world, especially because of its simplicity. It is said that the Temple Wall is the only place in the world where the shechinah—the divine presence discussed elsewhere in this book—still dwells.

Prayer services are constantly starting there, morning, noon, and night. Individuals can come to the Wall and pray, or they can join *minyanim*, groups of 10 or more male Jews who will pray as an instant, makeshift community. The Western Wall is the place to be on Friday night in Jerusalem, as thousands of Jews come to welcome the Sabbath with prayer, dancing, and song. It is an unforgettable experience.

Mystical Moments

The sanctity of the Western Wall is delineated in a popular Israeli song. One refrain reads, "There are people with hearts of stone, and stones with hearts of people."

Devine Devarim

minyanim   groups of 10 or more male Jews who pray as an instant, makeshift community.

You can now tour a segment underneath the Western Wall. If you are facing the Wall, the entrance to this tour site will be at your left. You will be able to visit underground passages alongside the Temple Mount that are truly striking, as they show you archeological discoveries dating back hundreds and hundreds of years. It is an astonishing sight to see the surface of the earth matched up against huge stones. You'll find yourself wondering how on earth those stones could have been moved into place. Visiting the tunnels offers an astonishing view of the construction of the Temple and the history of the region.

The tour concludes in the Arab Quarter, and Israeli soldiers will transport you back to the Jewish Quarter, depending on tensions in the region.

Walls of the Old City

One of the most exciting things to do in Jerusalem is to walk along the parapets of the walls of the Old City of Jerusalem. These walls were built by the Turks in the sixteenth century and are a striking and memorable site for any visitor to Jerusalem. It is impossible to forget the beauty of the walls, especially when they are viewed at night. Many visitors do not realize that it is possible to take a self-guided tour along the top of the walls of the Old City. This is a wonderful way to visit and truly get to know the Old City of Jerusalem.

The Jewish Quarter

This portion of the Old City of Jerusalem came into Jewish hands following the Six Day War of 1967. Today, it is a luxurious neighborhood with beautiful apartments overlooking or near the Western Wall and many other centuries-old synagogues and holy sites. You can also find religious bookstores, pizza stands, small grocery markets, and anything else you need for your visit.

The Jewish Quarter is well worth wandering around—you never know who or what you'll find. In years past, Jews frequented without any fear the fascinating *shouk*, or market, of the Arab Quarter adjacent to the Jewish Quarter. While the Arab Quarter is no less picturesque as in years past, there are times when Jews feel comfortable visiting there and there are times when they do not. You may want to ask around about the political climate of the day before you venture into the Arab Quarter.

High Spirits

A rabbi called his son in to help him upgrade his software on his computer. The son laughed when he saw that his father wanted to put some pretty hefty programs on his now archaic machine.

"You can't run this on your computer!" he laughed. "You need at least 486 megahertz and 16 megs of RAM to work efficiently."

His father remained calm and motioned for him to continue installing the software. "God will provide the RAM, my son."

The Dome of the Rock

The site on which the First and Second Temples stood is sacred not just to the Jews but also to the Arabs, who built two of their holiest mosques there. These two mosques are gorgeous and well worth your visit, with two caveats. The first has to do with the political situation. You may want to find out whether Americans—especially Jewish Americans—are welcome at the time of your visit. The second consideration is that religious Jews will not visit either of those mosques, not because they are mosques per se but because they are located on the ground that may have included the Holiest of Holies, the area of the First and Second Temples visited only by the high priest and only on Yom Kippur. No religious Jew would want to take a chance on accidentally wandering into that area, so for that reason observant Jews tend not to visit the Temple Mount.

Inside the larger of the two mosques, the Dome of the Rock, is a very large rock that the Moslems believe Mohammed used as a jumping off point for his ascension to heaven. According to Moslem tradition, it is also the place where Abraham sacrificed Isaac. If you do venture inside the mosque and examine the stone, you will see that large parts of it have been chipped away. Apparently those chippings were souvenirs of visiting crusaders 600-800 years ago.

Spiritual Citations

"The only thing I cannot forgive the Arabs for is that they forced our sons to kill their sons."

The Via Dolorosa

Jerusalem is holy not just to Jews and Moslems but also to Christians, for it is here that Jesus lived part of his life and, according to the Christian Bible, died on the cross. The Via Dolorosa winds through the Arab Quarter of Jerusalem, and it is not uncommon to see Christian children carrying a large cross and reenacting the last steps or stations in the journey of Jesus to his crucifixion.

Mea Shearim

This Orthodox Jewish neighborhood not far from the Old City is one of the most traditional religious neighborhoods in the world. If you step into the alleys away from the auto traffic on its heavily congested and, for the most part, narrow streets, you will feel as though you have been transported back nearly 3,000 years. You will see the city children rushing off to school, adults heading to work or to the house of study and prayer, and merchants selling all manner of Judaica. It is truly a fascinating place. One of the best known sights of Mea Shearim are the banners requesting in Hebrew and English that women who visit the neighborhood dress modestly, in keeping with the mores of the residents.

High Spirits

A mayor of a small Israeli town was taking a stroll with his wife. When the couple passed by a construction site, one of the workers yelled, "Hey there, Rachel!"

The mayor was shocked to see his wife wave back. "You know that guy?"

The wife smiled. "A few years before I met you, I was engaged to him."

The mayor put his arm around his wife. "Good thing you married me. Otherwise you'd be married to a construction worker."

Rachel removed his arm from her shoulder. "Actually, if I'd married him, he'd now be mayor!"

Shrine of the Book

This small white monument on the grounds of the Israel Museum is designed to look like the top of a Torah scroll. Here you will find actual fragments from the Dead Sea Scrolls found half a century ago in caves near Qumrun, which we will discuss shortly. These scrolls shed light on the life of Jews in the first century C.E., when the Romans were invading and when fringe groups of Jews, such as the *Essenes*, flourished in the regions not far from the Dead Sea and the city of Jerusalem.

Devine Devarim

Essenes a Jewish sect who led a rather ascetic life nearly 2,000 years ago. Their short-lived span was most likely due to their practice of celibacy, which required them to earn converts as their only means of increasing their population.

It is astonishing to look upon these fragments and realize that they had been kept in earthenware jugs for approximately 1,900 years until their accidental discovery by a shepherd boy darting in and out of the caves. One wonders what other jars might exist in those caves containing other scrolls and secrets from two millennia ago.

Yad Vashem

This is the Israeli memorial to Holocaust victims, and it is a tragic and powerful reminder of the cruelty inflicted on Jews and others during World War II. The name "Yad Vashem" is taken from the prophet Isaiah, who promised a memorial to those who suffered in God's name.

Yamin Moshe

This upscale Jerusalem neighborhood lies across a small valley from the Old City and affords a magnificent view of the walls of the Old City, especially at night. The area is named for Moses Montefiore, a visionary who sought to build the land of Israel more than a century ago. A windmill stands guard in Yamin Moshe, a quixotic reminder of Montefiore's vision for Jerusalem.

Beyond Jerusalem's Borders

Lest you think that all of Israel's spirituality is maintained strictly within the borders of the city of Jerusalem, let's now visit ten locations elsewhere in the country that are also of deep spiritual significance to Jews.

Qumrun

This archaeological site takes you into the lives of the Essenes, a monastic Jewish community that flourished almost 2,000 years ago. The Essenes lived separate and apart from bustling Jerusalem in order to devote their lives to spiritual contemplation. They are also known for their deep concerns with physical purity and would actually bathe numerous times a day in order to remain spiritually pure. From Qumrun you can look up to the hills where the Dead Sea Scrolls were found in 1946.

Jericho

Not far from Qumrun is the ancient city of Jericho, perhaps one of the oldest cities in the world. It is possible today to visit Jericho, now under the control of the Palestinian Authority, and see archaeological excavations dating back 15,000 years. The great archaeologist Katherine Kenyon lived and worked here.

> **Spiritual Citations**
>
> "Who has inflicted this upon us? Who has made us Jews different from all other people? Who has allowed us to suffer so terribly up till now? It is God that has made us as we are, but it will be God, too, who will raise us up again. If we bear all this suffering and if there are still Jews left, when it is over, then Jews, instead of being doomed, will be held up as an example."
>
> —Anne Frank

Masada

You can walk or take a cable car to the top of the this mountain, a redoubt for Jews who were seeking to avoid the Roman occupation in the first century C.E. Masada is famous because of the mass suicide of the Jews that took place here; they took their own lives rather than submit to Roman subjugation and, most likely, slavery.

From the top of Masada it is still possible to see the outlines of where the Roman legions encamped while besieging the mountain. On the far side of the mountain it is also possible to view the giant ramp of dirt and stone the Romans built in order to conquer the mountain and crush the Jewish rebellion. It is a truly moving and powerful sight.

Hebron

To the south of Jerusalem lies the sacred city of Hebron, famous from the time of Abraham as the burial place first of his wife Sarah, and eventually of Abraham himself, Isaac and Rebecca, and Jacob and both of his wives. This burial place, the tomb of the *machtalah*, is a site holy to both Jews and Moslems. Hebron has been the scene of almost continuous confrontation between Jewish and Arab residents, especially in the time since the Yom Kippur Intifada began. You may want to consult your Israeli friends before you venture in Hebron, because it is not a place you want to be at the wrong time.

High Spirits
Q. What was the first thing Eve did when Adam came home each day?
A. Counted his ribs.

Biet El

Not far north of Jerusalem—less than an hour's drive—lies the village of Biet El, a Jewish settlement approximately 20 years old. Biet El is surrounded by the Judea Hills, and the view from its synagogue alone is worth the trip. You can get a very clear sense of the isolation and even the bravery of the Jewish settlers in the lands that came into Jewish possession after the 1967 war.

Sefat

This holy city in the north of Jerusalem was home to many of the leading kabbalists over the centuries and remains a palpably spiritual environment. Often shrouded by clouds, this hilltop town has synagogues dating back to the nineteenth century as well as a lovely artists' quarter.

Much of Turkish, Arab, and Jewish history in the region can be traced in this one town; a crusader fortress lies at the top of the city, Turkish buildings still stand, and the armistice line—a staircase—drawn between the Arabs and Jews in 1948 takes a visitor down from the main part of the town into the centuries' old cemetery where some of Judaism's leading sages are buried.

The Golan

The Golan Heights, won from Syria in the 1967 war, are well worth a visit, even though they lie at a distance of several hours from Tel Aviv or Jerusalem. In the Golan, you can find archaeological sites of Jewish villages dating back 2,000 years, which the Israeli government uses as an invitation of the legitimacy of the Israeli presence in the Golan. It is also quite striking to visit the two hilltops adjoining Syria; from these hilltops you—and a lot of high-tech listening equipment—look down on the plains of Syria. It gives you a very powerful indication of the geopolitical realities of the Middle East.

Spiritual Citations

"Being a Jew is like walking in the wind or swimming: you are touched at all points and conscious everywhere."
—Lionel Trilling, U.S. critic

Museum of the Diaspora, Tel Aviv

This museum offers glimpses into Jewish history dating back thousands of years. There are recreations of temples and synagogues from all ages and from all parts of the world. There are all sorts of ritual objects on display. The net effect is to remind the visitor that the key implements of the Jewish Sabbath—candlesticks, wine glass, challah cover—have barely changed, except in outward design, over the millennia, providing a tangible reminder of the continuity of the Jewish religion.

Jaffa

The court area outside Tel Aviv, this lovely area is a perfect spot for winding down with a relaxing dinner after having taken in the previous 18 spiritual sites. There are a lot of wonderful restaurants with great water views. Normally, the rule of thumb is that the better the view, the worse the restaurant. Fortunately, this does not hold true in lovely, cobblestone-paved Jaffa.

Eilat

Okay, there's nothing especially spiritual about Eilat—it's just a nice beach town. What's fascinating is that as you lie on the beach, to your left is Saudi Arabia and to your right is Egypt—something to think about as you work on your tan. If the toplessness of the beaches distracts you enough, you may never realize that Saudi Arabia and Egypt lie so close at hand. Eilat is just for fun.

There you have it—20 sites of admittedly varying levels of spirituality that will give you a very broad view of Jewish spirituality, Middle Eastern history, and the continuity of the Jewish people. I hope you enjoyed the trip!

The Least You Need to Know

♦ A visit to Israel is something most Jews hope to accomplish at least once in their life.

♦ Visiting Israel is considered a display of solidarity with the Jews who live there.

♦ The Western Wall is the most holy of sites in all of Israel.

♦ Israel's spiritual sites also offer insight into other world religions and local history.

27

Is Judaism Spiritual?

In This Chapter

- ◆ A personal spiritual moment
- ◆ A trip to the 1970s Soviet Union
- ◆ The Soviet "refuseniks"
- ◆ Final thoughts

Is Judaism spiritual? Despite all the evidence we have seen, despite all the different aspects of Jewish mysticism and spirituality, the question remains: Is Judaism spiritual? Can it still satisfy the deepest longings of adherents? Can a Jew find a satisfying, ongoing spiritual experience in Judaism, or is it necessary to turn, as so many have in recent decades, to other faiths?

If you were to add up all the elements that we've seen in this book—Bible stories, the giving of the Torah, blessings, informal and formal prayer, Kabbalah and Zohar, gematria, shechinah, the afterlife, and the Messiah—is the result sufficient for a satisfying spiritual life?

Before we answer that question directly, let me relate a true story.

A Moscow Sabbath

In December 1979, as Russian troops and tanks rolled into Afghanistan, I was a 21-year-old college senior making a visit with a student group to what was then called the Soviet Union. When we flew into Moscow on a dark December night, we saw at the airport a man who looked like a Hasidic rabbi of old. He had a medium-length gray beard, a wide-brimmed, black hat, and a long black coat. Many of us in the group were Jewish, but none of us dared speak to him. We had heard that we could get people in trouble merely by entering into a conversation with them.

A week later, our group was in Leningrad. That Saturday morning, I arose early and made my way through the darkened streets—that far north, the sun does not rise until nine in the morning in the wintertime—to the main synagogue of Leningrad. My visit to the Leningrad synagogue occurred against the background of oppression of Soviet Jewry and the era of the "refuseniks." Jews who sought official permission from the Soviet government to emigrate to Israel were routinely denied, and were subsequently fired from their jobs for seeking to leave Russia. Since they were no longer employed, they were breaking the law. (In the Soviet Union, it was illegal not to hold a job.) Thus, they became subject to charges of "hooliganism," the term the Soviet Union used to describe the unemployed. It was a dicey time for the Jews of Russia.

When you're 21, rules don't mean much, and I simply wanted to attend religious services. I'll never forget the experience of rounding the corner and finding myself face to face with the great gates of the Leningrad Synagogue. They loomed up as if out of a movie. The grandeur of the gates, and the massive synagogue towering behind them, reminded me that there was a time when Jews in pre-Soviet Russia possessed enough money and political power to build such an architectural wonder. It also reminded me that my great-great-grandparents had come from Russia to the United States. Perhaps they had prayed in this very building.

Devine Devarim

siddur   a prayerbook.

refusenik   a Jew in the former Soviet Union who sought official permission from the government to emigrate to Israel but was routinely denied and subsequently fired from his jobs.

I went inside and took a seat. One of the most powerful memories of that day was that the youngest person in the congregation besides myself could not have been younger than 70 years old. Although I was to learn that there were young Jews practicing traditional Judaism, none dared show their face in a synagogue for fear of prosecution or loss of their job. The other thing I remember is that the old men were staring at my boots. I had good, solid, American boots on, and they offered great protection against the Soviet winter. Few, if any, of the men in the synagogue could have afforded anything like the boots I wore, not that they could have found anything of such good quality in Russian stores.

The service continued, and I followed along in the prayer book that one of the members gave me. One of the fascinating things about traditional Judaism is that the prayers have not changed much at all in the last 700 years, and a prayer book dating back 2,000 years could be used, with a few changes, in any orthodox synagogue in the world today. Praying out of a *siddur*, prayer book, that could have been used in any city across the globe and back through the centuries gave me a sense of connectedness to the Jewish people that I had never before experienced.

A few moments before the Torah reading in the middle of the service, a side door opened, and none other than the rabbi from the Moscow airport, dressed exactly the same way, suddenly appeared. I was surprised to see him again.

> **High Spirits**
>
> The best joke I heard in Russia came from our Intourist guide, who said, as we passed KGB headquarters, "That's the tallest building in Moscow, because you can see Siberia from the basement."

I was even more surprised when he addressed me in unaccented English after my *aliyah*, my invitation to say blessings before and after the reading of the Torah scroll. It turned out that the rabbi was from the east coast of the United States and traveled frequently to Russia to distribute literature and speak to the refusenik Jews who were attempting to practice Judaism.

After the service, the rabbi invited me back to his hotel room for lunch and we ended up spending the entire day together, talking about Judaism and the state of Jews behind the Iron Curtain. He asked me what I was doing for kosher food. At the time, I had been observant for about four or five months, and my level of kashrut was only moderate. I told him the truth: I was only eating three things: bread, chocolate, and ice cream. (Incidentally, and probably not coincidentally, I was the only person in my entire group not to have stomach problems, most likely because I wasn't eating the prepared food.)

The rabbi gave me a box of matzah and a can of Chicken of the Sea tuna fish. When I brought these items back to my hotel room that night, my roommate commented that this was probably the only can of Chicken of the Sea and the only box of matzah for 6,000 miles.

Going Underground

The rabbi gave me a lot more than matzah and tuna fish. He gave me the telephone number of the leader of the refusenik community in Moscow. He made clear to me that I was only to call this individual from a pay phone—that I was not to call him from a hotel telephone, since all of the telephones in every hotel frequented by foreigners were monitored. If I were to call the fellow from my hotel, I would be putting him at risk.

When I arrived in Moscow a few days later, I found a pay phone on the street and made the call. The individual on the other end of the line told me to be at a particular subway station in Moscow at 3 P.M. on Friday. There I would be met by another member of the Jewish Underground, who would take me to his apartment, where I would join a group of others for the Friday night Sabbath meal.

You can imagine my excitement at this private bit of spycraft in which I was engaging. The next few days passed slowly until it was time for me to make my way to the subway station. In true John LeCarre fashion, I took a series of different trains, in various directions, hoping to shake any KGB tail who might have been following me.

The Cold War was still at its peak, and I was under no impression that American Jews deviating from their prescribed guided tour of Moscow would be warmly tolerated. So I was a little bit afraid as I made my way to the subway station to which I had been directed and my assignation with the other member of the group.

At the top of the stairs, he was waiting for me. A bearded man in his early 30s. A refusenik. A member of the Moscow Jewish Underground. I was not hard to pick out in the crowd—my American boots alone probably gave me away. We walked a few blocks through the snow to his apartment building. He shared a two-bedroom apartment with an entire family of five—the family had one bedroom, and he had the other bedroom. Living space was at a premium in Moscow, especially for the unemployed. When my host sought to leave the country, he was instantly fired from his university job.

When I entered his home, stacked as it was with Jewish texts, I was immediately set to work peeling potatoes. "The rabbis of the Talmud wrote that every Jew should take part in the preparation for the Sabbath," my host explained, as he gave me a paring knife and a moderately large stack of potatoes. We talked as I peeled and he cooked.

Before long, eight other young Muscovite Jews arrived at the apartment. We conducted a Friday night service—the same one that can be found in any traditional congregation around the world then, now, or 10 centuries earlier. My host made *kiddush*, pronouncing the blessings over the wine inaugurating the Sabbath day. Then we washed our hands and listened to my host make the motzie, the prayer over the two braided loaves of bread. Where one found *challahs* in the middle of Moscow, I'll never know.

Devine Devarim

kiddush the pronouncement of the blessings over the wine that inaugurates the Sabbath day.

challah the traditional yeast-leavened, twisted bread eaten on the Sabbath and on holidays.

The Jews at the table were as interested in my life in America as I was in theirs. One of them showed me a passport in which the Russian word *zhid*, or Jew, was stamped. This wasn't 1929—this was 1979, and yet if you were Jewish, your Soviet passport indicated as much. In the Soviet Union, passports were not just for travel. They were a required document any time you applied for a job or did virtually anything that involved the government. Your Jewishness was not something you could escape from.

None of the Russians around the table had grown up understanding or speaking Hebrew. In fact, many of their parents did not know that they were learning Hebrew, attending Friday night services or having anything to do with Judaism. Their parents would have been shocked and terrified had they known, my host explained to me. It was understood in the Soviet Union that nothing good could come from identifying publicly with Judaism.

What Is to Be Done?

My host explained to me that the Jews of Moscow had specific needs—blue jeans, specifically. A pair of jeans bought in the States for $30 could be resold on the Moscow black market for $150. "A pair of blue jeans could feed a family for a month," my host explained.

Another extremely desirable item was a cassette radio. With such a device, it was possible to listen to Kol Yisrael, the Voice of Israel short-wave radio broadcasts, and tape the Hebrew lessons that the radio station broadcast each day. I resolved to return the next Friday night with as much booty as I could convince my fellow Jews in the group to purchase or part with.

The next week, I returned with two friends and two sacks containing pairs of blue jeans that my traveling companions had brought to the Soviet Union, hoping to find Russian Jews to whom they could give those jeans. We also had some Cross pens, which were said to bring a high premium on the black market, various other articles of clothing, some Jewish books, a *tallit* (Jewish prayer shawl), and two combination tape recorder/short wave radios, perfect for listening to Kol Yisrael. I also gave my host my set of *tefillin*, a system of leather straps and boxes worn by Jewish men, and sometimes women, during morning prayer services.

I'll never forget the expressions of the Russian Jews around the table as my friends and I unloaded all this gear. They looked embarrassed by the gifts, and I'm sure they were extremely grateful. That Friday night dinner was one of the most serene, pleasurable experiences of my life.

> **High Spirits**
>
> "Let me tell you something that we Israelis have against Moses. He took us 40 years through the desert in order to bring us to the one spot in the Middle East that has no oil!"
>
> —Golda Meir

> **Spiritual Citations**
>
> "There is no Judaism without love and fear, wonder and awe, faith and concern, knowledge and understanding."
>
> —Abraham Joshua Heschel

That night, my friends and I walked back through the frigid Moscow streets to our hotel. We were accompanied by two Englishmen who were involved in the efforts to aid Soviet Jewry. Also accompanying us for the first quarter-mile or so were my host and one of the other Moscow Jews.

The reason the two Russians came out with us on this bitterly cold night was because of the story of Abraham, who began the tradition of Jewish hospitality, which involves not only welcoming guests, but also, as they leave, accompanying them on the first steps of their journey—a practice still observed in Jewish communities around the world. Our host had taken his house key and, by means of a paperclip, had turned it into a rudimentary tie tack. One of the Englishman pointed this out to us.

"Did you notice that?" he asked. "He didn't want to violate the Sabbath prohibition against carrying from the inside to the outside, so he turned his house key into a tie tack. They want to do it right so much that it could almost make you cry."

> ### High Spirits
>
> Two Mafia hitmen in Moscow were waiting for their target to come home. They were told he always arrived at 9 P.M. Nine came and went, and so did 9:15. At 9:30, one hitman turned to the other and said, "Gee, I hope nothing happened to him!"

The law to which the Englishman was referring derives from the Book of Exodus, when the manna descended from heaven six days a week, with a double portion on Friday, so the Jews would not have to go foraging for food on the Sabbath. Since it was not necessary to carry things from outside one's domain into one's home, a Sabbath prohibition was enacted making it forbidden to carry from a private domain into a public domain or vice versa. This was the law to which the Russian Jews still scrupulously adhered.

We went back to our hotel, and I never saw any of my Jewish Muscovite friends again.

Judaism Today

In many ways, the spiritual core of traditional Judaism does not seem to speak to the modern world. The Bible stories seem outdated and rather harsh in the way disputes and problems are handled. The messianic yearnings that so deeply moved the Jewish people even three centuries ago, when their lot in Christian Europe was bleak, seem outdated and almost corny. Gematria is an intriguing parlor game, but few people could derive enough satisfaction from determining and adding up the numerical values of Hebrew letters to satisfy any deep spiritual need.

The fact is that much of the spiritual and mystical components of Judaism that sustained generations of Jews pales in interest beside easier-to-read books like *Conversations with God*. While authors like Neale Donald Walsh, author of the aforementioned series, have made spirituality modern, relevant, and understandable, Judaism lags behind in a state of almost rigid user-unfriendliness. It's almost as though Judaism doesn't even care that other spiritual paths seem so much easier to travel.

And yet, for all its emphasis on study, Judaism, throughout its first thousand years, was not a primarily intellectual faith. The patriarchs were prophets—people who did not reach out to God through their own intellect but found God coming down, as it were, to interrupt their lives and interact with them. The patriarchs used their intellects to drive their emotional attachment to God. That can still be a model for our approach to spirituality. Judaism has always been a prophetic and emotional experience imbued with awe and joy.

Even today, the more deeply you delve into Judaism, the more you discover that it does speak to the way we live in the modern world.

My purpose in this book has been to blow the dust off the covers of books that might otherwise dissuade you from opening them, and to offer exposure to the honest core of spirituality and mysticism that Judaism has contained for millennia. However, true Jewish spirituality does not lie in the lonely study of esoteric texts. As you no doubt already know from this book, spirituality is never devoid from character. I'd like to add a new thought here: In Judaism, spirituality is never devoid of *contact with other Jews.*

Jewish law actually prohibits an individual from moving to a place where there is no Jewish school, Jewish baker, or Jewish slaughterer. Jews have understood from the beginning of their existence as a people that we derive meaning not just from texts, but also from our contact with others.

> **Spiritual Citations**
>
> "Maybe all one can do is hope to end up with the right regrets."
>
> —Arthur Miller

> **High Spirits**
>
> A man called his mother in Miami Beach and asked, "What's new?"
>
> She said, "I haven't eaten in 46 days."
>
> "Why not?" he asked.
>
> She replied, "So my mouth shouldn't be full of food when you called."

James Michener wrote in *The Source* that while Christianity is primarily about the relationship between the individual and God, Judaism is primarily about the relationship between an individual and his or her fellow human beings. Certainly, the 613 commandments are divided into two categories: those that relate to the relationship between God and man, and those that relate to human interaction. Yet perhaps the majority of traditional Judaism governs relationships between people—love and marriage, sex, business, and even our thoughts about and speech to one another.

In some ways, it's easier to have a relationship with God than with people, because somehow we can count on the fact that God will forgive us, excuse us our sins, ignore our weaknesses, and still love us the way a parent loves a child. The hard thing, Judaism recognizes, is getting along with our fellows. That's what Judaism is all about.

I don't mean to downplay the importance of the stories, events, teachings, beliefs, and aspirations we have covered in this book. Rather, I would like to suggest that they are only the beginning. I'm not sure that you can capture the feeling of Jewish spirituality or mysticism from any text, no matter how detailed or authentic. The best way to experience the mystical and spiritual nature of Judaism is to experience it for yourself, whether it be at communal services or through your own endeavors.

The Soviet Union that I visited is no more. More than a million Jews have left Russia behind to make homes in Israel and the United States. What became of the nine Russians with whom I shared a Sabbath table? I have no idea. I was not about to contact them after my visit—I was told that a letter from America could do absolutely no good. The good news is that they no longer have to study Judaism and Hebrew in a clandestine fashion; whether they live in Moscow, Tel Aviv, Jerusalem, or Brooklyn, my Russian friends now have the same level of freedom to explore their Jewish heritage.

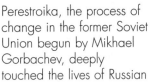

Mystical Moments

Perestroika, the process of change in the former Soviet Union begun by Mikhael Gorbachev, deeply touched the lives of Russian Jews, who became free to practice and study their religion and heritage. More than a million Russian Jews took the opportunity to emigrate to Israel and the United States.

A stranger once approached the great rabbi Hillel and asked him to explain all Judaism on one foot. Hillel, not wanting to be rude, told the man, "Do nothing to your fellow man that you would not want done to you. The rest is commentary. Now go and study."

In other words, Jewish spirituality is all about character—the way we treat others and the way we ourselves wish to be treated. This book is only the beginning; the rest is indeed commentary. Now go and study, and may your heart be ever a resting place for the shechinah, here and hereafter.

The Least You Need to Know

- Although some of the Biblical stories may seem out of place today, their morals still ring true.
- Even in recent years, Jews were still persecuted for their beliefs.
- Modern Judaism still holds true many traditional thoughts and beliefs.
- The only way to truly understand the spiritual aspects of Judaism is to experience it yourself.

Appendix A

For Further Reading

Bagint, Michael and Richard Leigh, *The Dead Sea Scrolls Deception*   A fascinating account of the discovery of the Dead Sea Scrolls at Qumrun near Masada, and the volley among scholars to keep each other from viewing the scrolls or releasing them to the public.

Berkovitz, Eliezer, *Faith After the Holocaust*   An extremely useful guide to understanding an approach to Jewish thought about the Holocaust.

Borowitz, Eugene B., *Choosing a Sex Ethic*   A reform rabbi explores the issue of sexuality and Judaism.

Boteach, Shmuley, *Kosher Sex: A Recipe for Passion and Intimacy*   Rabbi Boteach takes an entertaining—and enlightening—look at contemporary sex mores. It's a very enjoyable book.

Bunim, Irving, *Ethics from Sinai*   A three-volume translation and explanation of *prike avot*, epics of the father, one of the most widely known and studied aspects of the Talmud. Another great way to get into Talmud.

Chofetz Chaim, *Guard Your Tongue*   An English rendition of the classic book about avoiding gossip, written by one of the greatest Jewish minds of the twentieth century.

Golden, Harry, *Two Cents Plain*   A southern Jewish newspaper publisher's columns depicting the relationship between Jews and black and white America during the Civil Rights era.

Greenberg, Blu, *How to Run a Traditional Jewish Household*   An essential book for anyone seeking the answers that *bubbe* and *zadie* (grandma and grandpa) are no longer around to provide.

Ha-Levi, Yehuda, *The Kuzari*   This classic work tells the story of a Russian king who dreamt repeatedly that God was telling him that his thoughts were correct but his actions were incorrect. As a result, he interviewed a Christian, a Moslem, a great philosopher, and a rabbi, and actually settled on Judaism as the right path for himself and his people.

Heschel, Abraham Joshua, *Between God and Man*   A moving and beautiful philosophical study of Judaism written by one of the leading members of the conservative movement.

————.*The Prophets (Two Lions)*   An extraordinary guide to the life and thought of the individuals who had such a powerful effect on Jewish history.

————.*The Sabbath*   A beautiful, concise guide to the spiritual aspect of the Sabbath experience.

Horowitz, Edward, *How the Hebrew Language Grew*   An outstanding introduction to Hebrew.

Johnson, Paul, *History of the Jews*   Johnson, a noted British historian, does an outstanding job of presenting Jewish history in a fascinating light.

Kahati, Pincus, *The Mishnah*   An English translation of the Kahati edition of the core of Talmudic thought.

Kamenetz, Rodger, *The Jew in the Lotus: A Poet's Rediscovery of Jewish Identity in Buddhist India*   An account of the historical gathering of the Dalai Lama, his leading disciples, and some of the great rabbis of the modern world. A meditation on the similarities and differences between Judaism and Buddhism.

Kaplan, Aryeh, *The Aryeh Kaplan Anthology*   The collected works of one of the leading Jewish thinkers of the twentieth century.

Kaplan, Mordecai M., *Judaism as a Civilization*   Kaplan was trained in the orthodox movement, was a leading figure in conservative Judaism, and founded reconstructionism. His doctrine for what became the reconstructionist movement is found in this book.

Ki Tov, Eliyahu, *A Book of Our Heritage* (Nachman Bowman, translator) This is the best guide I've ever seen to the Jewish holidays.

Lamm, Maurice, *The Jewish Way and Mourning* An excellent one-volume compendium of Jewish customs related to death, burial, and mourning.

Levin, Michael, *What Every Jew Needs to Know About God* A brief introduction to Jewish theology. (And the author is a really nice guy!)

————.*Journey to Tradition* The story of a young man's "conversion" to Orthodox Judaism. (The author is a close personal friend!)

Luzzatto, Moshe Chaim, *The Path of the Just* and *The Way of God* Two excellent introductions to the philosophy of Jewish character.

Mindel, Nissan, *My Prayer* A guide, almost paragraph by paragraph, to the prayer services, both daily and Sabbath.

Munk, Elie, *The World of Prayer* A leading French rabbi offers an introduction to Jewish prayer.

Sachar, Howard Morley, *A History of Israel* A comprehensive one-volume history of the events leading up to the creation of the state of Israel and to the present day.

Sharansky, Natan, *Fear No Evil* The compelling account of the Russian Jewish refusenik-turned-Israeli cabinet minister.

Steinsalz, Adin, *The Thirteen-Petaled Rose* These are kabballistic tales of Rav Nachman of Bratslav, with Rabbi Steinsalz's expert commentary. An excellent "next step" in the study of Kabbalah.

————.*The Essential Comment* An extremely readable and easy-to-understand introduction to Talmudic thought. Highly recommended.

Wouk, Herman, *This Is My God* A great way to learn about the Jewish holidays.

Twenty Top Websites

Following is a list of extremely useful websites that will take you deeper into the issues we've explored in this book and also offer information on other aspects of Jewish life.

613.org   Listen to hundreds of hours of talks by the greatest rabbis of our time, all for free:

www.613.org/

Aish.com   Articles, lectures, Speeddating (online and real time), and more from this worldwide Jewish educational organization:

www.Aish.com

Alcoholism and Drug Addiction   The leading organization dealing with addiction among Jews:

www.jacsweb.org/index_ie.html

Calendar   The B'nai Brith organization offers a guide to Jewish holidays on the web:

bnaibrith.org/caln.html

Chabad Lubavitch   The home page for the Chabad Lubavitch Movement:

www.chabad.org/index.html

Conservative Judaism   The home page of the Conservative Movement:

www.uscj.org/

Daf Yomi Download English commentaries on the day's page of Talmud:

shemayisrael.co.il/dafyomi2/index.htm

Genealogy JewishGen, featuring *JewishGen Family Finder* (a database of over 200,000 surnames and towns), the Shtetl Seeker, and much more:

www.jewishgen.org/

Hebrew Bible and Talmud Texts Online Through Hebrew University, Israel (Hebrew font needed):

www.snunit.k12.il/kodesh/

Holocaust The United States Holocaust Museum:

www.ushmm.org/

Judaism 101 An online encyclopedia of Judaism:

www.jewfaq.org/

Judaism and Jewish Resources Andrew Tanenbaum's Outstanding List of Jewish Links:

shamash.org/trb/judaism.html

Kosher Food A guide to Kosher food, restaurants, Passover, and Kosher Alerts, from the Orthodox Union:

www.ou.org/kosher/

Passover Haggadah for Kids From Professor Eli Segal, a fun way to learn about Passover:

www.acs.ucalgary.ca/~elsegal/Uncle_Eli/Eli.html

Reconstructionist Judaism the home page for the reconstructionist movement:

www.jrf.org/

Reform Judaism the home page for the reform movement:

www.rj.org/

Singles The most talked about Jewish website for singles, with over 300,000 members:

www.jdate.com/jdDefault.asp

Soc.Culture.Jewish Newsgroup's Frequently Asked Questions and Answers About Judaism An outstanding resource:

shamash.org/lists/scj-faq/HTML/

Talmud   An extraordinary site with hyperlinks to explain all the different aspects of a page of Talmud:

www.acs.ucalgary.ca/~elsegal/TalmudPage.html

Yiddish   The Online "Virtual Shtetl" takes you inside the Yiddish language:

www.ibiblio.org/yiddish/shtetl.html

Glossary

Abishte   A Hasidic name for God.

adam kedmon   Original man.

aliyah   The honor of being called up to the Torah; also, the act of moving to the land of Israel; lit. going up.

amidah   The central part of the Jewish service, during which congregants stand and pray silently as a way of recreating the Temple service in their hearts and minds.

angel   From the Greek word meaning "messenger from God."

Aramaic   The common Jewish language 2,000 years ago.

Ashkenazim   Jews who settled in Eastern Europe.

atbash   Form of gematria in which the first letter of the Hebrew alphabet is transposed with the last, the second letter is transposed with the second to last, etc.

avinu malkaynu   A traditional Rosh Hashanah prayer that translates as "our father, our king" or "our parent, our ruler."

avodat haliv   Reciting prayers with belief and convictions; lit. service of the heart.

avodat hat'sfaytiyim   Reciting prayers one doesn't believe; lit. lip service.

Baal lashon hara   A repeat offender of lashon hara.

Bal Shem Tov   The founder of the Hasidic movement.

Bar/Bat Mitzvah   Originally, the age of maturity in the eyes of Jewish law (13 for boys, 12 for girls); today, the coming-of-age ceremony upon turning 13.

bechirat hofshi   Free will.

Beit ha'Mikdash   The proper name of the first and second Temples in Jerusalem.

Beit Haknesset   Synagogue.

Beit Midrash   A yeshiva study hall.

benoni   An average, ordinary Jew.

beracha   Blessing; pl. berachot.

bubbe   Affectionate term for grandma.

ch'et   Sin.

Chabad   Founded by Rabbi Shneur Zalman, perhaps the best-known branch of the Hasidic world known to secular and orthodox Jews; also Lubavitch Hasidus.

chait   Life.

challah   The traditional yeast-leavened, twisted bread eaten on the Sabbath and on holidays.

chavrusa   Spiritually committed Torah study partner.

chavurah   Gathering of spiritually committed Jewish friends.

chazzan   Prayer leader.

cofer ha-ikur   One who denies the basic point of Judaism that God exists and created the Torah.

daf yomi   The process of reading a page a day of the Torah, which comes out to be about seven and a half years; lit. a page a day.

davar   1. thing 2. word

davening   The traditional approach to Jewish prayer.

derech eretz   Respect.

din v'heshbon   A judgment and accounting for our lives before God.

drash   The textual analysis of text in which analogies and connections to other aspects of life can be found.

dvekut   The concept of adhering to God with joy; achieving piety and nobility of spirit through happiness, dancing, great fervor in prayer, and great enjoyment in the simple pleasures of life.

Esther   Jewish wife of King Ahasuerus who succeeds in convincing her husband not to follow Haman's plans to exterminate the Jews.

Exodus   The movement of the freed Jewish people out of Egypt and into the desert.

fahrbrengens   An all-night series of talks given by the late Lubavitcher Rebbi, Menachem Mendel Schneerson, at Brooklyn's Lubavitch headquarters.

farbissinie   Somebody who is depressed, moody, and just plain difficult to be around.

gam zu l'tovah   A concept that states that everything happens with a sense of ultimate good; lit. This too is for the best.

gematria   The system of replacing Hebrew letters with their equivalent number based on where the letters fall in the alphabet.

Germara   The compilation of commentaries on each of the laws and traditions contained in the Mishnah.

ghetto   A neighborhood in medieval European cities in which Jews were required to live.

ha'olam haba   The afterlife; lit. the world to come.

ha'olam hazeh   The world we live in, as compared to ha'olam haba.

Haftorah   A reading from the Prophets that follows the Torah reading during Sabbath morning services.

Haggadah   The scripture read at the Seder during the first two nights of Passover that recounts the plagues Moses brings upon Egypt and the Jewish Exodus.

halachah   Jewish law. Derived from the Hebrew word meaning "the way to go."

Haman   Advisor to King Ahasuerus who seeks to have the Jews exterminated. His plan is foiled, however, by the King's Jewish wife, Esther, and Haman is hanged. The Jewish victory is celebrated during Purim.

Hasid   An observant Jew and member of the Hasidic sect, one of the many groups that sprung up in the small towns of Eastern Europe in the eighteenth century. Hasidic men traditionally wear long black coats, side curls, and wide-brimmed black hats; var. Chassid.

Hechsherim   The little symbols on food packages that indicate that a particular item has been produced in accordance with Jewish dietary law. The most common *hechsher* is a U in a circle, which indicates that the food has the approval of the Orthodox Union, a leading body of orthodox rabbis. Other individual rabbis have different symbols to represent their own imprimatur, so a person who is careful about kashrut may accept hechsherim of some individual rabbis but not others.

hekdaish   The act of leaving all property to the temple instead of heirs.

Hillel   One of the greatest of the Talmud's authors.

Israel   Formerly the land of Canaan, now the Jewish state in the Middle East.

Israelite   A Hebrew; a Jew.

Jethro   Moses' father-in-law.

Kabbalah   A mystic, esoteric theosophy.

kashrut   The commandments and traditions regarding the preparation and serving of food and drink.

katagor   The "prosecutor" who lists a person's sins in the judgment of the soul after death.

kedusha   A morning prayer acknowledging the holiness of God; lit. holiness.

kelipot   In Kabbalah study, the shells of light that held individual sefirot in order to keep the emanations of God from intermingling.

Khazar   One of the tribes that comprised Russia in the eighth century.

kiddush   The pronouncement of the blessings over the wine that inaugurates the Sabbath day; lit. "declaration of holiness."

kipa   A small, round head-covering for men.

kittel   A white burial shroud worn by men on Yom Kippur that symbolizes the purity to which the soul is restored.

kohen   Priest; pl. kohenim.

kohen gadol   High priest.

Kol Nidre   Prayer recited on Yom Kippur.

Korach   Leader of an unsuccessful rebellion against Moses after the Exodus.

korait   The most severe punishment mentioned in the Bible, that of one's soul being cut off from one's people.

kosher   The Jewish laws relating to food and drink. Kosher is an adjective ("Don't eat that—it isn't kosher!"), and kashrut is the term for the overall system of laws regarding food.

Kuzari   Yehuda ha-Levi's book about the king of the eighth-century Khazars who converted, along with his entire people, to Judaism.

kvittel   Yiddish term meaning individual prayer; lit. "short letter"; pl. kvitlach.

lashon hara   Gossip.

lashon kodesh   Hebrew; lit. the holy tongue.

Levite   Member of the tribe of Levi, or one of his descendants.

maasei breishit   The creation of the universe.

maaser   In ancient Israel, the act of taking the first fruits of harvest to the Temple as an offering.

machloket   Argument.

Maimonides   Twelfth-century Egyptian Jewish codifier of law who wrote the Yigdal.

Makhzor   Prayerbook used during Rosh Hashanah and Yom Kippur.

mal'ach   An angel; lit. one who is charged with a mission; pl. malachim.

manna   1. the food, obtained by way of miracle, that the Jews lived on during their 40 years in the desert. 2. divine or spiritual nourishment.

Mashiach   The Jewish Messiah, who will rebuild the Temple in Jerusalem and usher in an era of world peace.

matzah   Unleavened bread traditionally eaten at Passover that originated from the Jews' hasty Exodus from Egypt.

Meah brachot   The practice of saying 100 blessings for God each day.

Menorah   The candelabra used in Hanukkah ceremonies; also the candelabra used in the first and second Temples in Jerusalem.

mezuzah   Parchment containing verses from Deuteronomy that is rolled up and hung outside a dwelling.

midrash   Rabbinical insights into Bible stories; also, collections of such insights are called by the same name.

mikdash ma'at   Miniature holy place carried by Jews in their hearts after the destruction of the second Temple.

mikva   A purifying bath, often used after sexual relations or after coming into contact with an impure substance.

minhag   A law that is specific to the customs of a particular group of Jews; pl. minhagim.

minyan An official quorum for prayer.

mishkan The prefab tabernacle that accompanied the Jews for their 40 years in the desert.

Mishnah The Torah laws given to Moses orally by God on Mount Sinai and the core of the Talmud; lit. repetition.

Mishnah Berurah The commentary on the Shulchan Aruch or guide to Jewish law, written by the Chafetz Chaim as a guide on behavior and practice, which is even today a staple in most observant Jewish homes around the world.

mitzvah Pl. mitzvot, the term used to describe a Divine commandment.

Moses Leader of the Jewish people out of slavery in Egypt.

motzi The blessing over bread.

motzi shame hara Slander; to give someone a bad name.

Mount Sinai Location where Moses and the Jewish people received the Torah from God.

musaf The additional amidah spoken on special service days (Sabbath, new moon, and festivals) in remembrance of and in recollection of the additional service once held in the Temple.

musar shmooze A rabbinical lecture on a character trait such as honesty, courtesy, friendliness, or respecting one's fellows.

Mussar The movement in Jewish education, begun by Rabbi Israel Salanter, that emphasized the development of character and ethics in addition to the usual concentration on Jewish law.

mysticism The practice of human beings reaching up to God.

nach The Hebrew acronym meaning *nivi'im* and *ketuvim*, the Prophets and the Writings.

ne'ilah The final hour of prayer on Yom Kippur.

niddah The guidelines regarding sexuality and marriage.

Og King of Bashon, a group that the Israelites defeated during their time in the desert.

parasha A weekly reading from the Torah; pl. parashiyot.

pardes The "garden" of connotations, created by using the first letter from each of the levels of meaning of the Bible. From this word comes the English "paradise."

Passover Holiday commemorating the night that God sent a plague on the firstborn of Egypt, but "passed over" the homes of the Jews.

pogrom   A mass murdering of Jews, usually ordered by the government.

Potiphar   The husband of the woman who tried to seduce Joseph, resulting in his being thrown in jail.

predicate theology   For those who do not believe in God, the practice of asking, "If there were a God, what would God want from us?"

prophecy   The words of God, spoken in Biblical times through the mouth of a devout believer.

prophet   One who is so attuned to God that God can actually speak through that person; there were thousands of such individuals in Biblical times, a small numbers of whose prophecies were recorded in the Bible.

prophetic religion   A religion founded when God speaks to one or more individuals; as opposed to a "mystical" faith that begins when individuals make a decision to contact and get to know God.

prosdor   The Talmudic word for this world, from the Greek for "entry hall." This world is considered just an entry hall to the palace, which is the afterlife or "world to come."

pshat   The most basic, literal interpretation of a Biblical text.

Purim   The holiday celebration marking the Jews' willing acceptance of the centuries-old laws of Mount Sinai, now that they have been saved from the clutches of Haman.

Rashi   Eleventh-century commentator of the Torah and Talmud whose words remain an integral part of scripture study.

rechillut   Gossip; repeating to A what B has said about A.

rebbe   A charismatic leader of the Hasidim.

refusenik   A Jew in the former Soviet Union who sought official permission from the government to emigrate to Israel but was routinely denied and subsequently fired from his or her job.

remez   A second layer of deeper textual meaning; lit. hint.

Rosh Hashanah   The Jewish New Year.

rosh yeshiva   The head of a Jewish school.

ruach hakodesh   The Holy Spirit.

Sabbath   *See* Shabbat.

sanegor   The "defense attorney" during the judgment of the soul after death.

sar   A princely angel who looks after a nation's interests and keeps God "informed" of what is happening with that nation.

Seder   The festive meal, celebrated at Passover, marked by the telling of the Exodus story or, today, the recounting of some other movement toward human freedom.

sefirot   In Kabbalah study, a series of 10 emanations, comprised of God's traits, that created the universe.

Sephardim   Jews descended from Spain or the Arab world.

Sforno   Fifteenth-century Biblical commentator, physician, and philosopher who lived around 1470–1550 in the northern Italian city of Bologna. "The Sforno," as the rabbi is colloquially called, is one of the most frequently read authors, even 500 years later.

Sh'ma   The line from Deuteronomy that summarizes the Jewish concept of spirituality and the monotheistic concept of God.

Shabbat   1. the Sabbath, or holy day. 2. The tractate consisting of 24 chapters of laws for the Sabbath.

shaliach   An emissary sent to make contacts in a local community, find donors, create a synagogue, and offer religious services, Sabbath and holiday meals, and classes, emphasizing traditional Judaism and especially the Lubavitch way; pl. shluchim.

Shavuot   The festival of the receiving of the Torah celebrated in late spring.

shechinah   The concept of trying to understand what it means to have God "dwelling" and "present" in the world; lit. the dwelling place of God.

shedim   According to Rabbi Chaim Luzzato, intermediate beings that exist between the spiritual and physical worlds.

shekel   1. in Biblical times, a unit of weight. 2. the currency of Israel.

Shemini atzeret   The eighth day of Sukkot, known as the "Zionist holiday."

shevirat ha'kelim   In Lurianic kabbalism, the moment during the creation of the universe when the kelipot shattered, scattering pure light everywhere; lit. the breaking of vessels.

shiva   The seven-day mourning period during which guests come to the house of the mourner.

shochet   A ritual slaughterer.

shofar   Ram's horn blown in remembrance during the Hebrew month of Elul, on the High Holy Days and in times of war.

shulchan aruch   The great code of Jewish law written by Rabbi Joseph Caro; lit. set table; in Judaism, the term is used to describe the belief that everyone organizes his or her spiritual life and religious practice as he or she sees fit.

shule   A Yiddish term for synagogue, derived from the German word for "school," since a synagogue or temple typically doubles as a schoolhouse.

siddur   A prayerbook, from the Hebrew word meaning "order" (similar to "Seder," the Passover meal).

Simchat Torah   The celebration of the law that concludes the New Year holiday season each fall and which marks the time where Jews both complete and begin to reread the Bible.

sinat hinam   Senseless hatred.

sod   The deepest level of contextual meaning containing the Bible's greatest secrets.

stiff-necked   The Bible's term for the Jewish people, who frequently resisted God's will with great stubbornness.

Sukkot   The feast of Tabernacles.

taharat hamishpacha   The laws governing family purity.

tallit   A Jewish prayer shaw; pl. talleisim.

Talmud   The great, vast compendium of Jewish law, lore, custom, and history.

Talmud chachim   Talmud scholar.

Tanya   The basic text of Chabad Chasidus.

tefilah   Prayer, in the sense of "attachment."

tefillin   A series of leather boxes and straps worn primarily by Jewish men during weekday morning services.

teshuva   Repentance, lit. "turning to God."

Tisha B'av   The day the first and second Temples were destroyed. In subsequent years, persecutors have chosen this day to inflict further punishment on the Jews as a way of intensifying an already grim day. For example, the Jews were expelled from Spain on Tisha B'av in 1492, and during World War II, the Nazis performed many of their most sadistic actions against the Jewish population; lit. the ninth day of the Hebrew month of Av.

Toiter Chassidim   "Dead" Hasidim, so named because they are the only group that has never sought to replace their rebbe, Rabbi Nachman of Bratslav, with another individual.

Torah   The first five books of the Bible. Also referred to as the Pentateuch or the Five Books of Moses.

Tosafot   The commentaries written in the twelfth and thirteenth centuries that expounded and further clarified Rashi's original texts.

Tsuris   A Yiddish term meaning nuisance or annoyance.

Tu B'shuvat   The New Year of the Trees, a holiday that generally occurs in February, the planting season in the Holy Land. Jewish children traditionally mark the occasion by "purchasing" trees in memory of loved ones through the Jewish National Fund.

tzaddik   A righteous person.

tzaddik v'ralo   A righteous person to whom evil occurs.

tzimtzum   Withdrawal; a term from Lurianic Kabbalah.

yarmulke   The Yiddish word for a kipa.

yeshiva   An institution of Jewish learning.

yetzer hara   An evil inclination in a person's character.

Yigdal   The 13 principles of faith, written by Maimonides, that are still sung each week at the conclusion of Sabbath services.

Yisrael   The name by which the Jewish people are known; lit. to wrestle with God.

Yom Kippur   The holiday during which Jews cleanse their souls for the New Year after having asked forgiveness from individuals we have harmed.

zadie   Affectionate term for grandpa.

Zohar   A kabbalistic text whose name is derived from the Hebrew word for "illumination."

Index

C

F

G

I

Museum of the Diaspora, 263
Qumrun, 261
Sefat, 262
violence concerns, 255-256
Tree of Life, The, 152
trip to Moscow (personal story of author), 265-270
Tu B'Av, 252
Tu B'shuvat, 192
tzaddik, 38
tzedakah (charitable giving), 242-243
tzibbur, 38

ushpizin, 245

V

Via Dolorosa, 259
violence of Israel, 255-256

W-X

walls of the Old City (Jerusalem), 258
websites
613.org, 277
Aish.com, 277
Alcoholism and Drug Addiction, 277
Calendar, 277
Chabad Lubavitch, 277
Conservative Judaism, 277
Daf Yomi, 278
Genealogy, 278
Hebrew Bible and Talmud Texts Online, 278
Holocaust, 278
Judaism 101, 278
Judaism and Jewish Resources, 278

Kosher Food, 278
Passover Haggadah for Kids, 278
Reconstructionist Judaism, 278
Reform Judaism, 278
Singles, 278
Western Wall, 257-258
will
free will, 35
God's will, 32-33
work restrictions (Sabbath), 225-228

Y

Yad Vashem, spiritual sites, 260
Yamin Moshe, spiritual sites, 260-261
yeshiva, 13
yetzer hara, 138
Yigdal, 28
Yisroel, Rabbi Shimon ben, 5
Yitzhak, Rabbi Levi, 131-133
Yom Kippur, 82
living the way angels live, 243
ne'ilah, 244

Z

Zalman, Rabbi Shneur, 133-134
Zionism, 7
Zohar, 154-156

Poor Man Should pray
Rich man give alms
_____

Gossip
_____

Moses / Joseph + the Coat of many colors
|
Exodus   what happened ?

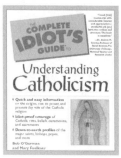

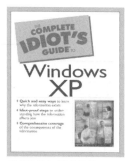
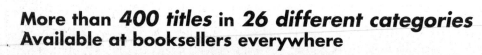